New Casebooks

HAMLET

New Casebooks

New Casebooks

HAMLET

WILLIAM SHAKESPEARE

EDITED BY MARTIN COYLE

MACMILLAN

First published 1992 by
MACMILLAN PRESS LTD
Houndmills, Basingstoke, Hampshire RG21 6XS
and London
Companies and representatives
throughout the world

ISBN 0–333–54127–8 hardcover
ISBN 0–333–54128–6 paperback

A catalogue record for this book is available
from the British Library.

12 11 10   9   8   7   6   5   4
03 02 01 00 99 98 97 96

Printed in Great Britain by
Mackays of Chatham PLC
Chatham, Kent

Contents

Acknowledgements

The editor and publishers wish to thank the following for permission to use copyright material:

Nigel Alexander, extract from *Poison, Play, and Duel: A Study in Hamlet*, Routledge and Kegan Paul (1971), by permission of the author;

Catherine Belsey, extract from *The Subject of Tragedy: Identity and Difference in Renaissance Drama* (1985) Methuen & Co., by permission of Routledge;

Stephen Booth, 'On the Value of *Hamlet*' from *Reinterpretations of Elizabethan Drama*, ed. Norman Rabkin (1969), by permission of Columbia University Press;

James L. Calderwood, extracts from *To Be or Not To Be: Negation and Metadrama in 'Hamlet'* (1983), by permission of Columbia University Press;

Peter Davison, extracts from *Hamlet: Text and Performance* (1983), by permission of Macmillan, London and Basingstoke, and Humanities Press International, Inc.;

Philip Edwards, 'Tragic Balance in *Hamlet*', *Shakespeare Survey*, 36 (1983), by permission of the author;

Marilyn French, extract from *Shakespeare's Division of Experience* (1982), copyright © 1981 by Marilyn French, by permission of Jonathan Cape Ltd and Charlotte Sheedy, Literary Agency, Inc. on behalf of the author;

John Hunt, 'A Thing of Nothing: The Catastrophic Body in

Hamlet', *Shakespeare Quarterly*, 39, No. 1 (Spring 1988), by permission of *Shakespeare Quarterly*;

David Leverenz, 'The Woman in Hamlet: An Interpersonal View', *Signs*, 4 (1978), by permission of University of Chicago Press;

Elaine Showalter, 'Representing Ophelia: Women, Madness and the Responsibilities of Feminist Criticism', from *Shakespeare and the Question of Theory*, eds P. Parker and G. Hartman (1985), Methuen & Co, by permission of Routledge;

Rebecca Smith, 'A Heart Cleft in Twain: The Dilemma of Shakespeare's Gertrude', from *The Woman's Part: Feminist Criticism of Shakespeare*, eds Carolyn Ruth Swift Lenz, Gayle Greene and Carole Thomas Neely (1980), by permission of The University of Illinois Press;

Leonard Tennenhouse, extract from *Power on Display: The Politics of Shakespeare's Genres* (1986), Methuen & Co., by permission of Routledge.

Every effort has been made to trace all the copyright holders but if any have been inadvertently overlooked the publishers will be pleased to make the necessary arrangement at the first opportunity.

General Editors' Preface

The purpose of this new series of Casebooks is to reveal some of the ways in which contemporary criticism has changed our understanding of commonly studied texts and writers and, indeed, of the nature of criticism itself. Central to the series is a concern with modern critical theory and its effect on current approaches to the study of literature. Each New Casebook editor has been asked to select a sequence of essays which will introduce the reader to the new critical approaches to the text or texts being discussed in the volume and also illuminate the rich interchange between critical theory and critical practice that characterises so much current writing about literature.

The series itself, of course, grows out of the original Casebook series edited by A. E. Dyson. The original volumes provide readers with a range of critical opinions extending from the first reception of a work through to the criticism of the twentieth century. By contrast, the focus of the New Casebooks is on modern critical thinking and practice, with the volumes seeking to reflect both the controversy and the excitement of current criticism. Because much of this criticism is difficult and often employs an unfamiliar critical language, editors have been asked to give the reader as much help as they feel is appropriate, but without simplifying the essays or the issues they raise.

The project of New Casebooks, then, is to bring together in an illuminating way those critics who best illustrate the ways in which contemporary criticism has established new methods of analysing texts and who have reinvigorated the important debate about how we 'read' literature. The hope is, of course, that New Casebooks will not only open up this debate to a wider audience, but will also encourage students to extend their own ideas, and think afresh about their responses to the texts they are studying.

John Peck and Martin Coyle
University of Wales, Cardiff

Introduction

MARTIN COYLE

This collection of essays has two main aims. The first of these is to provide students with a range of modern essays on *Hamlet* written by contemporary critics and dealing with various aspects of the play. Naturally the essays do not cover every aspect of the text, but they do take in a large number of topics from character and tragedy through staging, theme and language, to politics and ideology. The hope is that the volume will not only inform and interest but also stimulate and provoke discussion both about the play and about the problems it raises.

The second aim of this collection has to do with modern theories of criticism. The last fifteen or so years have seen the development of a considerable number of new theories of criticism which bear upon the important question of how we read literary texts. While this questioning of the place and role of criticism has led to something of a renaissance in literary studies and in particular in modern critical theory, it has also created an obvious danger. And that is to leave students standing on the edge of things unsure what is going on. What this collection therefore attempts to do is to bring together a range of essays that as well as discussing diverse aspects of *Hamlet* also illustrate the workings of some of these new critical ideas and show them in practice. Thus, for example, the penultimate essay, by Leonard Tennenhouse, which discusses ideas of power and *Hamlet*, is written from the perspective of New Historicist criticism (a term I discuss below). Not all the essays, however, fall into the category of modern critical theory. The collection starts, in fact, with three essays that are very largely traditional in their emphasis. The reason for this is two-fold. First, it would be misleading to suggest that everybody agrees with the new criticism or that traditional criticism has somehow mysteriously died. Indeed, almost the opposite has happened, with traditional critics vigorously defending their position and attacking what they regard as the crude rhetoric and alien jargon of their opponents.

The second reason for including several different critical viewpoints is more pragmatic. And that is that it seemed helpful to place more traditional approaches to *Hamlet* alongside new readings of the play so that readers can more accurately gain a sense of the difference between them and see what is at stake in the current debate about criticism. Inevitably such a debate is bound to involve abstract ideas, but the essays themselves, it is worth stressing, are not abstract in this way. Rather, as we shall see, they are all in their different ways concerned with the central issues of *Hamlet*. Like all good criticism, they are curious about the play, about what happens on stage, and about the meaning of what we see and hear.

I

The first three essays, by Philip Edwards, Peter Davison and Nigel Alexander, as I noted above, belong very broadly to traditional criticism. Though very different from each other in important ways that need to be recognised – traditional criticism is no more monolithic than poststructuralism or feminism – the essays nevertheless share certain assumptions which link them to each other and to the views of earlier critics. (The original Casebook, edited by John Jump, contains an admirable selection of the earlier criticism of *Hamlet* through from the eighteenth century to the 1960s.[1]) Perhaps central to these assumptions is the idea that *Hamlet*, whatever problems of interpretation it presents, is ultimately a unified work of art which offers its readers or audience a coherent vision of life. This vision is embodied in the figure of Hamlet and in the play's complex dramatic world. The business of the critic is to explore this world and in particular Shakespeare's use of character, language and staging to construct a remarkable revenge tragedy about the problem of how to act in the face of evil. In other words, what we are concerned with as critics in looking at *Hamlet* is the moral and intellectual impact of the play, with its shape and design as an artefact that deals with a recurrent human dilemma.

This view of the function of criticism and of what literature is about (the central experiences of life that we share with characters) is probably the one most readers are familiar with and would agree with. It also continues to dominate Shakespeare criticism in one form or another, partly at least because it underpins most editions of Shakespeare's plays. Most editions of *Hamlet* offer a traditional critical perspective on the play, a perspective that focuses on the morality of the Ghost's commands, the moral condition of the court, Hamlet's behaviour and actions, the play's values and its tragic nature. This is also the case with Philip Edwards's interesting essay, 'Tragic Balance in *Hamlet*', which is the first essay printed below. (Edwards is the editor of the New Cambridge edition of *Hamlet*; the essay printed here is developed further in his Introduction to the play.[2]) In essence, Edwards argues that twentieth-century criticism has eroded the tragic quality of *Hamlet* by lessening sympathy for its hero, but in particular by losing sight of the play's religious framework. The problem Hamlet faces, Edwards argues, is that he cannot be sure the Ghost is a symbol of divine justification, and he cannot be sure it is not. Edwards's point is that, for Hamlet, the possibility of a divinely authorised violence – a divinely authorised revenge which will cleanse Denmark and restore order – still exists and has not yet been replaced by our own modern scepticism. In this sense the play occurs at 'a point of terrible balance' even as that possibility, the possibility of actions being ratified by heaven, is disappearing. Edwards does not defend Hamlet's 'failure', but he does ask us to see that his 'mission'[3] is not necessarily wrong or tainted in the way many critics have suggested.

Edwards begins his essay by discussing some of the main trends in *Hamlet* criticism since the start of the twentieth century, so providing a useful overview of how traditional criticism has dealt with Hamlet's character. By contrast Peter Davison's piece, taken from his short but lively book on *Hamlet*, draws attention to three important points. The first of these is the distinction between text and performance, between the words on the page and their realisation on the stage. Nowhere is this distinction greater, Davison writes, 'than in the matter of comedy'. This is the second of Davison's points: that *Hamlet* contains a great deal of comedy and humour – some of it verbal, some of it visual, some low, some ambiguous – which is 'a determinant of Hamlet's nature and a key to the tonal quality of the play'.[4] Finally, Davison notes that, like most plays since the Middle Ages, *Hamlet* does not separate the comic and the tragic but that they are both present simultaneously.

Davison's analysis rightly emphasises the need to see *Hamlet* as a play, as a piece of theatre to be performed. A similar emphasis is found in the third essay, by Nigel Alexander, taken from the opening chapter of his book *Poison, Play, and Duel*. Alexander argues that the action of *Hamlet* is built around the powerful symbols of poison, play and duel and that Shakespeare uses these to focus his audience's attention on the complex moral and psychological problems of violence and revenge. These problems are debated in Hamlet's soliloquies with their conflicting and contradictory attitudes and emotions. Alexander suggests that the play does not offer any conclusions about what is the right response to the questions it poses about human aggression, not because it is confused but because Hamlet is aware that 'more than one single set of answers exists'.[5] While Alexander's approach to Shakespeare is essentially thus the very traditional one of exploring Hamlet's divided mind, his stress upon the contradictions of *Hamlet* serves to link his analysis with more recent poststructuralist thinking about the play.

This, however, does not mean to say that there is not much difference between traditional criticism and its opponents. Much modern writing on Shakespeare is, in fact, deeply hostile to traditional criticism. This is not just a matter of choosing to come at the plays from a different angle or of using a different kind of critical language (though both of these are important), but instead involves a rejection of all that traditional criticism stands for. In particular, the break is with the values of what is termed 'liberal humanism': that is, those assumptions that emphasise individuality (either of the author or of the hero), that see human nature as unchanging and universal, and that define literature in largely moral terms and as outside or above politics.[6] It is these assumptions, and especially the final one – that literature is outside politics – that modern critical theory has challenged in a number of different ways, as the following sections seek to clarify.

II

The fourth essay in this collection, by Stephen Booth, is entitled 'On the Value of *Hamlet*. Paradoxically such a title would not be unsuitable for a very traditional essay proposing that *Hamlet* does indeed offer us a fixed, unchanging set of values or meanings. Booth's essay, however, proves the very opposite of traditional in its reading of the text. For one thing, Booth is not at all concerned with Shakespeare's intention in the play (the notion of authorial intention is dismissed by modern critical theorists as irrelevant since to speak of an author's intention is to imply that there is a single, authoritative, correct reading of the text which cannot be contested). Nor does character analysis or the idea that the purpose of literature (or criticism) is to reveal deeper truths figure in his argument. Instead the essay focuses on what the play does, how it constantly frustrates its audience's understanding and creates a sense of unease through its inconsistencies and contradictions. Booth illustrates this idea by looking closely at the play's opening and notes how we progress from a sense of lack of order in scene i with the appearance of the Ghost to an uncomfortable excess of order in scene ii with the appearance of the court.

Summarised thus, Booth's essay might seem much more remote from the text of the play than it actually is. Indeed, there can be few critics who get closer than Booth to the texture of the minute-by-minute unfolding of the play's opening scenes and how they work as theatre to produce their ambivalent, contradictory effect on us as audience. As I noted above, Nigel Alexander also points to the element of contradiction in *Hamlet*. What marks Booth's essay out as untraditional, however, is not simply its stress on contradiction, but rather its emphasis on the play's plurality, as, for example, in the first scene where we no sooner learn about the military threat to Denmark than the Ghost appears, at once raising further political questions but also suggesting *Hamlet* will be a revenge tragedy. Or, as in scene ii, where Claudius's first speech by its 'unnatural connections between moral contraries' produces 'double and contrary responses'.[7] But what also separates Booth's essay from traditional criticism and identifies it as radical is the extent to which it deliberately decentres Shakespeare, character and moral values as the focus of analysis and replaces them with critic, audience and language.

Booth's essay appeared in 1973 and has influenced a great deal of contemporary thinking about *Hamlet*. In its perception of the play's plural effects, the essay also anticipated something of the direction of criticism over the last fifteen years, following the development of structuralism in the early 1970s. Structuralist criticism describes the practice of those critics who analyse literature using the theories and models of modern linguistics; in a sense what they seek to show is how all literary texts are made up of a series of codes and conventions which we as readers interpret almost automatically. The most readable (and enjoyable) example of this sort of analysis occurs in the book *Mythologies* by the French structuralist Roland Barthes who discusses how all kinds of meanings are constantly brought into play in everyday life even in such things as food and clothes.[8] For structuralists there is nothing 'special' about literature in this regard. They are also opposed both to the view that literature expresses the feelings or views of its author and to the notion that the text is a mirror or imitation of reality. Rather the emphasis of structuralist criticism – itself almost synonymous with Barthes – is on the text as a signifying system (i.e. system of signs) made of writing and without any separable 'content' other than language itself.

While Booth's essay in these terms is (again broadly) structuralist, it does not use two closely related concepts that are central to most structuralist thinking. The first of these is the idea that linguistic signs (written or spoken words) consist of two inseparable parts, the 'signifier' and the 'signified' – for example, the word (signifier) 'crown' and the various meanings (signifieds) we conventionally recognise by that word such as 'royalty', 'power'. The point to grasp here is that the relationship between the word 'crown' and the meanings 'royalty' and 'power' is a product of linguistic convention, not of something in the world. This links up with the second concept. This is the idea of the gap between the word and the world, that words do not depend on reality for their meaning but rather that words determine the meaning of reality. Underlying structuralism are the linguistic theories of Ferdinand de Saussure in which this idea that meaning resides in language itself and nowhere else is of central importance because it draws attention to the conventional nature of language, to the fact that it is a structure that we learn, and which teaches us to order the world and reality.[9] It is this fact which gives structuralism its impetus, for it makes it possible to see literary texts as signifying systems – think, for example, of the Ghost and how it signals at once the ideas of revenge, of the supernatural, of kingship, of military valour.

Structuralism, however, was really just the first stage in a series of critical upheavals that swept literary studies in Britain and America. No sooner had critics grasped an understanding of structuralism than poststructuralism arrived. The difference between the two might be put this way: that while structuralism sees meanings as an effect of codes, systems, conventions, poststructuralism is much more radical and focuses instead on the plurality of meaning, and so in consequence on the very endlessness of language. More simply, poststructuralism, and especially what is termed deconstruction, focuses not (as in traditional criticism) on some central meaning in the text but rather on the lack of a centre of meaning, on plurality, gaps, inconsistencies, contradictions, on what is not said, on what seems marginal or incidental. Indeed, Jacques Derrida, the French philosopher who initiated deconstruction, argues there can be no final interpretation of the text, no final closing off of its possibilities.[10]

This brief summary of structuralism and poststructuralism may seem far removed from the concerns of *Hamlet*, but as the fifth essay, a short extract from James Calderwood's book *To Be and Not To Be* reveals, poststructuralist criticism can draw attention to the complex way in which language works in a text. Calderwood's analysis of Hamlet's advice to Gertrude in the closet scene focuses on its curious negative quality, something that runs through the whole play. In an intricate argument Calderwood goes on to suggest that this 'negative principle' is symptomatic of the breakdown of order and proper differences wrought by Claudius's actions. A very similar point, it is worth noting, is made by Philip Edwards in the opening essay. Like Edwards, too, Calderwood sees Hamlet's killing of Claudius 'as an act of restorative destruction'[11] but, whereas for Edwards Hamlet is seeking to restore the past to Denmark, for Calderwood Hamlet's action is to restore language and the word to their proper function.

Calderwood's approach might best be described as a combination of structuralism and deconstructionist ideas, though what he is particularly interested in is the self-reflexive or 'metadramatic' quality of *Hamlet* – that is, in the way *Hamlet* draws attention to itself as a play so that it seems only to be about itself; to be, in other words, metaphorically about drama.[12] While his argument might seem hard to follow in places, what is evident in Calderwood's discussion of the closet scene as in his book as a whole is that here we have a critic enjoying the ingenuity of his analysis and the cleverness of his writing. Both of these features belong to a certain strand or phase of structuralism and poststructuralism that has all but disappeared (structuralism itself had much more direct influence on novel criticism than on Shakespeare studies). Nevertheless, it is important to emphasise its legacy to the criticism that has followed. Nearly all modern contemporary radical criticism accepts the relationship proposed by Saussure between signifier and signified, accepts, that is, the conventional nature of language, just as it accepts the idea of plurality, contradictions, gaps, inconsistencies in texts. Where much recent criticism parts company with structuralism and deconstruction is in their lack of political awareness and political commitment.

In order to make that last point clearer we need to go on to the next group of essays and the issue of feminism. Before doing so, I want to add two further small notes to do with terminology. Sometimes the term 'poststructuralism' – often spelt with a hyphen – is used by critics (largely American) simply to mean 'deconstruction'. Other critics, I think correctly, mean by poststructuralism all radical criticism that begins where structuralism leaves off – that is, deconstruction, some forms of feminism, recent Marxist criticism and so on. The second term is the one I've been using above when speaking of the new criticism as against traditional criticism. This should not be confused with New Criticism, a movement of the 1950s and 60s practised by such well-known critics as Cleanth Brooks. New Criticism was really concerned with the close reading of texts. Close reading, however, is still very much the order of the day; none of the more recent critics I have mentioned above (or below) has abandoned that central principle of twentieth-century criticism, though they have changed how that close reading is done and why it is done. These changes are nowhere more evident than in feminist criticism.

III

Modern feminist criticism is usually said to begin in 1970 with Kate Millett's book *Sexual Politics*.[13] Millett's title itself suggests the sort of radical break with earlier criticism that is associated with feminism in its questioning of political, social and cultural issues. As with Marxist criticism and later New Historicism (see below), what distinguishes feminist criticism is the taking up of a political position which both challenges traditional ideas but also produces a new reading of the text and a new meaning for it in our own society. Here, though, once again there is need for a word of caution. Feminist criticism is not a single, uniform movement involving one limited perspective. Rather feminism is a series of critical positions and practices which is constantly developing and which has moved on enormously from its beginnings. Nevertheless those beginnings, those first principles, remain axiomatic and are perhaps worth clarifying a little. We might best define feminism as a criticism which is not just concerned with the obviously important issue of the representation of women in literature, but with changing women's position in society and freeing them from oppressive constraints. In other words, feminism's project lies beyond the confines of literature and involves a deep commitment to changing attitudes, values, everything that limits women to being only what our culture has meant by female. But equally feminism has as part of its project the recovering and rereading of women's literature and literary history as well as the analysis of texts and language to reveal how they exclude women from full participation in culture. Again, central to feminist criticism is the analysis of how literature supports patriarchal values through stereotyping and silencing.[14]

This, however, is some distance from earlier feminist readings of Shakespeare. Here, two books not included in this collection might serve to illustrate something of the early debate. In *Shakespeare and the Nature of Women* Juliet Dusinberre argues that the drama from 1590 to 1625 is feminist in sympathy and that Shakespeare 'saw men and women equal in a world which declared them unequal'.[15] In effect Dusinberre argues that Shakespeare was able to transcend the limits of patriarchy (male rule) and act as a mirror to the growing status of women in the Renaissance. Dusinberre's stance is obviously not that of the radical feminist and it might well be argued that her position is really the very traditional one that Shakespeare, as usual, 'got it right'. By contrast, Coppélia Kahn in her book *Man's Estate: Masculine Identity in Shakespeare* argues that Shakespeare's work is filled with 'problems of sexual identity, family relationships, and gender roles'. In particular, Kahn suggests that Shakespeare's plays 'reflect and voice a masculine anxiety about the uses of patriarchal power over women, specifically about men's control over women's sexuality'. This anxiety, paradoxically, grows out of men's indirect and covert dependence on women 'for the validation of their manhood',[16] so that throughout the plays we see Shakespeare's heroes ambivalently seeking to prove their masculinity and identity through violence. As might be evident from this very brief summary, Kahn's book offers a much more probing analysis of Elizabethan culture than Dusinberre's and suggests why feminist criticism has had such a strong impact on Shakespeare studies.

The first feminist essay included in this volume also belongs to the early debate and offers a fairly straightforward way into feminist criticism. The essay, by Rebecca Smith, takes Gertrude as its subject. Smith argues that the traditional depiction of Gertrude, as 'a sensual, deceitful woman' is false and that what her words 'actually create is a soft, obedient, dependent, unimaginative woman who is caught miserably' between Claudius and Hamlet. Because it is focused on a single character the essay might be misread as just another way of discussing character, a rereading of Gertrude's character defending her against other readings. Contemporary theory, it has to be said, is very wary of character-based argument of this sort since it appears to lead back to the early twentieth-century criticism of Shakespeare and, in particular, to the work of A. C. Bradley who, in his book *Shakespearean Tragedy* (1904), tended to treat the characters as if they were real people rather than dramatic figures in a play. However, Smith's essay takes a wider approach than mere character analysis, looking at the way Gertrude's character has been presented – for example, in film – and also drawing attention to just how little evidence there is in the text about her. Interestingly, Smith notes that, while Gertrude 'is a stimulus for and object of violent emotional reactions in the ghost, Hamlet and Claudius', what evidence there is in the text suggests not the stereotype of the temptress but instead the 'malleable, submissive' wife and mother.[17] It is only a short step from Smith's essay to seeing not just how *Hamlet* as a play constructs woman within very limited horizons, but also to realising how important a matter Gertrude's presentation on stage is.

If Rebecca Smith's essay focuses on women and stereotyping, Marilyn French's essay, taken from her book *Shakespeare's Division of Experience*, starts from a different perspective. French argues that Shakespeare's world was divided by cultural notions of gender so that what was orderly and rational was masculine and associated with authority and legitimacy, while that which was feminine was fluid and inconstant and associated with sex and pleasure. In the tragedies, however, this value system, which idealises 'chaste constancy' in woman and has a horror of female sexuality, begins to break down under the strain of its irrationality and contradictions. So for Hamlet, French suggests, 'there is no mean between chastity – pure, cold, and holy – and depravity in women'.[18] Similarly men are divided either into gods or beasts. These splits are reflected in Hamlet's language and behaviour as he confronts a world that is much more ambivalent and ambiguous than his absolutist values allow. Such a bald summary necessarily omits many of the stages of French's thesis which combines feminism with a whole series of ideas to produce a challenging reading of what happens in *Hamlet*.

The third feminist essay included below comes from Elaine Showalter, one of America's leading feminist critics. Showalter's piece on Ophelia is a wide-ranging discussion which takes as its centre the representation of Ophelia through the centuries. It is a fascinating piece of research which locates the character of Ophelia not in Shakespeare's text but in the endless reproductions of her by culture and society. Showalter concludes that the representation of Ophelia changes independently of the play, and depends not on any essential character of Ophelia but rather on attitudes towards madness and women. In this sense there is no true Ophelia, only an Ophelia produced by criticism. Such a conclusion is not at all at odds with either poststructuralism generally or deconstruction, which both emphasise the role of criticism in the production of meaning; but what Showalter also emphasises is how the text is a site of struggle. Feminist criticism, she argues, is not a matter of seeking to defend this or that character interpretation but of confronting male hegemony (rule), which reproduces Ophelia in culture in the image of its own ideas and values. It is perhaps worth adding here that this question of how Shakespeare is used by society is one that has attracted much interest in modern criticism generally. But it is also worth noting how much the study of Shakespeare gains from broadening out beyond the text in the way Showalter does.

Even though it is concerned with difficult concepts, Showalter's essay, like those of French and Smith, remains very approachable. The same holds good for David Leverenz's piece on 'The Woman in Hamlet' which was first published in the feminist journal *Signs*. The essay is concerned partly with the idealisation Hamlet makes of his father, but mainly with his struggles with the conflict between the language of public ritual and that of personal feeling. Like Coppélia Kahn, Leverenz draws upon contemporary psychology in his analysis of the play, arguing that *Hamlet* is a tragedy of frustration in which the hero's identity is stifled by 'structures of rule that no longer have legitimacy', structures such as patriarchal manliness and aggressive masculine roles that have no meaning. Hamlet delays taking revenge, Leverenz argues, because 'his real struggle is to restore his mother's validation of his feelings',[19] feelings which are not repressed sexual desire but which have been denied by the male world of *Hamlet*. That Hamlet does eventually act, Leverenz continues, that he does take up the role prescribed for him, is the real tragedy of the play.

Leverenz's essay suggests something of the very powerful influence psychology has had on modern readings of *Hamlet*. A similar emphasis upon the psychological problems of the play was evident in Nigel Alexander's essay earlier on, but with significant differences. Where Alexander's analysis relates Hamlet's divided mind to the moral questions posed by the play, Leverenz's essay sees Hamlet's struggle in terms of the psychological effect wrought by social roles on men and women. What Leverenz's essay also illustrates, however, is the sort of close connections there sometimes are between feminist criticism, psychological criticism and what, for want of a better term, we might call political criticism, the subject of the final section.[20]

IV

The final group of essays begins with two political approaches to criticism: Marxist and New Historicist. It is worth stressing straight away that the practitioners of these approaches (in common with most feminists) argue that all readings of all texts are political and that there is no such thing as an innocent or neutral reading. In particular, they vigorously oppose the 'common-sense' approach of traditional criticism, with its beliefs in a Shakespeare outside or beyond politics and in the unified text.[21] Instead, much of the writing in this last section – the extracts by Belsey and Tennenhouse – is informed by the poststructuralist notion of contradiction together with the idea of the text as a site of struggle in which we witness many of the political tensions of the Renaissance which eventually resulted in the civil war of 1642. But along with this stress on contradiction are other more specifically political concerns, especially the notions of power and authority.

The brief extract by Catherine Belsey comes from her book *The Subject of Tragedy* and focuses on the problem of revenge in *Hamlet*. 'Revenge', Belsey notes, 'is not justice' but rather 'an act of injustice on behalf of justice'. It is also at once 'in excess of justice'[22] – and so hellish – but desirable, in so far as it punishes murder. Such contradictions, Belsey continues, are ultimately part of a larger question about authority in the revenge plays of the Renaissance. What is, we might ask, the proper course of action against a king who is a regicide? Is it legal to take arms against Claudius? If so, who would justify such action? Can the subject (Hamlet) challenge the court (the political body) in his/her own right? Like other plays of the period, Belsey continues, *Hamlet* does not resolve such questions but instead seems both to condemn and endorse revenge.

Once more, it is worth noting the differences between a traditional reading such as Philip Edwards's and a Marxist reading such as Catherine Belsey's: that while both critics focus on the problem of violent action and authority, Edwards sees it as a moral problem, Belsey as part of the political crisis of Renaissance England as it moved out of Tudor absolutism (absolute power of the monarchy) into the capitalism that characterises our own modern age. That crisis, Belsey argues, sees 'the installation of the sovereign subject',[23] that is, the beginnings of the notion of the self as private, autonomous, as possessing an interior soul. This new figure, however, like Hamlet, as yet possesses no power to act: it is only later bourgeois culture that authorises the individual to act through its stress on the value of subjectivity.

The Subject of Tragedy is part of the shift of more recent theoretical criticism away from a concern with only the words on the page towards a concern with the history, politics and culture in which texts were situated. This shift also underlies so-called New Historicist criticism, a term coined by Stephen Greenblatt in 1980 which describes the critical standpoint of a number of American writers represented here by Leonard Tennenhouse. Where much modern criticism of the 1970s showed little interest in the context of Shakespeare's plays, New Historicist criticism attempts to read the plays back into history. Not history as a series of dates or great events but rather history as power, politics, ideology. In this view of history, however, the plays are not seen as simple mirrors of the times, as merely passive documents, but as theatrical displays of various strands or ideas about power and politics.[24]

In the particular extract on Hamlet given here, Tennenhouse seeks to show how the play represents a dilemma of power between Hamlet and Claudius. Hamlet's claim to power, Tennenhouse argues, derives from his position as son as well as from 'popular support',[25] while Claudius's comes from marriage and force. Tennenhouse goes on to explore the political implications of this conflict between the claims of blood and force, looking particularly at Hamlet's staging of The Murder of Gonzago, the play-within-the-play, and how its story of a nephew murdering an uncle serves to equate Hamlet's act of vengeance with Claudius's original crime as a violent assault on the state through its sovereign's body. Though not always easy to follow (Tennenhouse is interested in comparing Hamlet with Shakespeare's history or chronicle plays to see what ideas about power tragedies and histories share[26]), Tennenhouse's argument gives the play-within-the-play an important new perspective and also raises some interesting ideas about revenge and the role of the people in the play's conflict.

Unlike Tennenhouse's essay, the final essay in this collection, by John Hunt, 'A Thing of Nothing: The Catastrophic Body in *Hamlet*', is not a 'political' reading of the play. It starts from a long established area of Shakespeare criticism, the study of imagery – in this case body imagery. Hunt argues that what we get in *Hamlet* is a 'virtual anatomical catalogue . . . of the human form' and goes on (with not a little wit) to explore how the play's corporeal images constantly suggest the idea of 'nonbeing' lurking at the very centre of existence. After deconstructing the play's imagery in this way, Hunt turns in the second part of the essay to what he calls 'the great mystery of the play, Hamlet's quandary about how to act'. Here Hunt suggests that Hamlet can only act once he has learnt to accept 'physicality, with all its dissolute inconstancy',[27] to accept the body with all its weaknesses and limitations.

While Hunt's conclusion is very much in line with traditional thinking about Hamlet's apparent change or difference in Act V, his essay as a whole suggests some of the ways in which the insights and ideas of modern critical theory have begun to influence and even change traditional approaches to Shakespeare. Because modern critical writing is a different way of thinking it can, as Hunt shows, lead us back into new ways of seeing the text and new ways of understanding topics such as imagery or (as in Tennenhouse's piece) staging and devices like the play-within-the-play. What, though, Hunt's essay also reveals – as do all the essays in this collection – is that any discussion of *Hamlet* invariably leads to and is inextricably linked with the criticism of the play. *Hamlet* without criticism, it would seem, is almost unthinkable.

That, perhaps, would make a fitting conclusion for this introduction but for one final important point, which has to do with the text of *Hamlet*. All major editions of *Hamlet* (the Arden, the New Cambridge, the New Penguin, the Oxford, the Pelican, the Riverside, the Signet) include solid introductions both to the play and to its textual history. Sometimes, however, it is easy to miss the main point about this history, which is that there are three early texts of *Hamlet* and that these differ from each other in significant ways. *Hamlet* was probably written around 1600. In 1603 there appeared a printed version of the play, the so-called First Quarto (or Q1: quarto refers to the size of the page), but this version is generally regarded as corrupt or stolen and is much shorter than the *Hamlet* we are used to.[28] A Second Quarto (Q2) appeared in 1604/5. Then a third version of the play was printed in 1623 in the First Folio (F1), that is, in the first printing of Shakespeare's complete works (folio, like quarto, is a printer's term referring to size of page; a folio is twice the size of a quarto and was used for the printing of large volumes). Most editions rely on either Q2 or F1 as their base text, but often use readings – individual words or lines or even stage directions – from the other texts. The implications for criticism of this combining of texts are considerable. Not only are there three different versions of *Hamlet* (although Q2 and F1 have much in common, the latter does, for example, omit Hamlet's last soliloquy about Fortinbras in IV.iv), but the editions we study are themselves radically different from each other and are highly unlikely ever to have been acted in exactly the form we are given them by editors. Shakespeare's texts are, in fact, notoriously unstable and we have no incontrovertible evidence – that is no copy of Shakespeare's original drafts or 'foul papers' as they are called – that the texts we read bear out his intentions. What we read is an 'edition' of 'Shakespeare' based on an editor's critical understanding of the play, often containing amendments to previous editions. In addition, of course, we have performances of the play which themselves often offer us a 'new' *Hamlet*.

All of this in turn raises a number of complex issues. Since we do not know what Shakespeare wrote, what is the status of the modern texts we read? Whose values do they embody? Are they a reflection of the past or the present? But the problems go beyond these questions to much more basic matters. Is there, in fact, a text we can call *Hamlet*, or are there several *Hamlets*? As I noted above, the early texts of *Hamlet* – the two quartos and the folio – all differ from each other. Some modern editors (especially the Oxford Shakespeare[29]) argue that these differences are too significant to be ignored, that it is misleading to conflate the texts, and that such amalgamations, far from reflecting Shakespeare's original intentions, only produce a much more 'problematic' play by combining incompatible details from the separate versions.

This question of the text or texts of *Hamlet* has become one of the most controversial topics in recent Shakespeare studies. In many ways it reflects the debate about literature and criticism that I have outlined above: about whether what we read is the product of a single mind able to reveal to us something permanent about the nature of the human condition, or whether Shakespeare's plays are the products of a particular political and social culture which we have inherited and which we reproduce in our analyses; about whether there can be a single 'right' reading of Shakespeare's plays, or whether meaning – like criticism and the texts it discusses – is inevitably plural. But there is also a practical side to this information about texts and editing. It is included because several critics in the essays printed below refer to the various texts of *Hamlet* either in support of their argument or to clarify particular points. Again, it may well be that occasionally your edition of the play differs in detail from those quoted in the essays.

For what I hope are obvious reasons quotations in the essays have not been standardised, though the style of references has. Provisional titles have been given to some of the pieces. Footnotes have been kept in full because they can often be both informative and helpful. Suggestions for further reading appear at the end, while each essay is followed by a few brief notes about its argument. The essays themselves, I ought to point out, are not printed in chronological order, and the story I tell around them is not meant to exhaust their significance or to forestall other readings of them. Nor, indeed, is it intended to suggest that there is a sort of steady critical progression from Essay 1 to Essay 12, or that there is, after all, a collective critical orthodoxy, an agreed position on *Hamlet*. Rather what I have tried to convey is a sense of the different kinds of critical approach to Shakespeare that there are for you to choose from and which you might find productive to explore in your own analysis of the play.

NOTES

1. John Jump (ed.), *Shakespeare: 'Hamlet'* (London, 1968).

2. Philip Edwards (ed.), *Hamlet*, The New Cambridge Shakespeare (Cambridge, 1985).

3. See pp. 32, 27 below.

4. See pp. 37, 45 below.

5. See p. 55 below.

6. For a clear discussion of liberal humanism, see Catherine Belsey, *Critical Practice* (London, 1980), ch. 1.

7. See p. 65 below.

8. Roland Barthes, *Mythologies* (Paris, 1957; London, 1972).

9. For a fuller discussion of the relationship between modern linguistics and literature, see Ann Jefferson and David Robey (eds), *Modern Literary Theory*, 2nd edn (London, 1986), ch. 2.

10. Useful brief discussions of Derrida and deconstruction can be found in Ann Jefferson and David Robey (eds), *Modern Literary Theory*, 2nd edn (London, 1986), and Raman Selden, *A Reader's Guide to Contemporary Literary Theory* (Brighton, 1985).

11. See pp. 73, 77 below.

12. On 'metadrama' more generally in Shakespeare, see Calderwood's earlier book, *Shakespearean Metadrama* (Minneapolis, 1971).

13. Kate Millett, *Sexual Politics* (New York, 1970).

14. For a list of introductions to feminist criticism, see Further Reading, pp. 195–6.

15. Juliet Dusinberre, *Shakespeare and the Nature of Women* (London, 1975), p. 308.

16. Coppélia Kahn, *Man's Estate: Masculine Identity in Shakespeare* (Berkeley, 1981), pp. 3, 12, 17.

17. See pp. 80, 82, 92 below.

18. See pp. 102, 99 below.

19. See pp. 148, 149 below.

20. One reason for these close connections stems from the influence of the French philosopher and psychoanalyst Jacques Lacan on modern critical thinking. Lacan is discussed briefly in the notes to essays 8 and 10 (pp. 128, 158 below). For further reading on Lacan, see Raman Selden, *A Reader's Guide to Contemporary Literary Theory* (Brighton, 1985), pp. 80–4 and Ann Jefferson and David Robey (eds), *Modern Literary Theory*, 2nd edn (London, 1986), ch. 6.

21. On the relationship of 'common sense' to traditional criticism, see Catherine Belsey, *Critical Practice* (London, 1980), ch. 1.

22. See pp. 154, 157, 155 below.

23. See p. 158 below.

24. For a fuller discussion of New Historicism, see Hugh Grady, *The Modernist Shakespeare* (Oxford, 1991). On Cultural Materialism, a type of Marxist criticism which has much in common with New Historicism, see Jonathan Dollimore and Alan Sinfield (eds), *Political Shakespeare* (Manchester, 1985). On Marxist criticism see Ann Jefferson and David Robey (eds), *Modern Literary Theory*, 2nd edn (London, 1986), ch. 7.

25. See p. 160 below.

26. Behind Tennenhouse's argument lie the ideas of the French philosopher and historian Michel Foucault (see p. 166 below). A fuller discussion of Foucault can be found in Raman Selden, *A Reader's Guide to Contemporary Literary Theory* (Brighton, 1985), pp. 98-100.

27. See pp. 171, 168 below.

28. The First Quarto, often referred to as a 'bad' quarto because of the unreliability of its text, runs to 2154 lines. The Second Quarto has 3674 lines; the Folio text is 3535 lines. For these and other details, see Philip Edwards (ed.), *Hamlet*, The New Cambridge Shakespeare (Cambridge, 1985), p. 9.

29. G. R. Hibbard (ed.), *Hamlet*, The Oxford Shakespeare (Oxford, 1987).

1

Tragic Balance in 'Hamlet'

PHILIP EDWARDS

The breakdown in sympathy for Hamlet during the twentieth century seems to me a critical and cultural fact of some importance, and I believe it has inhibited a genuinely tragic response to the play.[1] Yet although the criticism of our time has eroded the tragic quality of *Hamlet*, one can see latent within that criticism the possibilities of a renewal which might bring the play back to us as tragedy. The twentieth-century view of the play developed as an antithesis to the view which prevailed in the nineteenth century. The new view that one envisages emerges as a synthesis of the two earlier views. I shall argue that this emerging view, though necessarily a product of our own times, could restore to *Hamlet* something of the tragic quality that may have belonged to the play in its own day.

The nineteenth-century view, the thesis with which we begin, received its latest and greatest expression in Bradley's *Shakespearean Tragedy* in 1904. It is a vision of a noble and generous youth who for reasons quite mysterious to himself is unable to carry out the sacred duty, imposed by divine authority, of punishing an evil man by death. It is a vision of paralysis and disablement, of ultimate victory bought at a terrible cost.

Against this I would set, rather obviously, G. Wilson Knight's powerful essay of 1930, 'The Embassy of Death' from *The Wheel of Fire*. Knight had important predecessors, of course, and he himself radically revised his account of the play. Nevertheless, the essay is central. Knight portrayed the Denmark of Claudius and Gertrude as a healthy, contented, smoothly-running community. Claudius is clearly an efficient administrator, and he has sensible ideas about not letting memories of the past impede the promise of the future. Hamlet, by contrast, is a figure of nihilism and death. He has communed with the dead, and been instructed never to let the past be forgotten. As a 'sick soul commanded to heal', he is in fact a poison in the veins of the community. Knight went so far as to say that 'Hamlet is an element of evil in the state of Denmark', 'a living death in the midst of life'. He is an alien at the court, 'inhuman – or superhuman ... a creature of another world'. Neither side can understand the other.

Claudius murdered his brother, and Hamlet's mission is the punishment of a murderer. Hamlet, Knight admitted, is in the right. And if he had been able to act quickly and cleanly, all might have been well. But which of the two, he asked, Claudius or Hamlet, 'is the embodiment of spiritual good, which of evil? The question of the relative morality of Hamlet and Claudius reflects the ultimate problem of this play.' He gave his own answer: 'A balanced judgement is forced to pronounce ultimately in favour of life as contrasted with death, for optimism and the healthily second-rate, rather than the nihilism of the superman; for [Hamlet] is not, as the plot shows, safe; and he is not safe, primarily because he is right.' So Hamlet is wrong to pursue that which is right. 'Had Hamlet forgotten both the Ghost's commands [that is, to remember the past and avenge the dead] it would have been well, since Claudius is a good king, and the Ghost but a minor spirit.'

Wilson Knight said 'The ghost may or may not have been a "goblin damned"; it certainly was no "spirit of health".' This sentence is the theme of much of the *Hamlet* criticism which followed. A great many critics have found an element of evil in the pact between the Ghost and Hamlet. Harold Goddard, in *The Meaning of Shakespeare* (Chicago, 1951), said of his ideas about *Hamlet* that he had been expounding them to students since the days of the First World War. The Ghost is the spirit of war and a symbol of the devil, corrupting Hamlet with his 'thirst for vengeance' and his instruction to kill. To kill whom? Claudius, a man who could have been shown the error of his ways. 'The King ... is no villain.' Shakespeare tempted us in the audience to want Claudius's death in order that we should become ashamed of ourselves and realise with Shakespeare that killing was evil. Hamlet loses in the end because he gives in to the Ghost and 'descends to the level of Laertes'.

L. C. Knights's *Approach to Hamlet* of 1960 was uncompromising in its hostility to the Prince and his mission. Hamlet is an immature person lacking 'a ready responsiveness to life' who is pushed by the Ghost to concentrate on death and evil. Shakespeare himself disapproved of revenge. This latter view achieved its most thorough and scholarly expression in Eleanor Prosser's *Hamlet and Revenge* of 1967. Here the Ghost's credentials are picked threadbare and Hamlet's identification with the bloodthirsty villains of revenge fiction is complete.

You may well say that, formidable though the battle-line of Wilson Knight, Goddard, Knights and Prosser may be, I am representing only one trend of mid-twentieth-century criticism. What of C. S. Lewis and Maynard Mack, and many others who cannot be said to share these views? It is more than a trend I am isolating; it is the common currency of *Hamlet* criticism to deplore, not Hamlet's failure to carry out his mission, but the mission itself. Although there are no beginnings in *Hamlet* criticism, I trace the movement back to the extraordinary lines of Mallarmé, in his essay of 1896 on Hamlet and Fortinbras which Joyce brought to our attention in *Ulysses*, and his more extended view in *Crayonné au théâtre* (1886).[2] Hamlet is the solitary, 'étranger à tous lieux où il poind'. He walks about, we remember, 'lisant au livre de lui-même'; he denies others by looking at them, and even without willing it spreads death about him. 'The black presence of the doubter causes this poison.'[3]

Many contemporary critics, unable to deny the damning evidence of Prosser but uneasy that the prevailing hostility towards Hamlet tends to make too little of Claudius's crime, have sought to restore a tragic balance to the play by stressing Hamlet's struggle to make a bad deed good. This is associated with the very widespread 'contamination' theory which we find in Maynard Mack. 'The act required of him, though retributive justice, is one that necessarily involves the doer in the general guilt.'[4] A searching and sensitive expression of this view is in Nigel Alexander's *Poison, Play, and Duel* (1967). The proof of the King's guilt does not solve Hamlet's problem. 'The question remains, how does one deal with such a man without becoming like him?' (p. 125).

The idea that Hamlet's problem is somehow to punish Claudius and yet transcend the sheer human violence and vindictiveness which such punishment entails goes back to 1839 and the once famous but now forgotten 'conscience' theory of Hermann Ulrici.[5] 'It cannot,' he said, 'be an entirely innocent and heavenly spirit that would wander on earth to demand a son to *avenge* his death.' Hamlet has to try to convert the 'external action' of revenge 'into one that is *internal*, free,

and truly *moral*'. The will to the deed must not be a matter of
external pressure, it must become 'voluntarily his own'. Ideally this
cannot be unless the 'moral necessity' of the deed can be seen to be
'the substance of the divine order of the universe'. Ulrici argues, very
interestingly, that Hamlet actually forces the issue of the sympathy of
divine power and arrogates to himself the role of providence. Here
again he anticipates much modern criticism. I cannot think, however,
that the neo-Ulricians have in fact rescued the play of *Hamlet* from
being the rather dismal story of blight which it is in great danger of
becoming.

At this point, I should like to summarise the four closely-related
areas in which the mid twentieth century most strongly diverged
from earlier opinion. The first is the authority of the Ghost; whether
he is an authorised emissary of heaven, or just the spirit of an
aggrieved king, or, at the extreme, a false spirit from hell. The second
area is the morality of his injunction – namely, to exact vengeance
for murder; the morality, therefore, of Hamlet's quest to kill
Claudius. The third area is the moral and indeed material condition
of Denmark and its court under Claudius. The fourth concerns
Hamlet himself, how we judge his actions and behaviour generally;
what we think of him as a man.

I personally cannot see a way forward in any discussion of *Hamlet*
that does not take as a point of departure that it is a religious play.
Bradley refused to call it this, but he acknowledged that the religious
element in the play gave it a distinctive tone among Shakespeare's
tragedies. Middleton Murry thought that Hamlet's fear of damnation was of tremendous and unrecognised potency in the play. I
agree. What Keats said of *King Lear* would have fitted *Hamlet*
better: 'the fierce dispute/Betwixt damnation and impassioned clay.'
George Herbert spoke of himself as

> A wonder tortur'd in the space
> Betwixt this world and that of grace.
>   ('Affliction', IV)

With characteristic reductiveness Hamlet asks 'What should such
fellows as I do, crawling between earth and heaven?' The setting of a
play which never moves from Elsinore is earth, heaven and hell.

> O all you host of heaven! O earth! what else?
> And shall I couple hell?
>   (I.v.92–3)

When Hamlet says he is prompted to his revenge by heaven and hell, he means he is involved in the whole supernatural world of good and evil and their eternal warfare.

Hamlet when we first meet him is in a state of despair. He longs for death, and would take his own life if suicide were not forbidden by divine decree. It is at this moment that Horatio and Marcellus burst in on him with news of an apparition, seemingly a visitant from beyond the grave in the likeness of his dead father. C. S. Lewis said 'The appearance of the spectre means a breaking down of the walls of the world.'[6] Of this equivocal figure, in the 'questionable shape' of his father, Hamlet passionately demands, 'What should we do?', a question which expands from the specific to become a general appeal for guidance, for a direction and a purpose in one's life. The Ghost's response indicates that the doings of a corrupt mortal world are integrated within an eternal world. What Gertrude has done will be taken care of: 'Leave her to heaven.' But Claudius for his crime is not to be permitted to continue among men and enjoy his booty of crown and queen: 'Bear it not.' What is unendurable to heaven is not to be endured by men. Evil is not ineradicable, and heaven may appoint an agent of its justice to pluck it out – Hamlet. Hamlet's reaction to this communication is like a conversion or a baptism. He ostentatiously wipes away all previous values, and dedicates himself as a new man.

> And thy commandment all alone shall live
> Within the book and volume of my brain,
> Unmixed with baser matter.
>
> (I.v.102–4)

'As a stranger give it welcome', he says to Horatio about the visitation. He identifies himself with the stranger. He becomes a stranger by adopting the garb of madness.[7] Like Bunyan's Christian, he considers himself a pilgrim and a stranger in his own city of Vanity Fair or Elsinore.

The French Marxist critic Lucien Goldmann scarcely mentioned Shakespeare in his 1955 study of Racine and Pascal, *The Hidden God*. But I found in it much food for thought about *Hamlet*. His theory of tragedy, for which he gives credit to the early work of Lukács, is based on the notion of Pascal that man has to wager that God exists, for he is a hidden God whose presence is not indisputably known and whose voice is not unequivocally heard. The tragic hero longs for clear directives to govern his action; he longs for absolutes, for an existence which he can value as authentic and uncompromising.

But the God to whom he looks, in whose existence he dares to believe, whom he longs to obey, is shrouded and hidden; his voice distorted and scarcely audible, his guidance and his requirements never clearly discernible. The world in which the hero lives, which he would contract out of if he could, is our own accustomed world with our ordinary values. Conspicuously, it is a world never ruled by absolutes, but by perpetual compromise, adjustment and expediency. In this world the hero demands justice, honesty, truth. In his vain efforts to live out what he perceives as the ideals of a higher order in a world which finds his conduct scandalous, offensive, and insane, lies tragedy.

The critical element in this tragic structure is the notion that God is neither absent nor obviously present. If God is dead, or if God is clearly known, the tragedy (Goldmann says) cannot exist. The special irony of the tragic hero's position is that the difficulty of trying to live out what God wants is compounded by the difficulty of *knowing* what God wants, or even whether He exists.

Hamlet seems to be precisely in the position which Goldmann postulates for the tragic hero. From the very first he insists on absolutes – 'I know not seems'. The voice he hears gives him his mission, which he rapidly expands into a cleansing of the world, a setting right of disjointed time. As the scourge and minister of heaven, he wilfully seeks his own salvation by flailing others with his tongue for their moral inadequacies and redirecting their lives as he moves forward to a killing which will re-baptise the state of Denmark.

What the scholarship of this century has taught us is that the status of the voice which Hamlet hears is from first to last uncertain. The ambiguity of the Ghost is of fundamental importance. Shakespeare uses the great perplexity of his age about the origin and status of ghosts to indicate the treacherousness of a sense of communion with a higher world. Hamlet's own sense of this treacherousness seems nearly always underestimated. It is at the very end of Act II, at the conclusion of the 'rogue and peasant slave' soliloquy, that Hamlet openly expresses his fear that 'the spirit that I have seen may be a devil'. But it is on his next appearance, in, 'To be or not to be', that he most fully and profoundly expresses a much wider scepticism. He is once again in the despair of Act I, again longing for the oblivion of death. Since that time he has been given a mission, which he eagerly seized as being heaven-sent, to renovate the world by a single act. Now he rejects such a possibility. The alternative courses which

Hamlet sets before himself in the first five lines of the soliloquy, asking himself which of them is the greater nobleness, are: to continue to endure the antagonisms of existence, or to escape from them in the only possible way, by the act of suicide. The only opposition which the individual can make against the mischances of existence is to take his life. No other act can end the sea of troubles. No other act can improve the condition of the world or the condition of its victims. By implication, the deed of revenge, as a creative act bringing earth nearer to heaven, is of no avail.[8] Whether Hamlet kills the King or not, Denmark will continue to be as it is, a place of suffering ruled by fortune. If there is a nobleness in continuing to live, it is a nobleness of suffering, not a nobleness of reforming and transforming the world. This is exactly the view on the alternative of living or taking one's life put by Schopenhauer in his essay 'On Suicide'.[9] Since no human act can improve the world and all acts contribute to its continued beastliness, Schopenhauer said that the only argument against suicide as a praiseworthy course must be that continued suffering is praiseworthy in itself.

If Hamlet rejects, at least as a means of saving mankind, the killing of the King, he refuses the alternative course through fear of damnation. The soliloquy which begins as a debate on nobleness ends in a contest of cowardliness. What is one most afraid of, the possibility of damnation for taking one's life, or the certainty of suffering on earth? It is conscience, the implanted sense of right and wrong, which makes us too cowardly to embrace a course which reason tells us is noble. And it is this same conscience, this worrying about the consequences of things and the way they look in the eye of eternity, which inhibits other 'enterprises of great pitch and moment' so that they 'lose the name of action'.

Although it is only by inference and by implication, the killing of the King is twice referred to in this great soliloquy. In the later reference we gather that Hamlet has not proceeded with revenge because his conscience cannot convince him that the act is good; in the earlier that, whether the act is good or bad, it cannot change the world. To call Hamlet's mood in 'To be or not to be' a pocket of pessimism, or to speak of his doubts about the Ghost as transient, is to mistake the man whom Shakespeare has drawn. As the play progresses, different surfaces of this many-faceted character catch the light, but the make-up of the whole remains much the same; there is much less 'development' in Hamlet than is often supposed.

Doubts or no doubts, he takes his revenge. Buoyed up by the

success of the ruse of the play and determined on action, he decides to spare the King as he prays, but moments later, finding him in the ignominious position of eavesdropper in Gertrude's closet, he kills him, and discovers it is Polonius he has struck. By this misdeed, he triggers off a new cycle of vengeance. By unwittingly killing Polonius, Hamlet unwittingly takes his own life.

The progress from this point to the final chance-medley is complex and intricate. I argued in a lecture in 1980[10] that the less complex version of the latter part of the play in the Folio may well represent Shakespeare's own decision to replace both the defiance of the 'hoist with his own petar' speech and the self-recrimination of 'How all occasions do inform against me' with a silence as regards Hamlet's inner thoughts which is as challenging and mysterious as the silence that lies between Acts I and II. If I am right, tremendous weight is thrown forward on to the account of what has been going on in his mind which he gives to Horatio on his return from the sea-voyage; an account most significantly expanded in the Folio.

In recognising 'a divinity that shapes our ends,/Rough-hew them how we will', Hamlet recognises, with a clear and conscious modification of his earlier sense of his own freedom and power, that he is subject to the control of a higher power which redirects him when his own blunders have impeded his progress. The recognition is Hamlet's; not necessarily Shakespeare's; not necessarily ours. He continues with an all-important speech, the full version of which is found only in the Folio.

> Does it not, think thee, stand me now upon –
> He that hath killed my king and whored my mother,
> Popped in between th' election and my hopes,
> Thrown out his angle for my proper life,
> And with such cozenage – is't not perfect conscience
> To quit him with this arm? And is't not to be damned
> To let this canker of our nature come
> In further evil?
>
> (V.ii.63–70)

To have this demand for assurance coming from Hamlet at this point in the play is extraordinary. Such anxiety can only be a measure of much perplexity. Once again, the theme is conscience and damnation. Conscience formerly made great enterprises lose the name of action; now it is conscience to raise one's arm against Claudius. Damnation formerly lay in wait for Hamlet if he took his own life, or killed the king at the behest of a devil-ghost. Now it would be his meed if he failed to stop a cancerous growth in human nature by allowing Claudius to go on living.

Hamlet says 'the interim is mine', in which to carry out what he sees as a holy resolve. But of course it isn't. The interim belongs to Claudius and Laertes. It is too late for Hamlet to act on his conviction. The first time, too much in fancied control of the world's destiny, he killed the wrong man; the second time he kills the King indeed, but not until he has his own death-wound.

There can be no question about the extent of Hamlet's failure. Quite apart from his responsibility for the deaths of Polonius, Ophelia and his schoolfellows, there is the simple, inescapable fact that the attempt to rid Denmark of its villain-king has left the country in a worse state than it was at the outset. The foreigner Fortinbras, whose threat to the kingdom opens the play, takes it over at the end without firing a single shot. Fortinbras is success as Hamlet is failure. Nor should we take much comfort from Hamlet's own development. Even if we think of his persistent cruelty to Ophelia and his overbearing self-righteousness towards Gertrude as passing stages in his emotional history, we yet face some awkward moments towards the end of the play. Any suggestion that the Hamlet who returns from the voyage is in some state of sanctity has to be resisted. Here again, there is a victory for the criticism of the twentieth century. There has been an anti-Hamlet lobby in every generation but it has become so strong that it is impossible for anyone who to any degree 'believes in' Hamlet to sentimentalise him.

There can be no question about the extent of Hamlet's failure. But tragedy must surely ask about the extent of his success. I have been looking at Hamlet as a somewhat fitfully inspired missionary. It is time to turn to the problem which has so engaged the criticism of the twentieth century, the quality of the mission itself. What do we say about the moral standing of the 'court party'? About the values which Hamlet seeks to reimpose on Denmark? And above all about the ethics of wishing to kill Claudius?

'There is nothing either good or bad but thinking makes it so.' What *is* Denmark like? If we don't see sin and crime at Elsinore we are not likely to feel that Hamlet's despair is anything but an illness, or his mission to cleanse the world other than obsession and delusion. I should like to quote a typical modern attempt to abstain from black-and-white answers to this question, by Michael Long, in *The Unnatural Scene* (1976). In portraying Denmark, says Dr Long,

Shakespeare shows 'no ruthless desire to track down viciousness'. No, it is 'a lucid presentation of very ordinary human failings as they prove catastrophically inept in the face of difficult moral demand. . . . The real "crime" in which all these characters are involved is that of participating without protest in a social normality which is hostile to the most essential needs of consciousness' (p. 140). We see the strong influence here of both Wilson Knight and L. C. Knights. I should also like to cite John Bayley's praise for Gertrude in *Shakespeare and Tragedy* (1981); he speaks of the 'innocence' in the play, which 'extends to Gertrude's marriage to Claudius, and his relations with her' (pp. 173–4).

This levelling of the score, as regards moral judgement, between Hamlet and those to whom he is opposed is characteristic of our century and our eagerness to see both sides of the question. We know too much to believe in villains and heroes. And even if we feel uneasy with this moral levelling as applied to the play of *Hamlet*, it is very hard not to feel more uneasy at the severity and sharpness of Hamlet's moral distinctions, at the stridency of his insistence on the beauty of his father's life and the ugliness of his uncle's. Everyone feels something excessive in his disgust at his mother's remarriage, in his charge of incest, and in his savage denunciation of his uncle as a usurper.

The question of the moral distinctions in the play seems to me of the very first importance in considering how far the criticism of our day may have blurred the tragic issue as it was presented to Shakespeare's audience. I agree entirely with Wilson Knight's words: 'The question of the relative morality of Hamlet and Claudius reflects the ultimate problem of this play.'

Three times during the course of the play Shakespeare brings the story of Cain and Abel to our minds.[11] There is the mention of 'the first corse' in II.ii; 'the primal eldest curse . . . A brother's murder' in III.iii; and 'Cain's jawbone, that did the first murder' in V.i. *Hamlet* is the story of two royal brothers, a kingdom and a queen, given to us as a reflection of the primordial disintegration of the human family in that first murder which resulted from and betokened man's separa-tion from God. In his book *Violence and the Sacred*, René Girard describes how the dissolution of cultural order comes about from the blurring of recognised distinctions and differences, and argues that the basic mythical presentation of this cultural dissolution is in terms of the rivalry of brothers, in fratricidal conflict over something they cannot share – a throne, a woman. The result of cultural dissolution, the 'sacrificial crisis' as Girard terms it, is that violence can no longer be contained, and overflows in the unending cycle of the vendetta.

The obliteration of differences and distinctions is what chiefly worries Hamlet; that Gertrude cannot distinguish between the two brothers, between Cain and Abel. 'Look here upon this picture, and on this!'

> This was your husband. Look you now what follows,
> Here is your husband. . . . Have you eyes?
>
> (III.iv.53, 63–5)

It is abundantly clear that Claudius seduced Gertrude in the old king's lifetime.[12] It is the thought that this complaisant woman was accustomed to sleep with either of two brothers which gives special force to the idea of 'incest'. The fierce refusal to accept the undiscriminating hospitality of Gertrude's loins is where the tragedy begins. Centuries later, the need to accept the undiscriminating hospitality of Molly Bloom's loins is where Joyce's *Ulysses* ends. In between lies the Romantic revolution during which Byron presented Cain as a much misunderstood figure.

'He that hath killed my king and whored my mother.' Here is plain speaking!

> A murderer and a villain
> A slave that is not twentieth part the tithe
> Of your precedent lord, a vice of kings,
> A cutpurse of the empire and the rule,
> That from a shelf the precious diadem stole
> And put it in his pocket –
>
> (III.iv.96–101)

Here is a forthright recognition of distinctions!

The sense of distinction which Hamlet apprehends to be weakening has now disappeared, as I think my quotations from Wilson Knight, Michael Long, and John Bayley show. I could adduce many, many more, including those at the edges which tell what a poor fish the old king was, probably an alcoholic and possibly impotent. But, as I say, we are all in this. We can't possibly share Hamlet's sense of values. Hyperion to a satyr? A man's a man for a' that. But nor could Shakespeare necessarily or unequivocally share Hamlet's sense of values. It is in the moment of the weakening and questioning of distinctions that he writes his play. What Shakespeare could not do was to repudiate Hamlet's sense of values. We, having gone right down the road that Shakespeare was on, have turned the corner, and can't see the place where the play happened, the place where blurring has just begun, and might *perhaps* be stopped.

To restore to his mother her sense of difference, to eliminate the man who obliterates distinctions and dares, by murder, to claim the protection of the divinity that hedges a king, to restore to Denmark its beauteous majesty – this is the mission of Hamlet, who, in doing this, can see himself as the scourge and minister of heaven itself. In a scheme of things in which the distinctions between persons are ratified by heaven, the killing of Claudius is as far removed from the brutal poisoning of the former king as can be. It would belong in an area of sacredness which is totally foreign to us. An act of cleansing and not one of pollution, it would have the sanctity of a sacrificial offering. [13]

That there can be a distinction between a violence which purifies, and is acceptable, and all other forms of violence, which are out-lawed, must seem to us the most dangerous concept possible. Only among terrorist circles are differences of kind among acts of violence accepted. We don't accept capital punishment if only because as Saul Bellow's hero put it, 'Nobody's hands are clean enough to throw the switch'. [14] But, difficult though it is for us, unless we can see *some* sense in an idea of authorised violence, there can be little hope of recapturing the tragic sense of the play *Hamlet*. Oddly enough, the nineteenth century, which had its own scruples about capital punish-ment, seems to have had too little doubt about divinely-sanctioned violence in *Hamlet* (apart from Ulrici and his followers of course) and to that extent *they* diminished the tragic balance of the play. Claudius ought to be killed, they felt: it was some terrible paralysis which prevented Hamlet from doing the deed. G. K. Chesterton saw the way things were going and in an essay of 1923 leapt to the defence of the older view. We could no longer apprehend the play, he claimed, because we had ceased to believe in punishment, and had substituted pity in its stead. 'The sort of duty that Hamlet shirked is exactly the sort of duty that we are all shirking; that of dethroning injustice and vindicating truth.' [15]

This disarming simplicity has as little to do with what we find in the play of *Hamlet* as has the opposing view that the execution of Claudius is too horrid even to contemplate. The only person who holds a simple view about punishing Claudius is the Ghost. 'How-somever thou pursues this act, / Taint not thy mind.' This revenge he asks for is a straightforward business, demanding courage and will, like meeting the challenge of old Fortinbras, all those years ago.[16] But for Hamlet nothing is simple or straightforward. His rage to re-establish the world of distinctions and sanctions which he fears is disappearing never quite certainly finds either its divine justification or its true way of proceeding. Throughout the play, to everyone, his language is teasing, riddling, punning, looking two ways at once, never directly serious or directly jesting. In almost everything he says, he reveals his incapacity for or refusal of single vision and single valuation. Hamlet's commitment to killing the king wavers constantly; he tries out the avenger's script, he clearly prefers to chasten his mother, and (for me most significantly) at the second visitation actually fears that the Ghost's presence may convert his 'stern effects' and substitute tears for blood. Because of the impossibility of total conviction, great enterprises lose the name of action. But ''tis not so above. *There* is no shuffling.' Is there a line of communication from that higher region where uncertainty doesn't reign, authorising conduct which, though it seems terrible, brings the values of heaven into a corrupt Denmark? The play of *Hamlet* takes place within the possibility that there is – in the symbol of the Ghost. Neither positive that there is, nor positive that there is not.

I have for several years suggested to my students that the central dilemma in *Hamlet* is that which Kierkegaard describes, concerning Abraham and the intended sacrifice of Isaac, in his work *Fear and Trembling*. Abraham believed that he had heard God and in obedience was prepared to murder his beloved son. This indeed is faith. It is the idea of the wager again – betting that there is a God – and that trusting in what we hear enables us to fulfil a demand of the absolute, although we outgo the laws of worldly ethics.

Kierkegaard tries out many scenarios for the intense but skeletal drama provided in Genesis. What would Isaac say when he heard Abraham's explanation of his extraordinary conduct towards him? 'So you were prepared to kill me because a voice told you to?' And so on. There *can* be no certainty. Isaac was not killed, but Abraham was ready and willing to kill him. Either he was a murderer, or he was an obedient child of God. Faith, says Kierkegaard, is 'a paradox which is capable of transforming a murder into a holy act well-pleasing to God'. But, he asks, 'If the individual had misunderstood the deity – what can save him?'

The *mistaken* conviction of the individual that he can be above the universally accepted ethics of society, Kierkegaard calls the 'demoniacal'. He speaks of 'the knight of faith who in the solitude of the universe never hears any human voice, but walks alone with his dreadful responsibility'. Dreadful, because he may be eternally lost, for following the demoniac and not the divine. Either way, he seems mad to the world; at the very least, the world 'denounces as presumption his wanting to play providence by his actions'.[17]

The literary criticism of the past fifty years, with its challenge to the conduct of Hamlet and the authority of the Ghost, has unintentionally moved the play right into the point of terrible balance described by Kierkegaard. Is Hamlet's sense of mission divine or demoniac? A former pupil of mine objected to my use of Kierkegaard concerning a play written when theology was dominated by Luther. It was Wittenberg Hamlet was studying at. William Tyndale, who visited Luther at Wittenberg, will do just as well.

> FAITH, is the believing of God's promises, and a sure trust in the goodness and truth of GOD; which faith justified Abraham, and was the mother of all his good works which he afterwards did. Good works are works of God's commandment, wrought in faith ... Jacob robbed Laban his uncle; Moses robbed the Egyptians; and Abraham is about to slay and burn his own son; and all are holy works, because they are wrought in faith at God's commandment. To steal, rob, and murder, are no holy works before worldly people; but unto them that have their trust in God they are holy, when God commandeth them. Holy works of man's imaginations receive their reward here, as Christ testifieth, Matt. vi.

'Holy works of man's imaginations' are what Kierkegaard would call 'demoniac' activity. Stephen Greenblatt, whose *Renaissance Self-Fashioning* directed me towards Tyndale, stresses the violence with which, in the Reformation debates, each side accused the other of creating God in their imaginations. I quote from Tyndale again.

> These are they which Jude in his epistle called dreamers, which deceive themselves with their own fantasies. For what other thing is their imagination, which they call faith, than a dreaming of the faith, and an opinion of their own imagination wrought without the grace of God?[18]

Both Horatio and Hamlet understood what Tyndale meant by 'imagination'. 'He waxes desperate with imagination', says Horatio; that is, with self-created ideas of what the Ghost is. And Hamlet fears that if he can't confirm the Ghost's story, 'my imaginations are as foul / As Vulcan's stithy', that is, that he has been building his views of heaven's decrees on a mental image and not on truth.

The practical effects of Hamlet's purifying violence are disastrous. Claudius sought to protect his kingdom and did it efficiently against the attacks of both Fortinbras and Laertes. Hamlet comes in, an alienated, savage, destructive force, and Denmark passes into foreign hands. Against the tangible misery which he causes have to be set the intangible values of salvation and damnation which govern his entire conduct – values which are not only intangible but unverifiable, and may belong in the end to men's imagination.

It has been my contention that the tragic value of the play *Hamlet* has become enfeebled through two successive, antithetical waves of criticism, and that the possibility of renewing that tragic value lies not in trying to refute or wipe away mid twentieth-century criticism but in acknowledging it, absorbing it and moving on from it with reinforcement from the nineteenth-century criticism it had tried to replace. I should make it clear that so far as I am concerned the twentieth-century critic (who, of course, like Yeats's Fisherman is 'a man who does not exist') has not only refused to follow the old-fashioned custom of identifying with Hamlet, he has positively rejected him. In Nietzschean terms, the twentieth century has completely upset the equilibrium of Apollo and Dionysus by putting all the weight on the Apollonian side. The maintenance of social order takes precedence of all else, and Hamlet is a disturbing nuisance wrecking the social fabric by trying to bring back the past. 'Claudius is a good king, and the Ghost but a minor spirit.' The all-important question for me is, what *kind* of sympathy do we need to find for Hamlet in order to restore an equilibrium which I believe could have been Elizabethan, but which I think you will not easily find in nineteenth- or twentieth-century criticism?

Doubts about the Ghost, doubts about the ethics of revenge, doubts about the nastiness of Claudius, and doubts about the niceness of Hamlet, are a legacy of modern times which we need to hold fast to. But when the doubts become positive scepticism, we are as lost as we were when we supposed that the Ghost was guaranteed, that revenge was good, that Hamlet was noble and Claudius a rotter.

Shakespeare, it may be said, looked at the past not only nostalgically but sentimentally. Yet those of his heroes who try to restore or even preserve the past, and oppose the future, Richard II, Brutus, Coriolanus, have an ineffectuality and a woodenness about them which betoken a grim historical realism on Shakespeare's part. It is in *Hamlet* above all of Shakespeare's plays that I find superbly and movingly presented an openness towards both past and future in which the possibility of restoration is balanced against the futility of trying. And this is not entirely because of the unbelievable interest of the mind which contemplates the task of bringing back the majesty of beauteous Denmark. It is also because of the great transcendental hypothesis which is the framework of the play, and the context in which past and future are seen. The sense of an order of distinction among people which is ratified in heaven, the sense that there is a communication between heaven and earth, the sense that there *can* be a cleansing act of violence which is both a punishment and a liberation, these are as powerfully present in the play as is the conviction that these things do not exist. Hamlet's groping attempt to make a higher truth active in a fallen world fails hopelessly. But just suppose we can entertain the *possibility* that he was within reach of a higher truth. 'What should we do?' he asks the Ghost. And of Horatio he asks, 'Is't not to be damned to let this canker of our nature come in further evil?' Wilson Knight, in that brilliant early essay of his, recognised the alien and inhuman prophet that Hamlet essentially is. And he repudiated him. Hamlet vexed and troubled the world and failed to change it for the better. But he continues, or he ought to continue, to vex and trouble us with the suspicion, and the fear, that although he never got there, he may have been after something worth having. It is not faith we need to understand *Hamlet*, but doubt about our own scepticism. We need just enough questioning to keep alive the openness of Hamlet's question to Horatio. 'Is't not to be damned to let this canker of our nature come in further evil?' And to be able to respond also to that other remark of his:

> There are more things in heaven and earth, Horatio,
> Than are dreamt of in your philosophy.

From *Shakespeare Survey*, 36 (1983), 43–52.

NOTES

[In this opening essay Philip Edwards raises many of the issues that have dominated traditional criticism of *Hamlet*: the Ghost, the moral ambiguity of its commands, the moral status of the court, Hamlet's behaviour and actions. The thrust of Edwards's argument is that twentieth-century critic-ism, by losing sympathy for Hamlet, has also lost sight of the play's tragic impact. Hamlet's quest, Edwards argues, is not simply to kill Claudius but to restore Denmark to its past order and values. Here the ambiguity of the

Ghost is central: Hamlet cannot be sure the Ghost is a symbol of divine intervention, of divine authority to act, but neither can he be sure it is not. Edwards contends that in order to make sense of *Hamlet* as a tragedy we need to have some sympathy for Hamlet's attempt, however disastrous, to 'make a higher truth active in a fallen world', his attempt to change the world for the better, but that we also need to remain open to the questions he asks about salvation and damnation. In addition to providing a very useful review of previous traditional criticism of *Hamlet*, Edwards's essay raises a number of important ideas about tragedy and the moral and intellectual framework of the play. Ed.]

1. This article originated in a series of three public lectures delivered at the University of Otago, Dunedin, New Zealand, in 1980. In its present form, it is a slightly modified version of a lecture given at the International Shakespeare Conference at Stratford-upon-Avon in August 1982.

2. Martin Scofield discusses these views in *The Ghosts of 'Hamlet'* (Cambridge, 1980), pp. 25–6.

3. Mallarmé, *Oeuvres complètes* (Paris, 1945), pp. 300–2, 1564.

4. 'The World of *Hamlet*' (1952), reprinted in *'Hamlet': A Casebook*, ed. J. Jump (London, 1968), pp. 86–121.

5. Hermann Ulrici, *Shakespeare's Dramatic Art*, trans. L. D. Schmitz (1876), vol. 1, pp. 86–121.

6. C. S. Lewis, 'Hamlet, the Prince or the Poem?' *Proceedings of the British Academy*, 28 (1942), 139–54; 148.

7. I owe this point to Hiram Haydn, *The Counter-Renaissance* (New York, 1950), p. 626.

8. Compare A. J. A. Waldock, *'Hamlet': A Study in Critical Method* (Cambridge, 1931), p. 87: 'The feeling that vengeance (or anything) is worth while presupposes an active belief in life. Hamlet . . . has almost lost that belief.'

9. Schopenhauer, *Essays and Aphorisms*, ed. R. J. Hollingdale (Harmondsworth, 1970), pp. 77–9.

10. Given at the International Association of University Professors of English meeting at Aberdeen, August 1980. [The argument may be found in Philip Edwards's New Cambridge edition of *Hamlet* (Cambridge, 1985), pp. 15ff. Ed.]

11. Compare Rosalie Colie, *Shakespeare's Living Art* (Princeton, 1974), p. 230.

12. Unless the Ghost is a liar of course; and he doesn't lie about the murder. See I.v.42–6, 55–7. Also J. D. Wilson, *What Happens in Hamlet*, 3rd edn (Cambridge, 1951), pp. 292–4.

13. See the opening chapter of René Girard's *Violence and the Sacred* (1972; trans. Patrick Gregory, Baltimore and London, 1977), on the distinction between legitimate and illegal violence in primitive society.

14. Saul Bellow, *The Dean's December* (New York, 1982), p. 180.

15. G. K. Chesterton, *Fancies versus Fads* (London, 1923), p. 33.

16. On the 'absurdly simplified command' of the Ghost, see G. K. Hunter, 'The Heroism of Hamlet', in *'Hamlet'*, Stratford-upon-Avon Studies, 5, ed. J. R. Brown and B. Harris (London, 1963), p. 104, and John Masefield, *William Shakespeare* (London, 1911), p. 161.

17. Kierkegaard, *Fear and Trembling*, trans. W. Lowrie (New York, 1941), pp. 64, 71, 90, 95.

18. William Tyndale, *Doctrinal Treatises*, Parker Society (1848), pp. 407, 53.

2

The Comedy of 'Hamlet'

PETER DAVISON

Nowhere is the distinction greater between text and performance than in the matter of comedy. It is not simply that what makes one person laugh leaves another unmoved, but rather the difficulties of recognising as comedy what on the printed page seems uncomic; secondly, imagining the stage business that makes lines comic; and thirdly, not finding comedy where none exists. Performance can help enormously, but performance itself depends on the text or upon received tradition; for this, the passage of time hardly helps.

In the pirated edition of *Hamlet* of 1603, some lines were added to those written by Shakespeare. Most modern editions omit these but the New Penguin edition includes them, as Shakespeare's, at III.ii.43–53. Despite the New Penguin editor's argument, it is more likely that the actor who first played Hamlet, Richard Burbage, has himself done what, in the part of Hamlet, he is telling the clowns not to do: that is, he *ad libs*. As it is most unusual for a straight actor to *ad lib*, then or now, this looks very much like Burbage's riposte to his good friend Shakespeare. Because it is Burbage *ad libbing*, the audience will assume that these are lines he is supposed to say as part of his role in the play, so that only members of the company would realise the nature of the 'joke'. There is nothing a modern performance can do to revivify this moment. But one can go further.

Hamlet – or Burbage, if this conjecture is correct – tells how the gentlemen playgoers write down in their notebooks jests of comedians with a limited repertoire and then call out the punch-lines before the clown can get to them in his stories. And he gives examples of these 'jests': 'Cannot you stay till I eat my porridge?'; 'You owe me a

37

quarter's wages'; 'My coat wants a cullison', and 'Your beer is sour'. Now, by working very hard one can raise a slight laugh – a titter as Frankie Howerd would say – by the time the third or fourth of these is reached, but such laughter as transpires derives more from the performer's technique than from the lines themselves. One of these catch-phrases appears in a jest book of the time and also in a single play (*A Yorkshire Tragedy*, 1606), but even in the context of a play it would not raise a laugh today. Recognising the comic from the printed page, especially for plays of an early period or different culture, can obviously be very difficult.

Now I have glided over comedy and what rouses laughter as if they were the same, which, of course, they are not. Ben Jonson, Shakespeare's contemporary, went so far as to argue that 'the moving of laughter is a fault in comedy, a kind of turpitude, that depraves some part of a man's nature without a disease'. This may be to take things too far, but it warns usefully against assuming that comedy must automatically be funny and that what is funny is necessarily of the genre, Comedy. This is important to bear in mind when considering comedy and the use of humour in *Hamlet*.

There are other problems. Take, for instance, this little exchange:

> **Guildenstern** But we both obey,
>   And here give up ourselves in the full bent
>   To lay our service freely at your feet,
>   To be commanded.
> **King** Thanks, Rosencrantz and gentle Guildenstern.
> **Queen** Thanks, Guildenstern and gentle Rosencrantz.
>   (II.ii.29–33)

Rarely, if ever, do commentators say anything about this passage in editions of the play; its meaning, so far as the words go, is plain enough. But is it meant to raise a laugh, as it has on occasion at Stratford? How is it to be performed? Richard David, contrasting the National Theatre production of 1976 with that at the Roundhouse in the same year, remarked (referring first to the National):

> Rosencrantz and Guildenstern, constantly sweeping off their hats in an exaggerated unison to signify their compliance with Claudius's commands, become a pair of faceless automatons very different from the subtly diversified and ten times more dangerous false friends at the Roundhouse. And we were treated again to the corny old joke of making the Queen's repetition of Claudius's acknowledgment – 'Thanks, Rosencrantz and gentle Guildenstern' – with the names reversed, a correction, with the suggestion that the two were so

indistingishable that the King has mistaken one for the other. At the Roundhouse, King and Queen were in full agreement as to the identities of their guests, and Gertrude's reversal of the names was merely an elegant courtesy to ensure that each was accorded equal precedence.

Two totally different ways of interpreting these innocuous-seeming lines. (Although the Gielgud/Burton production did not strive for a laugh here, one was to be heard from the theatre audience of the filmed stage-play.) Note also the different effect of meaning in its broader, not merely verbal sense, of Rosencrantz and Guildenstern's business with their hats.

The treatment of the Ghost raises rather trickier problems. There is no doubt that the Ghost ought to thrill even a blasé, sophisticated modern audience. Often it doesn't; the key to doing so may be found in something Charles Marowitz wrote in the Introduction to his *College Hamlet*: 'What is frightening about a ghost is not its unearthliness, but its earthliness: its semblance of reality divorced from existence.' Given that this is successfully achieved (and note how the RSC's Ghost in 1965 was much larger than life-size), what is one to make of the swearing to silence sequence in I.v?

Hamlet insists that Marcellus and Horatio swear that they will not reveal what they have seen that night. He demands they swear upon his sword. It is worth noting in passing that in performance the physical nature of the sword can give force to its dual imagery. It is at once a warlike object, in its way representative of the war background to the play (the very 'source of this our watch' being Fortinbras's 'post haste and romage in the land' [I.i.106–7]), and its hilt forms a crucifix upon which they will swear and which is used to dramatic effect in this manner at other points in the play.[1] In this way the 'necessary business' of the play in performance can fruitfully bring out the essential ambiguities of the language. Thus in Hamlet's urgency with Horatio and Marcellus:

> **Hamlet** Never make known what you have seen tonight.
> **Horatio** and **Marcellus** My lord, we will not.
>   **Hamlet**   Nay, but swear't.
>   **Horatio**   In faith,
>   My lord, not I.
> **Marcellus**   Nor I, my lord – in faith.
> **Hamlet** Upon my sword.
> **Marcellus**   We have sworn, my lord, already.
> **Hamlet** Indeed, upon my sword, indeed.
>   (I.v.144–8)

There are three, possibly four, stages to this brief dialogue. First, Horatio and Marcellus promise not to reveal what they have seen (l.145); Hamlet then demands they swear to that, which they do, Marcellus repeating Horatio's 'in faith' almost as an afterthought so that the everyday 'i'faith' becomes what it originally was, an attestation of faith. This is still not enough for Hamlet: they must, in the third stage, swear upon his sword. Now if the sword is presented blade first, his demand carries with it an element of threat. Marcellus protests they have already sworn (l.147). Hamlet's reply repeats the word 'indeed' (in contrast to his companions' use of 'in faith'). How is this said? Threateningly? More significantly, what business accompanies this line? If Hamlet were, as a fourth stage in this short sequence, to reverse his sword on this line, presenting the hilt, with its religious implications foremost in sight and mind, the whole tenor of the incident would change direction.

But now there is a further change of tone. What follows has all the potentialities for *low* comedy, almost burlesque – of which Burton made the most, and to which the audience responded with loud laughter.

> *The* **Ghost** *cries under the stage*
>
> **Ghost**   Swear.
> **Hamlet**   Ha, ha, boy, sayst thou so? Art thou there, truepenny?
>   Come on. You hear this fellow in the cellarage.
>   Consent to swear.
>   . . .
> **Ghost**   (*beneath*) Swear.
> **Hamlet**   *Hic et ubique?* Then we'll shift our ground.
>   . . .
> **Ghost**   (*beneath*) Swear by his sword.
> **Hamlet**   Well said, old mole! Canst work i'th'earth so fast?
>   A worthy pioneer! Once more remove, good friends.
> **Horatio**   O day and night, but this is wondrous strange!
>   (I.v.149–52, 155–6, 161–4)

At least three characteristics of this passage require comment: the stage movement necessitated by the words and its effect; Hamlet's badinage; and the significance of certain words.

The Ghost certainly strikes apprehension in Hamlet's colleagues; e.g. Barnardo's

> How now, Horatio? You tremble and look pale.
> Is not this something more than fantasy?
>   (I.i.53–4)

To critics such as Maynard Mack, 'the ghost is the supreme reality, representative of the hidden ultimate power, in Bradley's terms – witnessing from beyond the grave against this hollow world'. To producers such as Peter Hall in 1965, the Ghost assumed super-human proportions, standing from 8 to 12 feet high depending which theatre critic one read. It was big enough to require a trolley to move it and a double so that rapid exits and entrances could be made at opposite sides of the stage. Gielgud's Ghost in 1964 was inspired by the words 'Stay, illusion' (I.i.128). The audience saw only a huge shadow of a helmeted head with shoulders, supposedly cast by a figure off-stage, and heard Gielgud's recorded voice, at first husky but gradually becoming less so. The actors addressed the figure supposedly off-stage, the shadow being behind them. However, as the shadow was actually cast by a projector also behind the actors, and as a pillar stood between the actors and the screen, part of this 'shadow' was illogically obscured at times. And, surely, ghosts do not cast shadows!

Hamlet's jocular familiarity with the Ghost – 'truepenny', 'this fellow in the cellarage', '*Hic et ubique?*' (Here and everywhere?), 'old mole', 'worthy pioneer' – contrast strangely with a figure representative of 'supreme reality' and so fearsome to Hamlet's friends. It may be that he is anxious to disguise from his colleagues just how seriously he takes the Ghost's behests, but this explanation needs to be considered in the context of the stage movements. Those movements are demanded by the language as those on-stage seek to locate the old mole who can tunnel through the earth so fast. The movements of Horatio and Marcellus may represent their fear as they seek to escape the Ghost; or it may be in response to the Ghost's demands so that they make their oaths above the position whence he intones 'Swear'. How this is realised in performance depends upon the director's understanding. The voice of the Ghost is often artificially modified to make it more sepulchral. The total effect is – or should be – a curious combination of the fearsome and the comic.

The scene can be played wholly seriously, but that is to miss an essential element. Olivier achieved this in the film by cutting out virtually the whole of this section, having his Ghost utter 'Swear' only once. Certainly the scene should not slip into burlesque. Both the comic and the fearful were achieved in the 1976 Roundhouse production, according to Richard David. Delicate control ensured that the 'farcical extravagance aggravated by the marvellous adroitness with which the "old mole" was made to move underground, never got out of hand'. Helen Gardner once brought out the relationship between the fearful and the comic by a very neat modern parallel. She pointed out that Reilly, the all-knowing psychiatrist in T. S. Eliot's *The Cocktail Party*, is also treated ambiguously. Eliot, she explains, 'has been able to exploit for comic purposes our ambivalent feelings about "mind doctors"'. We have no difficulty in seeing psychiatrists simultaneously as a power, a threat, and comically; so is the Ghost in I.v. Those conflicts of modes were as 'normal' to an Elizabethan audience as those exploited by T. S. Eliot in our day.

This tonal ambiguity matches to perfection − or rather, realises dramatically in performance − the uncertainties attendant on the Ghost for Hamlet and us. Shakespeare keeps prompting our uncertainty by his choice of words and his requirements for stage movement. It should also be noted that Hamlet is *already* acceding to one of the Ghost's demands: making Horatio and Marcellus swear secrecy. Hamlet says the Ghost is honest, but it is heard under the stage (in the cellarage) − and 'under the stage' was the location of hell in the Elizabethan theatre. The early stage directions specifically require that the Ghost cry from under the stage. 'Old mole' might be a nickname for the devil; 'pioneer' (or a sapper) was certainly used for devils who travelled through the earth. And a devil is by no stretch of imagination 'honest'. Thus do tonal and verbal uncertainties reflect the duality of the stage movement. This conflict of tones in I.v. is to be found throughout the play, for example in Hamlet's behaviour towards Ophelia at the play (III.ii.121−44, 254−61) and in his response to questions asking the whereabouts of Polonius after he has murdered him (IV.iii.16−30).

English drama since the Middle Ages has notoriously defied conventions of dramatic decorum so generally accepted on the Continent, especially those that insist upon the separation of the comic and the tragic. Thus, in certain medieval cycles of plays telling the story of Christian salvation, notably those associated with Wakefield and York, even the Crucifixion of Christ is presented in a context of rough humour. Paradoxically, in a more secular age we may find it difficult to laugh at a scene of such cruelty, but in its own day an audience would have been able to respond simultaneously to the suffering and the comedy. The function of such comedy was to draw the audience's laughter and thus to place each spectator on the side of the torturers or knights crucifying Christ. Thus those watching the spectacle, if tempted to laugh, become as guilty as those perpetrating the act. This use of comedy still flourished in Shakespeare's day. The religious cycles did not die out, as some drama histories suggest, but were stopped forcibly by Queen Elizabeth's government because of their association with 'the old faith', Roman Catholicism. By a strange coincidence, the year the first professional theatre was built in London (when Shakespeare was twelve years old) saw the imprisonment in the Tower of the authorities who had permitted such a cycle to be performed at Chester. Shakespeare and his contemporaries, and their audiences, were capable of responding simultaneously to the comic and that which aroused pain (that is, to the pathetic, from the Greek *páthos*, suffering).

In recent years, with the advent of Arden, Beckett, Orton, Osborne and Pinter, something of that capacity has been restored to us and companies such as the RSC and the National have been adept at realising this conflict of emotions in performance. Anthony Sher's Fool in the RSC 1982 *King Lear* is a notable example. What seemed to Voltaire to be vulgar and barbarous has been rediscovered for what it was originally intended to be: a dramatisation of the essential conflict of emotions and forces within us which demands of us a judgement. To oversimplify very considerably, we judge through the correctness of our responses (for example, when and what to laugh at), whether, in Lafeu's words, we are making 'trifles of terrors, ensconcing ourselves into seeming knowledge' when we should instead be submitting to 'an unknown fear'.

Hamlet uses comedy in a masterly way in direct line with that medieval tradition. This is particularly to be seen in the use of *comédie noire* (a term derived from Anouilh's plays of the 1930s and 1940s): that grotesquerie found in I.v, III.ii, IV.iii, and the scene between Hamlet and the Gravedigger in V.i. The humour of *Hamlet* is much more varied than this, however. There are at least three characters who could be classed as comics, especially were the play not a tragedy: Polonius, Osric and the First Gravedigger. Polonius is not the fool that Osric is, and some productions present him seriously or (as did Peter Hall) show his fooling as a mask to his political cunning. All, however, are focal points of comedy. Osric's play with his hat (and in some productions, that of Rosencrantz and Guildenstern: see above) would not be out of place in a modern pantomime. (It was particularly noticeable in the Gielgud/Burton modern rehearsal-dress production that Osric, exceptionally, had a showy, befeathered hat to flourish.) There is repartee (II.ii.206–9, 213–15); music-hall cross-talk comedy (V.i.120–7); riddles and conundrums (V.i.41–59, 127–34); clowning (obviously Osric and the Gravediggers, but note also Hamlet's forcing of a recorder upon Guildenstern [III.ii.353–79], and, of course, his advice to the clowns [III.ii.37–43]; irony (a

nice example being Hamlet's 'Thrift, thrift, Horatio. The funeral
baked meats/Did coldly furnish forth the marriage tables' [I.ii.180–
1]: Burton got a good laugh on 'Thrift, thrift'); bawdy (especially
and paradoxically in the scenes with Ophelia); the absurd (Polonius's
'pastorical-comical' speech [II.ii.395–40], and his conversation with
Hamlet about the shapes of clouds [III.ii.383–90]); and, inevitably,
much wordplay, two examples of which must suffice: 'A little more
than kin, and less than kind!' (I.ii.65); and 'Conception is a blessing.
But as your daughter may conceive . . .' (II.ii.184–5). Quite often the
humour is used in a way wholly appropriate to comedy. This is
particularly apparent in the Polonius, Osric and Gravedigger scenes;
but even such a line as 'A little more than kin, and less than kind' has
to be spoken as an aside: the device as typical of comedy as the
soliloquy is of tragedy. The aside prompts an intimate relationship
between character and audience; our support is actively solicited.
Thus we are prompted to see things from Hamlet's point of view and
must be alive to judging whether we always agree with that.

Just as there are many kinds of humour, so does it perform many
functions in the play. The biting satire scourges – such satire was
then much in fashion; its apparent misplacement (in the Ghost and
Ophelia scenes) may prompt unease and uncertainty in us; it
counterbalances to some extent the brooding on death; in Act V the
comedy is a means for dramatising a rejuvenated Hamlet come to
terms with obsessive thoughts of mortality, rather than – as the
famous eighteenth-century editor, Steevens, described this element in
a letter to David Garrick – a farce entitled 'The Gravediggers; with
the pleasant humours of Osric, the Danish Macaroni'. (Steevens in
his edition, 1778, also considered that Hamlet killed the King to
revenge himself, not his father.)

If Polonius, Osric and the First Gravedigger are focal points of
comedy, it is nevertheless Hamlet who is always involved in humour
of every kind. For a character whom we take to be so brooding, so
introspective, as black as the clothes he traditionally wears, this is
remarkable. It is not simply to be explained by Timothy Bright's
association of wit with melancholy.[2] Hamlet's humour is properly to
be termed wit, and that word 'wit' should be considered not solely as
a word for a kind of comedy but as retaining something of its
original Anglo-Saxon meaning: 'intelligence', from the verb, *witan*,
'to know'. Hamlet's wit is a mark of his intellectual superiority. His
very university, perhaps fortuitously, implies the same idea – Wittenberg. Hamlet's wit, his power of mind, takes expression in both his

attempt to puzzle out the meaning of life and death, and in his humour.

Getting a grasp of the humour of the play (and, for a tragedy, it is often a very funny play) is therefore especially important for any production. Humour is a determinant of Hamlet's nature and a key to the tonal quality of the play as a whole. As so many of the characters are a source, or a focus, of comedy, it is noticeable that this does not apply to Claudius and Gertrude. *Hamlet*, especially through its use of comedy, demands that an audience make judgements and ensures that it 'thinks through the skin', as it were, so uniting feeling and thought. This is one reason for the play's sustained power over centuries and across cultures. It is not possible to understand *Hamlet*, nor present it adequately on the stage, without coming to terms with the comedy. Vivian Mercier, writing of Samuel Beckett's drama, distinguished two kinds of humour: the macabre, and the grotesque. 'Oversimplifying', he said, 'these two types of humour help us to accept death and to belittle life.' That might well be applied to the use of humour in *Hamlet*.

From Peter Davison, *'Hamlet': Text and Performance* (London, 1983), pp. 24–33, 22–3.

NOTES

[This extract from Peter Davison's book on *Hamlet* focuses on the importance of thinking about plays not just as texts but as something to be performed on stage. In particular, Davison looks here at the question of comedy in *Hamlet*, using as examples both the Rosencrantz and Guildenstern scenes and the Ghost scenes. This leads Davison on to a discussion of the tragicomic nature of Renaissance drama and the various functions of comedy in the play. Like Philip Edwards in the opening essay, Davison alerts us to some of the qualities of *Hamlet* that mark it out as belonging to a culture different from our own, but also to how the advent of twentieth-century theatre has helped illuminate the mixed mode of the play. Like Edwards, Davison writes from a broadly traditional perspective, but the most distinctive quality of his approach is his stress on the differences between a play as a text and a play as theatre. All quotations in the extract are from the New Penguin edition of *Hamlet*, ed. T. J. B. Spencer (Harmondsworth, 1980). Ed.]

1. [Peter Davison later notes (p. 71) how at the beginning of IV.ii, in the 1965 RSC production, Hamlet knelt before 'the sword with which he had

just killed Polonius . . . seemingly in prayer, the hilt once again forming a crucifix'. Ed.]

2. It is easy for us to misunderstand the word 'melancholy' today. In Elizabethan times the word was related to the theory of the four humours which were thought to control human temperament. Patrick Cruttwell has likened this melancholy to the temperament of the scholar, the meditative man. Hamlet has recently been studying at Wittenberg University (attended by Luther and Marlowe's Dr Faustus) and he intended to return there. Melancholia was, however, fashionable in Shakespeare's time in a way that meditativeness is certainly not today. It could, perhaps, be but a pose. Not long before Shakespeare began writing there was published in London *A Treatise on Melancholy*, written by Timothy Bright. Although some scholars (such as Harold Jenkins) have thought 'the influence of Bright on Shakespeare's conception of Hamlet has been much exaggerated', some of Bright's description, if it does not show influence, reveals a strikingly similar view. According to Bright, in human beings melancholy 'breedeth a jealousy of doubt in that they take in deliberation, and causeth them to be the more exact and curious in pondering the very moments of things. . . . Such persons are doubtful, suspicious, and thereby long in deliberation.' The melancholic's dreams are fearful and (particularly intriguing) his house, 'except it be cheerful and lightsome, trim and neat', seems like a prison or dungeon (see II.ii.241–50). But most significant in the light of our possible misconception of the melancholic as one of a morose and bitter nature, is Bright's assertion that 'Sometime it falleth out that melancholy men are found very witty', as Hamlet assuredly is. [I am grateful to Professor Davison for suggesting the inclusion of this material from pp. 22–3. Ed.]

3

Poison, Play, and Duel

NIGEL ALEXANDER

Hamlet is a play of ideas. The problems of Hamlet exist for an audience as the result of the dramatic presentation of a number of complex intellectual and emotional questions. These moral and political problems are realised within the context of a murder story which involves three families, and an entire state, in a deeply disturbing conflict of love and hate. This discord is enacted in physical and psychological conditions which force an audience towards a definition of the terms of courage, honour, and revenge which the characters use as justification for their actions. The spectator's attention is particularly focused upon these problems through the character of Hamlet, Prince of Denmark.

In a remarkable series of speeches and soliloquies Hamlet, torn by conflicting emotions and divided against himself, asks the tormented and tormenting questions which create the special quality of the play. It is necessary, however, for the critic and the director to observe that the difficulties and doubts experienced by his protagonist are only one of the dramatic methods used by Shakespeare to draw the necessary questions of the play to the attention of his audience. There is a distinction between Hamlet's problems and the problem of *Hamlet*.

The actors who play any of the characters in *Hamlet* may bring a wide range of personal resources and experience to the interpretation of their roles. No such licence, however, can be permitted to the company which intends to present *Hamlet*. They must perform three difficult theatrical tasks supremely well. They must make the way in which the spirit of the dead King walks on to the stage strike the audience as both natural and unnatural. The Ghost must be theatrically acceptable and yet clearly outside normal experience. Their next task is to simulate their own profession and mimic the reception of a court performance as part of the dramatic action. The audience in the theatre must be made to grasp the distinction, and the relationship, between the play and inner-play; between the 'poison in jest' (II.ii.229) played by the actors and the acts of poison performed by the characters. Finally, they must produce a difficult and exciting stage fight. This stage business must be managed in such a fashion that the exchange of rapiers, and the rapid succession of deaths by poison, seem a dramatic and logical conclusion to the Ghost's original revelation of murder by poison.

The dramatist has laboured to establish this connection for his actors. The Ghost gives Hamlet an account of a single death by poison. The inner-play presents the physical act of poisoning twice, once in dumb show and once accompanied by speech. In the final duel four of the main characters die by poison. Shakespeare deploys all the resources of his exceptional sense of theatre, and all the imaginative power of his language, to assist the players in this performance of poison, play, and duel. There are many ways of playing Hamlet, but no performance of *Hamlet* can succeed if it ignores the way in which the repetition of these powerful symbolic actions is designed to dominate and determine the language and the physical behaviour of all the characters on stage. It is this design which will catch the imagination of the audience.

When the play opens Claudius has obtained the crown of Denmark by secretly poisoning the King his brother. One month after the funeral and coronation he has married Gertrude, the wife of his dead brother and the mother of Hamlet. A Ghost, in the shape of the dead King, appears on the battlements of the castle of Elsinore. It discloses the crimes of Claudius, and commands Hamlet to revenge his father's murder. In the play Hamlet's problems develop from the fact that he does not immediately obey this command by killing the King his uncle.

Hamlet is unable to explain this delay and frequently reproaches himself in bitter terms for his failure to kill the King. At a crucial stage of the action, and in the seventh and last of his soliloquies, Hamlet can say (IV.iv.43–6):

> **Hamlet**   I do not know
> Why yet I live to say 'This thing's to do',
> Sith I have cause, and will, and strength, and means,
> To do't.

It is hardly surprising that the question of Hamlet's delay has assumed such critical importance. It is so evidently a problem for Hamlet.

It is here that Hamlet's problems differ in marked fashion from the problem of the play. To accept Hamlet's self-reproaches, and look for some reason, explained or unexplained, which prevented him from killing the King is to accept an important, although generally unstated, assumption. It accepts that the most natural, or the best, solution to the problem of murder and violence in Denmark should be a swift and, if necessary, violent retaliation or revenge. Hamlet never questions the necessity and duty of avenging his father's murder. The duty of revenge, however, is presented in more than one dramatic fashion during the course of the play. The play which Shakespeare wrote does ask its audience to examine and question the assumption made so readily by so many of Hamlet's critics – the assumption that Hamlet's only proper response to the news that his father has been murdered in secret is to become a secret murderer.

The play is not a series of random scenes but an ordered and highly controlled pattern. The metaphorical and symbolic language is used to expand, define, and interpet the physical actions of the characters. Within this poetic pattern of action and language the theme of violent death followed by equally violent revenge and retaliation is repeated in different circumstances by different players. As death answers to death in the play the audience are required to examine the nature of this act of violence. The play is more than a murder story: it is an examination of the kind of response provoked by murder.

Fortinbras, Hamlet, and Laertes all know that their fathers have been killed. All, in their own fashion, revenge their deaths. The desire for vengeance is seen as part of a continuing pattern of human conduct. The way in which that desire is fulfilled or frustrated in the play forces the audience to examine this fashion of human behaviour and the effect that it has upon the lives and fortunes of all of the characters. The varied ways in which individuals meet the challenge of their common humanity are compared and contrasted. The audience are entertained because they are being asked to see, and feel, and understand a little more about the hidden springs of action which are supposed to drive the characters. In being asked to look into the mirror of a stage play and define their own attitudes and sympathies to what they see, they are being given the opportunity to recognise, and perhaps comprehend, something about their own personalities. *Hamlet* is a masterpiece because it is designed to provide intense and unusual possibilities of self-recognition.

The play's pattern of violence is not confined to sons who have lost their fathers. The death of Polonius affects Ophelia as well as Laertes. She is unable to stand the strain imposed by her father's death. Her reaction is violent but it is violence which is turned against herself. Driven insane by the shock, she drowns in circumstances which lead some of the characters to suggest that she has committed the ultimate self-violence of suicide. Her death confirms Laertes in his desire for revenge. That desire, however, makes him a willing instrument of the King. Claudius, too, is engaged in retaliation. He is anxious to counter what he feels to be a threat to his life and throne from Hamlet. He therefore engages Laertes in a plot to murder Hamlet secretly and with the help of poison. Their joint attempt to revenge themselves upon Hamlet succeeds – but it also leads to the death of the Queen and to their own destruction.

As they move passionately but unwittingly to their deaths, Laertes and Ophelia appear to exemplify in conduct the alternative courses of action considered by Hamlet in his soliloquy, 'To be, or not to be' (III.i.56). Ophelia chooses 'not to be' and finds refuge from 'the heart-ache' (III.i.62) of human existence in madness and death. Laertes chooses 'to be' and takes up arms in order to end his troubles by killing his enemy. In this desperate endeavour he meets his own death – knowing that 'I am justly kill'd with mine own treachery' (V.ii.299).

Revenge, madness, and possible self-destruction are all debated passionately in Hamlet's soliloquies. Hamlet's awareness of the possible paths before him, his intense consideration of the issues and their consequences, is only part of the dramatist's larger awareness of the problem. *Hamlet* dramatises a number of possible human responses to direct and indirect aggression. It is therefore concerned with the kind of internal psychological pressures which may destroy not only an individual or a society but the human species. The play does not solve this problem. In dramatising his characters' response and reaction to this situation Shakespeare suggests a number of uncomfortable questions which are usually overlooked by those critics who feel that the problems of Hamlet exist only to provide Shakespeare with an excuse for his dramatic illusion.

The court of Denmark is bound together by the usual ties of kinship and hierarchic social order which can be traced in human society from the 'primitive' tribe to the 'advanced' industrial corporation. The structure of this particular society is influenced by the fact that its present King obtained the crown by murdering his brother.

The play dramatises the way in which Claudius attempts to conceal this fact. Although he is legally and socially accepted as King of Denmark he could hardly count upon the support of his society if the true facts were known. In the course of the play the 'natural' bonds of the society of Denmark are broken in almost every conceivable fashion. As the characters, both men and women, respond to the intolerable pressures created by violence and treachery they become themselves violent and treacherous.

As the play proceeds it becomes clear that Hamlet's problem is not only to combat the violence and treachery with which he is surrounded but to try to control the violence within himself – even when that violence seems 'natural' or even laudable in his situation. The exercise of this control is as necessary, and as difficult, in the twentieth century as it was at the beginning of the seventeenth. It is not surprising that audiences have seen mirrored in Shakespeare's play their own most fundamental problems and ineradicable fears.

It is also not surprising that the play has provoked an enormous moral and critical debate about the nature and fitness of Hamlet's own response to his situation. Critics continue to debate whether Hamlet's conduct is 'normal', 'moral', 'weak', 'selfish', or 'aggressive' because the play forces questions of motive and human responsibility upon the attention of its audience. The play does not solve the riddle of the universe. It does compel its critic to reveal, and sometimes to question, his own concealed assumptions and attitudes to the human predicament. The continuance of this debate is a natural consequence of the play's artistic design and a tribute to Shakespeare's own analysis of the problems. Hamlet's problems are not accidental. They have been created for him by the dramatist.

The moral and psychological questions which grip the attention of the spectator can only exist upon the stage because, in the version of *Hamlet* which was played between 1599 and 1601, Shakespeare had discovered new and brilliant solutions to old intractable dramatic problems. These new solutions made the performance of *Hamlet* as important an event for the Jacobean drama as Marlowe's *Tamburlaine* had been for the Elizabethan. The director, and the critic, of the play must distinguish carefully between the problems presented by the play, which are moral and psychological, and the dramatic and technical problems which Shakespeare solved in order to be able to present his play. The moral problems of *Hamlet* exist because Shakespeare discovered a way in which they could be dramatically expressed.

As a work of dramatic art *Hamlet* is created by five major technical triumphs. These may be listed simply as Shakespeare's use of the Ghost, the device of presenting *The Murder of Gonzago* before the court, the way in which the themes of love and death, involving both Gertrude and Ophelia, are united in the graveyard scene, the way in which the final duel unites the military imagery and the imagery of poison, and, finally, the entire creation of the mind and consciousness of Hamlet. By these methods Shakespeare dramatises the past, provides dramatic conflict in the present, and prepares a satisfying, but unexpected, future resolution of that conflict.

These are not simple matters but artistic problems of great difficulty and complexity. Hamlet's soliloquies, for example, are one of the most interesting features of the play. Their recurrent themes are conscience, and a consciousness of the human condition which involves an awareness of oblivion and death. Yet Hamlet never steps forward to provide the spectators with a suitable synthesis of safe opinions on these subjects. The soliloquies conspicuously fail to solve the riddle of the universe because they contradict each other. They fail to provide any easily assimilable explanation of Hamlet's own motivation. They express, above all, an appalling awareness of frustration and failure. This uniquely observed dramatisation of Hamlet's feelings of personal inadequacy has caused many commentators to assume that anything so strongly expressed must represent the real truth about the character.

The fact that Hamlet feels inadequate does not necessarily mean that he is inadequate. One of the questions raised by the play is precisely what response is adequate in the conditions of Elsinore. Critical attention is usually concentrated upon Hamlet's divided mind and the suggestion is sometimes made that it represents some deep division or sense of personal inadequacy within the dramatist. This fails to observe that the extended presentation of Hamlet's troubled consciousness allows Shakespeare to solve one of the most difficult of his artistic problems.

One of the most helpful critical accounts of this problem is given by Henry James in the preface written for the New York edition of *The Spoils of Poynton* – although the passage quoted actually refers to *A London Life*:

> We may strike lights by opposing order to order, one sort to another sort; for in that case we get the correspondences and equivalents that make differences mean something; we get the interest and the tension of disparity where a certain parity may have been in question. Where it

may *not* have been in question, where the dramatic encounter is but the poor concussion of positives on one side with negatives on the other, we get little beyond a consideration of the differences between fishes and fowls.[1]

It is evident that one order opposes another in the conflict between Hamlet and Claudius. Hamlet describes it as a duel between 'mighty opposites' (V.ii.62). Under pressure, Claudius naturally resorts to the language of 'divine right' to defend his position as King of Denmark. The cry of 'treason' is still raised at the end of the play when Hamlet stabs the King.

This natural opposition between King and Prince is complicated by two further factors. The audience knows that Claudius obtained the crown by murdering the King of Denmark. In using the language of divine right to sanction his acts as King, Claudius is also implying the possibility of a divine retribution for the act which made him King. It is then possible to regard Hamlet as the agent of this divine retribution. It is equally possible to regard him as a man who has been betrayed by a demon in the shape of his father into an act of damnable impiety. It is clear that this encounter involves more than a poor concussion of positives with negatives.

The contrast between Hamlet and Claudius, however, is only an introduction to the play's major conflict. This takes place in Hamlet's mind. The progress of this mental battle can be traced clearly in the seven soliloquies. Their function in the pattern of the play is to make clear the exact nature of the division in Hamlet's mind. For this reason the soliloquies are not consistent. They vary according to Hamlet's contradictory moods and warring passions. They are not, therefore, a series of wholly positive statements in Hamlet's favour. They present, with an almost mathematical precision, a coherent and logical account of 'the correspondences and equivalents that make differences mean something' in Hamlet's consciousness.

This may be demonstrated briefly by a consideration of Hamlet's fifth and sixth soliloquies. Up to this point the soliloquies have been filled with Hamlet's memory of his father and with his attempt to understand the nature of his own position and role of avenger. He has questioned his own apparent inability to act. Now, on his way to his mother's closet (III.ii.378), and standing behind the figure of the praying King (III.iii.73), he presents a totally negative image. He no longer mentions conscience. His words provide a complete vocabulary and grammar of intent for an avenger of blood.

It appears to be the duty of exacting a complete and damnable revenge which prevents him from stabbing the King. Yet the seventh soliloquy (IV.iv.32) returns to a consideration of the earlier problems of conscience and consciousness. Hamlet again debates the questions of honour and action. This soliloquy might be considered to modify the hymn of hate expressed in the fifth and sixth – except that it closes with the words (IV.iv.65–6):

> **Hamlet** O, from this time forth,
> My thoughts be bloody, or be nothing worth!

The feeling of failure and frustration, which Hamlet himself recognises, is created by this rapid alternation between the language of blood revenge and the language of conscience. These contradictory attitudes can only be reconciled or explained away if the critic chooses to ignore one or more of the soliloquies. Any attempt to resolve the dilemma in this way ignores the problem which has been deliberately created by Shakespeare.

Hamlet is at one moment the Prince who holds in his hand the skull of Yorick, the King's Jester, and uses it to remind himself and the audience of man's mortality. Conscious of his own intelligence, Hamlet naturally questions his place in a universe which may appear at one and the same time to be a 'majestical roof fretted with golden fire' (II.ii.298) and 'a foul and pestilent congregation of vapours' (II.ii.301). At another moment he is a man who hates the King with such determined and implacable loathing that he becomes an avenger who hopes to reach beyond the grave and damn his enemy's soul to eternal hell fire.

These attitudes are difficult to reconcile. They may easily coexist in the same mind. If they do, and it becomes necessary to act on one view or the other, they will create a profound mental disturbance and conflict which cannot be solved by the easy application of moral formulas. It is not possible to be a courtier who is a scholar from Wittenberg and at the same time a courtier who is totally consumed by the passion of blood revenge. Hamlet is a scholar from Wittenberg who is determined to become an avenger of blood. He is consequently judged, by critics of the play, as an over-zealous scholar who proves himself an inadequate avenger, or an inadequate scholar who, neglectful of the doctrines for which the University of Wittenberg was famous throughout Europe, proves himself to be an over-zealous and damnable avenger.

The conflicting accounts of Hamlet's character are themselves evidence that his mind presents a more subtle conflict than 'the poor concussion of positives on one side with negatives on the other'. There is a sense, and I believe it to be a powerful and deeply rooted sense, in which any audience of *Hamlet* longs for the Prince to act in final and decisive fashion against the King. There is also a sense in which an audience must recoil before the entire macabre masque of vengeance – especially when vengeance becomes associated with the techniques of eternal sadism.

Faced with the experience of these contradictory emotions on the part of the protagonist and the audience, it is perhaps natural to conclude that the dilemma is insoluble and that 'the experience of Hamlet, then, culminates in a set of questions to which there are no answers'.[2] It would be a mistake, however, to imply that Shakespeare is content to solve his dramatic problem by representing Hamlet's divided mind and to leave his audience in the same confusion as his characters.

Hamlet's mind is at war with itself because he is aware that more than one single set of answers exists to the problems which face him. These problems, the necessary questions of the play, do not admit of any 'final' or 'ultimate' solution. They must, however, be solved to the extent that in order to act, men have inevitably to judge between particular beliefs and values. The other characters in the play do not hesitate to act because they are sure of their own values and beliefs. Fortinbras and Laertes act because they believe that certain actions are right or honourable. Claudius acts because, although he is aware that his conduct is neither right nor honourable, he intends to survive. Hamlet, as subject as they are to the instinctive pull of human passion, is dramatised as a man who is not only aware of problems which have escaped the notice of the other characters, but is engaged in a search for the right answers.

The dramatist is inevitably involved in moral problems. It is not his task to present his audience with instant recipes for the correct regulation of life or conduct. The kind of art which does present instant recipes is, as Bertolt Brecht and William Burroughs insist, a branch of the international narcotics traffic. The play asks its audience if they are entirely confident that they know that their own answers are right – or whether anyone can know what the right answers are. The play of *Hamlet* culminates in a series of questions to which the audience must find answers. The answers that each individual finds are an expression, a revelation, and a definition of his human personality. This play should also make the spectator wonder if the personality which he has revealed to himself is entirely adequate.

From Nigel Alexander, *Poison, Play, and Duel: A Study in Hamlet* (London, 1971), pp. 1–10.

NOTES

[This extract comes from the introductory chapter of Nigel Alexander's study of *Hamlet* which centres on the moral and psychological problems of the play. In this opening section, Alexander focuses on the play's symbolic design, in particular its symbols of poison, play and duel, and how these are used by Shakespeare to direct the audience's attention towards the central themes of revenge and conscience embodied in the struggle between Hamlet and Claudius. The play's major conflict, however, Alexander suggests, takes place in Hamlet's mind, but more especially in his soliloquies which 'vary according to Hamlet's contradictory moods and warring passions'. The function of the soliloquies, Alexander suggests, is 'to make clear the exact nature of the division in Hamlet's mind' between bloody revenge and conscience, between his awareness of man's mortality and his implacable loathing of Claudius. The soliloquies, however, Alexander continues, do not resolve the problems of the play but rather confront us with a series of choices and judgements about what is the right way to act. Such a conclusion is very much in line not only with contemporary traditional criticism but also with more recent critical thinking on *Hamlet* which similarly stresses the play's interrogative nature, how it confronts its audience with questions. All quotations in the extract are from *William Shakespeare: The Complete Works*, ed. Peter Alexander (London and Glasgow, 1951). Ed.]

1. Henry James, *The Art of the Novel: Critical Prefaces by Henry James*, ed. R. P. Blackmur (New York, 1934), p. 132.

2. Norman Rabkin, *Shakespeare and the Common Understanding* (New York, 1967), p. 9.

4

On the Value of 'Hamlet'

STEPHEN BOOTH

It is a truth universally acknowledged that *Hamlet* as we have it –
usually in a conservative conflation of the second quarto and first
folio texts – is not really *Hamlet*. The very fact that the *Hamlet* we
know is an editor-made text has furnished an illusion of firm ground
for leaping conclusions that discrepancies between the probable and
actual actions, statements, tone, and diction of *Hamlet* are accidents
of its transmission. Thus, in much the spirit of editors correcting
printer's errors, critics have proposed stage directions by which, for
example, Hamlet can overhear the plot to test Polonius' diagnosis of
Hamlet's affliction, or by which Hamlet can glimpse Polonius and
Claudius actually spying on his interview with Ophelia. Either of
these will make sense of Hamlet's improbable raging at Ophelia in
III.i. The difficulty with such presumably corrective emendation is
not only in knowing where to stop, but also in knowing whether to
start. I hope to demonstrate that almost everything else in the play
has, in its particular kind and scale, an improbability comparable to
the improbability of the discrepancy between Hamlet's real and
expected behaviour to Ophelia; for the moment, I mean only to
suggest that those of the elements of the text of *Hamlet* that are
incontrovertibly accidental may by their presence have led critics to
overestimate the distance between the *Hamlet* we have and the
prelapsarian *Hamlet* to which they long to return.

I think also that the history of criticism shows us too ready to
indulge a not wholly explicable fancy that in *Hamlet* we behold the
frustrated and inarticulate Shakespeare furiously wagging his tail in
an effort to tell us something, but, as I said before, the accidents of

our texts of *Hamlet* and the alluring analogies they father render *Hamlet* more liable to interpretive assistance than even the other plays of Shakespeare. Moreover, *Hamlet* was of course born into the culture of Western Europe, our culture, whose every thought – literary or non-literary – is shaped by the Platonic presumption that the reality of anything is other than its apparent self. In such a culture it is no wonder that critics prefer the word *meaning* (which implies effort rather than success) to *saying*, and that in turn they would rather talk about what a work *says* or *shows* (both of which suggest the hidden essence bared of the dross of physicality) than talk about what it *does*. Even stylistic critics are most comfortable and acceptable when they reveal that rhythm, syntax, diction, or (and above all) imagery are vehicles for meaning. Among people to whom 'It means a lot to me' says 'I value it', in a language where *significant* and *valuable* are synonyms, it was all but inevitable that a work with the peculiarities of *Hamlet* should have been treated as a distinguished and yearning failure.

Perhaps the value of *Hamlet* is where it is most measurable, in the degree to which it fulfils one or another of the fixable identities it suggests for itself or that are suggested for it, but I think that before we choose and argue for one of the ideal forms toward which *Hamlet* seems to be moving, and before we attribute its value to an exaggeration of the degree to which it gets there, it is reasonable to talk about what the play *does* do, and to test the suggestion that in a valued play what it does do is what we value. I propose to look at *Hamlet* for what it undeniably is: a succession of actions upon the understanding of an audience. I set my hypothetical audience to watch *Hamlet* in the text edited by Willard Farnham in *The Pelican Shakespeare* (Baltimore, 1957), a text presumably too long to have fitted into the daylight available to a two o'clock performance, but still an approximation of what Shakespeare's company played.

The action that the first scene of *Hamlet* takes upon the understanding of its audience is like the action of the whole, and most of the individual actions that make up the whole. The first scene is insistently incoherent and just as insistently coherent. It frustrates and fulfils expectations simultaneously. The challenge and response in the first lines are perfectly predictable sentry-talk, but – as has been well and often observed – the challenger is the wrong man, the relieving sentry and not the one on duty. A similarly faint intellectual uneasiness is provoked when the first personal note in the play sets up expectations that the play then ignores. Francisco says, 'For this relief much thanks. 'Tis bitter cold, / And I am sick at heart' (I.i.8–9). We want to know why he is sick at heart. Several lines later Francisco leaves the stage and is forgotten. The scene continues smoothly as if the audience had never focused on Francisco's heartsickness. Twice in the space of less than a minute the audience has an opportunity to concern itself with a trouble that vanishes from consciousness almost before it is there. The wrong sentry challenges, and the other corrects the oddity instantly. Francisco is sick at heart, but neither he nor Bernardo gives any sign that further comment might be in order. The routine of sentry-go, its special diction, and its commonplaces continue across the audience's momentary tangential journey; the audience returns as if *it* and not the play had wandered. The audience's sensation of being unexpectedly and very slightly out of step is repeated regularly in *Hamlet*.

The first thing an audience in a theatre wants to know is why it is in the theatre. Even one that, like Shakespeare's audiences for *Richard II* or *Julius Caesar* or *Hamlet*, knows the story being dramatised wants to hear out the familiar terms of the situation and the terms of the particular new dramatisation. Audiences want their bearings and expect them to be given. The first thing we see in *Hamlet* is a pair of sentries. The sight of sentries in real life is insignificant, but, when a work of art focuses on sentries, it is usually a sign that what they are guarding is going to be attacked. Thus, the first answer we have to the question 'what is this play about?' is 'military threat to a castle and a king', and that leads to our first specific question: 'what is that threat?' Horatio's first question ('What, has this thing appeared again to-night?' [I.i.21]) is to some extent an answer to the audience's question; its terms are not military, but their implications are appropriately threatening. Bernardo then begins elaborate preparations to tell Horatio what the audience must hear if it is ever to be intellectually comfortable in the play. The audience has slightly adjusted its expectations to accord with a threat that is vaguely supernatural rather than military, but the metaphor of assault in which Bernardo prepares to carry the audience further along its new path of inquiry is pertinent to the one from which it has just deviated:

> Sit down awhile,
> And let us once again assail your ears,
> That are so fortified against our story,
> What we two nights have seen.
>
> (I.i.30–3)

We are led toward increased knowledge of the new object – the ghost – in terms appropriate to the one we assumed and have just abandoned – military assault. Bernardo's metaphor is obviously pertinent to his occupation as sentinel, but in the metaphor he is not the defender but the assailant of ears fortified against his story. As the audience listens, its understanding shifts from one system of pertinence to another; but each perceptible change in the direction of our concern or the terms of our thinking is balanced by the repetition of some continuing factor in the scene; the mind of the audience is in constant but gentle flux, always shifting but never completely leaving familiar ground.

Everyone onstage sits down to hear Bernardo speak of the events of the past two nights. The audience is invited to settle its mind for a long and desired explanation. The construction of Bernardo's speech suggests that it will go on for a long time; he takes three lines (I.i.35–8) to arrive at the grammatical subject of his sentence, and then, as he begins another parenthetical delay in his long journey toward a verb, 'the bell then beating one', *Enter Ghost*. The interrupting action is not a simple interruption. The description is interrupted by a repetition of the action described. The entrance of the ghost duplicates on a larger scale the kind of mental experience we have had before. It both fulfils and frustrates our expectations: it is what we expect and desire, an action to account for our attention to sentinels; it is unexpected and unwanted, an interruption in the syntactical routine of the exposition that was on its way to fulfilling the same function. While the ghost is on the stage and during the speculation that immediately follows its departure, the futile efforts of Horatio and the sentries (who, as watchers and waiters, have resembled the audience from the start) are like those of the audience in its quest for information. Marcellus' statement about the ghost is a fair comment on the whole scene: ''Tis gone and will not answer' (I.i.52), and Horatio's 'In what particular thought to work I know not' (I.i.67) describes the mental condition evoked in an audience by this particular dramatic presentation of events as well as it does that evoked in the character by the events of the fiction.

Horatio continues from there into the first statement in the play that is responsive to an audience's requirement of an opening scene, an indication of the nature and direction of the play to follow: 'But, in the gross and scope of my opinion, / This bodes some strange eruption to our state' (I.i.68–9). That vague summary of the significance of the ghost is political, but only incidentally so because the audience, which was earlier attuned to political/military considerations, has now given its attention to the ghost. Then, with only the casual preamble of the word *state*, Marcellus asks a question irrelevant to the audience's newly primary concerns, precisely the question that no one asked when the audience first wanted to know why it was watching the sentries, the question about the fictional situation whose answer would have satisfied the audience's earlier question about its own situation: Marcellus asks 'Why this same strict and most observant watch/ So nightly toils the subject of the land' (I.i.71–2). Again what we are given is and is not pertinent to our concerns and expectations. This particular variety among the manifestations of simultaneous and equal propriety and impropriety in *Hamlet* occurs over and over again. Throughout the play, the audience gets information or sees action it once wanted only after a new interest has superseded the old. For one example, when Horatio, Bernardo, and Marcellus arrive in the second scene (I.ii.159), they come to do what they promise to do at the end of scene i, where they tell the audience that the way to information about the ghost is through young Hamlet. By the time they arrive 'where we shall find him most conveniently', the audience has a new concern – the relation of Claudius to Gertrude and of Hamlet to both. Of course interruptions of one train of thought by the introduction of another are not only common in *Hamlet* but a commonplace of literature in general. However, although the audience's frustrations and the celerity with which it transfers its concern are similar to those of audiences of, say, Dickens, there is the important difference in *Hamlet* that there are no sharp lines of demarcation. In *Hamlet* the audience does not so much shift its focus as come to find its focus shifted.

Again the first scene provides a type of the whole. When Marcellus asks why the guard is so strict, his question is rather more violent than not in its divergence from our concern for the boding of the ghost. The answer to Marcellus' question, however, quickly pertains to the subject of ours: Horatio's explanation of the political situation depends from actions of 'Our last king,/ Whose image even but now appeared to us' (I.i.80–1), and his description of the activities of young Fortinbras as 'The source of this our watch' is harnessed to our concern about the ghost by Bernardo, who says directly, if vaguely, that the political situation is pertinent to the walking of the ghost:

> I think it be no other but e'en so.
> Well may it sort that this portentous figure
> Comes armèd through our watch so like the king
> That was and is the question of these wars.
>
> (I.i.108–11)

Horatio reinforces the relevance of politics to ghosts in a long speech about supernatural events on the eve of Julius Caesar's murder. Both these speeches establishing pertinence are good examples of the sort of thing I mean: both seem impertinent digressions, sufficiently so to have been omitted from the folios.

Now for the second time, *Enter Ghost*. The re-entrance after a long and wandering digression is in itself an assertion of the continuity, constancy, and unity of the scene. Moreover, the situation into which the ghost re-enters is a careful echo of the one into which it first entered, with the difference that the promised length of the earlier exposition is fulfilled in the second. These are the lines surrounding the first entrance; the italics are mine and indicate words, sounds, and substance echoed later:

> **Horatio**   *Well, sit we down,*
> And let us hear Bernardo speak of this.
> **Bernardo**   Last night of all,
> *When yond same star* that's *westward* from the pole
> Had made his course t' illume that part of heaven
> Where now it burns, Marcellus and myself,
> The bell then beating one –
>
> *Enter Ghost.*
>
> **Marcellus**   *Peace, break thee* off. *Look where it comes again.*
>
> (I.i.33–40)

Two or three minutes later a similar situation takes shape in words that echo, and in some cases repeat, those at the earlier entrance:

> **Marcellus**   *Good now, sit down,* and tell me he that knows,
> *Why this same st*rict and most observant watch,
> So nightly toils the subject of the land . . .
>
> . . . .
>
> *Enter Ghost*
>
> *But soft, behold, lo where it comes again!*
>
> (I.i.70–2, 126)

After the ghost departs on the crowing of the cock, the conversation, already extravagant and erring before the second apparition when it ranged from Danish history into Roman, meanders into a seemingly

gratuitous preoccupation with the demonology of cocks (I.i.148–
65). Then – into a scene that has from the irregularly regular
entrance of the two sentinels been a succession of simultaneously
expected and unexpected entrances – enters 'the morn in russet
mantle clad', bringing a great change from darkness to light, from
the unknown and unnatural to the known and natural, but also
presenting itself personified as another walker, one obviously re-
levant to the situation and to the discussion of crowing cocks, and
one described in subdued but manifold echoes of the two entrances
of the ghost. Notice particularly the multitude of different kinds of
relationship in which 'yon high eastward hill' echoes 'yond same star
that's westward from the pole':

> But look, the morn in russet mantle clad
> Walks o'er the dew of yon high eastward hill.
> Break we our watch up . . . .
>
> (I.i.166–8)

The three speeches (I.i.148–73 – Horatio's on the behaviour of
ghosts at cockcrow, Marcellus' on cocks at Christmas time, and
Horatio's on the dawn) have four major elements running through
them: cocks, spirits, sunrise, and the presence or absence of speech.
All four are not present all the time, but the speeches have a sound of
interconnection and relevance to one another. This at the same time
that the substance of Marcellus' speech on Christmas is just as
urgently irrelevant to the concerns of the scene. As a gratuitous
discussion of Christianity, apparently linked to its context only by an
accident of poulterer's lore, it is particularly irrelevant to the moral
limits usual to revenge tragedy. The sequence of these last speeches is
like the whole scene and the play in being both coherent and
incoherent. Watching and comprehending the scene is an intellectual
triumph for its audience. From sentence to sentence, from event to
event, as the scene goes on it makes the mind of its audience capable
of containing materials that seem always about to fly apart. The
scene gives its audience a temporary and modest but real experience
of being a superhumanly capable mental athlete. The whole play is
like that.

During the first scene of *Hamlet* two things are threatened, one in
the play, and one by the play. Throughout the scene the characters
look at all threats as threats to the state, and specifically to the
reigning king. As the king is threatened *in* scene i, so is the audience's
understanding threatened *by* scene i. The audience wants some solid

information about what is going on in this play. Scene i is set in the dark, and it leaves the audience in the dark. The first things the play teaches us to value are the order embodied in the king and the rational sureness, purpose, and order that the play as a play lacks in its first scene. Scene ii presents both the desired orders at once and in one – the king, whose name even in scene i was not only synonymous with order but was the regular sign by which order was reasserted: the first confusion – who should challenge whom – was resolved in line 3 by 'Long live the king', and at the entrance of Horatio and Marcellus, rightness and regularity were vouched for by 'Friends to this ground. And liegemen to the Dane'. As scene ii begins it is everything the audience wanted most in scene i. Here it is daylight, everything is clear, everything is systematic. Unlike scene i, this scene is physically orderly; it begins with a royal procession, businesslike and unmistakable in its identity. Unlike the first scene, the second gives the audience all the information it could desire, and gives it neatly. The direct source of both information and orderliness is Claudius, who addresses himself one by one to the groups on the stage and to the problems of the realm, punctuating the units both with little statements of conclusion like 'For all, our thanks' and 'So much for him' (I.ii.16, 25), and with the word 'now' (I.ii.17, 26, 42, 64), by which he signals each remove to a new listener and topic. Denmark and the play are both now orderly, and are so because of the king. In its specifics, scene ii is the opposite of scene i. Moreover, where scene i presented an incoherent surface whose underlying coherence is only faintly felt, this scene is the opposite. In scene i the action taken *by* the scene – it makes its audience perceive diffusion and fusion, division and unification, difference and likeness at once – is only an incidental element in the action taken or discussed *in* the scene – the guards have trouble recognising each other; the defence preparation 'does not divide the Sunday from the week', and makes 'the night joint-labourer with the day' (I.i.76, 78). In scene ii the first subject taken up by Claudius, and the subject of first importance to Hamlet, is itself an instance of improbable unification – the unnatural natural union of Claudius and Gertrude. Where scene i brought its audience to feel coherence in incoherence by response to systems of organisation other than those of logical or narrative sequence, scene ii brings its audience to think of actions and characters alternately and sometimes nearly simultaneously in systems of value whose contradictory judgments rarely collide in the mind of an audience. From an uneasiness prompted by a sense of lack of order, unity, coherence, and continuity, we have progressed to an uneasiness prompted by a sense of their excess.

Claudius is everything the audience most valued in scene i, but he is also and at once contemptible. His first sentences are unifications in which his discretion overwhelms things whose natures are oppugnant. The simple but contorted statement, 'therefore our . . . sister . . . have we . . . taken to wife', takes Claudius more than six lines to say; it is plastered together with a succession of subordinate unnatural unions made smooth by rhythm, alliteration, assonance, and syntactical balance:

> Therefore our sometime sister, now our queen,
> Th' imperial jointress to this warlike state,
> Have we, as 'twere with a defeated joy,
> With an auspicious and a dropping eye,
> With mirth in funeral and with dirge in marriage,
> In equal scale weighing delight and dole,
> Taken to wife.
>
> (I.ii.8–14)

What he says is overly orderly. The rhythms and rhetoric by which he connects any contraries, moral or otherwise, are too smooth. Look at the complex phonetic equation that gives a sound of decorousness to the moral indecorum of 'With mirth in funeral and with dirge in marriage'. Claudius uses syntactical and rhetorical devices for equation by balance – as one would a particularly heavy and greasy cosmetic – to smooth over any inconsistencies whatsoever. Even his incidental diction is of joining: 'jointress', 'disjoint' 'Colleaguèd' (I.ii.9, 20, 21). The excessively lubricated rhetoric by which Claudius makes unnatural connections between moral contraries is as gross and sweaty as the incestuous marriage itself. The audience has double and contrary responses to Claudius, the unifier of contraries.

Scene ii presents still another kind of double understanding in double frames of reference. Claudius is the primary figure in the hierarchy depicted – he is the king; he is also the character upon whom all the other characters focus their attention; he does most of the talking. An audience focuses its attention on him. On the other hand, one of the members of the royal procession was dressed all in black – a revenger to go with the presumably vengeful ghost in scene i. Moreover, the man in black is probably also the most famous actor in England (or at least of the company). The particulars of the scene make Claudius the focal figure, the genre and the particulars of a given performance focus the audience's attention on Hamlet.

When the two focuses come together ('But now, my cousin Hamlet, and my son –') Hamlet's reply (I.ii.65) is spoken not to the king but to the audience. 'A little more than kin, and less than kind' is the first thing spoken by Hamlet and the first thing spoken aside to the audience. With that line Hamlet takes the audience for his own, and gives himself to the audience as its agent on the stage. Hamlet and the audience are from this point in the play more firmly united than any other such pair in Shakespeare, and perhaps in dramatic literature.

Claudius' 'my cousin Hamlet, and my son' is typical of his stylistic unifications of mutually exclusive contrary ideas (cousin, son). Hamlet's reply does not unify ideas, but disunifies them (more than kin, less than kind). However, the style in which Hamlet distinguishes is a caricature of Claudius' equations by rhetorical balance; here again, what interrupts the order, threatens coherence, and is strikingly at odds with its preamble is also a continuation by echo of what went before. Hamlet's parody of Claudius and his refusal to be folded into Claudius' rhetorical blanket is satisfying to an audience in need of assurance that it is not alone in its uneasiness at Claudius' rhetoric. On the other hand, the orderliness that the audience valued in scene ii is abruptly destroyed by Hamlet's reply. At the moment Hamlet speaks his first line, the audience finds itself the champion of order in Denmark and in the play, and at the same time irrevocably allied to Hamlet – the one present threat to the order of both.

From *Reinterpretations of Elizabethan Drama*, ed. Norman Rabkin (New York, 1969), pp. 137–51.

NOTES

[Stephen Booth's influential essay on *Hamlet*, from which this extract is taken, runs to some 40 pages and is, unfortunately, too long to print in full here. What Booth is interested in is the 'poetics' of *Hamlet* – that is, the play's systems of value, its patterns and effects – and this he explores by looking at the play's major features: the opening with the Ghost; the court and Claudius; and, of course, Hamlet's soliloquies. Though he does not use the term, Booth's approach might best be described as structuralist – certainly his argument, that the first scene of *Hamlet* 'provides a type of the whole' play, is characteristically structuralist in its searching out of a structural pattern. So, too, is his emphasis upon what happens to the audience of *Hamlet* as it finds its focus constantly being changed, and his stress upon how Hamlet's soliloquies are ordered and reasonable and, at the same time, illogical and contradictory. In this opening part of the essay Booth is particularly concerned with discussing how the first scenes of the play work upon the audience and skilfully combines close analysis of the text with a sense of the play as drama. All quotations in the essay are from *The Pelican Shakespeare*, ed. Willard Farnham (Baltimore, 1957). Ed.]

5

Verbal Presence: Conceptual Absence

JAMES L. CALDERWOOD

In a classic article on *Hamlet* some years back Maynard Mack first called attention to the fact that Hamlet's world 'is preeminently in the interrogative mood. It reverberates with questions, anguished, meditative, alarmed'.[1] Many of these are questions of fact or identity – 'Who's there? . . . Have you had quiet guard?' (I.i.1, 10). Some are questions of value: 'And yet, to me, what is this quintessence of dust?' (II.ii.320). And some focus upon meaning, or more often upon the absence of it:

> What may this mean . . .?
> (I.iv.51)
> What means your lordship?
> (III.i.107)
> Will they tell us what this show meant?
> (III.ii.141)
> Alas, sweet lady, what imports this song?
> (IV.v.27)
> What should this mean? . . .
> Or is it some abuse, or no such thing?
> (IV.vii.48–9)

The voices asking within the play for meanings seem to speak for the play itself, calling for interpretation. Very few critics have been able to resist that call; and of those who have hearkened to it fewer still have escaped the feeling expressed by Laertes in reply to

68

Claudius' query about the meaning of Hamlet's letter: 'I'm lost in it, my lord' (IV.vii.55).

As a maker of mazes in which we all lose ourselves Shakespeare exhibits a truly Daedalean cunning. However, if he does not always let us out of his mazes, at least he often advertises where the entrances are and graciously asks us in. His curious thriftiness with names, for instance – his unwillingness to spend more than the name of 'Hamlet' on the old king, the young prince, and the play itself – seems to address us with sly innocence, asking 'What might this mean, my lords?' Unable to resist so gentle an invitation, in Part I, I set off into the labyrinths of the play, working blithely down corridors of names toward the distant sound of shuffling hoofs.

I offered in Part I a fairly positive, determinate, 'centred' interpretation of the play. In Part II, I want to suggest some of the ways in which the play resists positive interpretation, especially by its employment of the negative mode. Perhaps the most enticing entrance to this winding matter appears near the end of the Closet Scene when Gertrude, having been fairly thrust through by the verbal daggers of her son, asks Hamlet 'What shall I do?' and is told:

> Not this, by no means, that I bid you do:
> Let the bloat king tempt you again to bed,
> Pinch wanton on your cheek, call you his mouse,
> And let him, for a pair of reechy kisses
> Or paddling in your neck with his damned fingers,
> Make you to ravel all this matter out,
> That I essentially am not in madness
> But mad in craft.
>
> (III.iv.188–95)

Why, we can hardly help wondering, such paradoxical advice? Why the conspicuous double negative and the loathsome imagery when Hamlet might simply have said 'Tell the King I am truly mad'? To be sure, Gertrude's moral retardation calls for extreme remedies, as the entire Closet Scene has demonstrated, and it may be that the very oddness of Hamlet's advice helps it take root, since in the following scene when the King asks 'How does Hamlet?' Gertrude affirms that he is 'Mad as the seas and wind, when both contend/ Which is the mightier' (IV.i.7–8). Unfortunately, it is not clear whether Gertrude is deliberately deceiving the King here, as Hamlet asked, or simply reverting to her complacent assumption throughout the Closet Scene that 'not [her] trespass, but [Hamlet's] madness [was speaking]' (III.iv.146).

But perhaps Hamlet is not so much instructing Gertrude in that speech as engaging in a type of word-magic. Seeking to control an uncertain future as well as an unreliable mother, he forecasts a repugnant scene of betrayal and, by enclosing it within the frame of the double negative, erases it. If this is Hamlet's intent, his task would be made easier were he a devotee not of drama but of a non-verbal art like sculpture. Then he could fashion replicas of Gertrude and Claudius in bed and, like a primitive with effigies of his enemy, destroy them. Or, to come at the matter more directly, which of course is not Hamlet's style, he might simply wait for a moment when effigies and words are both unnecessary, as he contemplated doing in the Prayer Scene:

> When he is drunk asleep, or in his rage,
> Or in the incestuous pleasure of his bed,
> At game a-swearing, or about some act
> That has no relish of salvation in it—
> Then trip him ...
> (III.iii.89–93)

Claudius and Gertrude in bed are hardly the same as effigies of Claudius and Gertrude in bed, but both are alike at least in their destructibility. As part of non-verbal reality, both are positive presences that can be, not negated, but eliminated. Commenting on Bergson's 'The Idea of Nothing' in *Creative Evolution*, Kenneth Burke says:

> Bergson points out that there are no 'negative' conditions in nature. Every situation is positively what it is. For instance, we may *say* 'The ground is *not* damp'. But the corresponding actual conditions in nature are those whereby the ground is dry. We may say that something 'is not' in such and such a place. But so far as nature is concerned, whatever 'is not' here is positively somewhere else: or, if it does not exist, then other things actually occupy all places where it 'is not'.[2]

Things in nature and replicas of them in the visual arts are condemned either 'to be or not to be'. So too with things a bit out-of-nature, like the Ghost. Gertrude exemplifies Burke's final statement perfectly when Hamlet, staring at the Ghost, cries to her 'Do you see nothing there?' and she says 'Nothing at all, yet all that is I see' (III.iv.131–2). If the Ghost is not there for Gertrude, then other things occupy the space where it 'is not'. Lacking the duplicity of the negative, kings, queens, effigies, even ghosts cannot both be *and* not be the same time. That is a delicate skill possessed only by words.

Negation, that is, introduces a paradox into language: the verbal presence of conceptual absence. Such a paradox probably goes unnoticed in a sentence like Hamlet's 'It is not nor it cannot come to good' (I.ii.158), because 'It' in the first clause and the 'coming to goodness' of 'it' in the second clause have an imageless pallor to begin with, even before the bleach of the three negatives is added. But in constructions where the negated term is more vivid, the negative itself may fade into abstractness. 'If you would form an idea of nothing', Burke observes, 'you require an image – and, as Bergson points out, an image must be of something'.[3] Even in a simple negative like 'The castle does not exist' the logical explosiveness of 'not', which should blow the pretentious castle out of existence, is itself nullified in some degree by the fact that the castle is at least vaguely imaginable and the 'not' is not.

But the paradox of negation is at its most duplicitous in Hamlet's advice to his mother. Here the double negative functions as a conceptual eraser of all that follows it. This suggests how tenuous and vulnerable language is in the presence of the negative. Any sentence, of whatever mass and charge its rhetorical forces, can be ambushed and slain by a single 'not'. On the other hand, language cannot survive without the negative, which is, Burke argues, 'the essential distinction between the verbal and the non-verbal',[4] and which ensures that names are not things, as Plato said, and that signifiers are not signifieds, as Saussure said.[5] However, if language cannot survive without the negative, words can. Hamlet's repugnant images not only resist erasure but take on a verbal presence so graphic and memorable as almost to erase the double negative itself. We may register the logic of Hamlet's 'Not this, by no means' and discount the existence of what he then describes, but we can by no means vitiate the life of his utterance or annul our imaginative experience of it. Inspirited by poetic imagery, Hamlet's words about the 'bloat king' are more durable than the king himself. You can, after all, kill kings. Even Hamlet in his own good time can kill a king. You can also kill speech: kill the king and his speech dies with him. What you cannot do, it seems, is kill words, for your only weapon is other words. Killing words with words is like observing electrons through an electron microscope. In their quantum shyness the electrons will not reveal themselves fully (position and velocity at once) even to their own subatomic kind, nor will words yield outright to other words. The result is a linguistic version of Heisenberg's Uncertainty Principle.

Negation, then, could be regarded as a suicidal impulse within a language that, like the Everlasting, has fixed his canon 'gainst self-slaughter. The negative cannot destroy without at the same time creating something to destroy. In doing so, it gives life to what it kills.

Let me return to Hamlet's advice to Gertrude a bit further on. Thinking of negation as a logocidal impulse should sidetrack us for the moment to Hamlet's 'To be or not to be' speech, where his own impulse to suicide encounters the negative.

> Who would fardels bear,
> To grunt and sweat under a weary life.
> But what the dread of *something after death*.
> The *undiscovered country* from whose bourn
> No traveller returns, puzzles the will
> And makes us rather bear those ills we have
> Than fly to others *that we know not of?*
> (III.i.77–83)

Life, whose repellence makes suicide inviting, encounters Not Life, that which 'we know not of', which repels Hamlet even more forcibly. It is not the presence of death that Hamlet fears. He is truer to the nature of the negative in this respect that Claudio in *Measure for Measure*, who in his famous speech to Isabella first says 'Ay, but to die, and go we know not where' and then graphically shows that he *does* know where:

> To lie in cold obstruction and to rot;
> This sensible warm motion to become
> A kneaded clod, and the delighted spirit
> To bathe in fiery floods, or to reside
> In thrilling region of thick-ribbed ice;
> To be imprisoned in the viewless winds,
> And blown with restless violence round about
> The pendent world: or to be—worse than worst—
> Of those that lawless and incertain thought
> Imagine howling—'tis too horrible!
> (III.i.118–28)

Claudio's imagination is well stocked with images of death. Hamlet's, on the other hand, is prodigal toward life:

> the whips and scorns of time.
> The oppressor's wrong, the proud man's contumely,
> The pangs of despised love, the law's delay,

> The insolence of office, and the spurns
> That patient merit of the unworthy takes ...
> (III.i.71–5)

As in Hamlet's advice to Gertrude, the world of Not-Being, which would destroy the world of Being through the act of suicide, gives it instead a verbal life rank with repugnant images.

Claudio is repelled by vivid images of what death *is*. For him death is not negative but a positive presence, a region of strange and horrible experiences into which the spirits of the dead are cast. Hamlet, on the other hand, is repelled by images of what life is. If he gives death a kind of presence as a 'country', it is nevertheless an 'undiscovered country', a 'something' so undefinable as to be a nothing. What he fears is not so much death as life-in-death:

> Perchance to dream! Ay, there's the rub:
> For in that sleep of death what dreams may come.
> When we have shuffled off this mortal coil,
> Must give us pause. There's the respect
> That makes calamity of so long life.
> (III.i.66–70)

Hamlet is not afraid that death will erase life but that it will not do so sufficiently – that death's nightmares will be simply an intensification of life's bad dreams. Life, though lost, may be found again in death, even as in his speech the imagery of life retains its vigour beside the negative debility of 'that we know not of'. There's the respect that makes calamity, and words about calamity, of so long life. For however specious it may be for the philosopher to reify the negative – and the risks he takes in regarding *le néant* in this fashion are exemplified by the fate of Polyphemus at the hands of 'Nobody' – for the poet, 'Not To Be' inevitably entails 'To Be'.

To return to our textual crux: what, then, is Hamlet doing in his speech of advice to Gertrude? Many things, no doubt – some of them contradictory, some of them hard to distinguish from what Shakespeare is doing by means of Hamlet's speech. After all, the negative principle 'Not This', which in poetic employ becomes 'Not This But Nevertheless This', would appear to license contradictions, ambiguities, multiplications of meaning. One could argue that Hamlet is indulging a voyeuristic Oedipal imagination within the self-exonerating safety zone of the double negative. Or that he is sublimating in repugnant but at least non-murderous language the matricidal impulses that were frustrated earlier in the scene by the arrival of the

Ghost. Or that he is trying through magical force of speech to control the future. Or, to the contrary, that he is negating his own negations. His repellent images, that is, may be intended, not only to make Gertrude recoil into goodness, but also to express his own futility in a world so replete with evil that goodness itself withdraws into the unexpressive vacancy of 'Not this, by no means'.

Pursuing this latter line, we might regard Hamlet's speech as a reaction (by Hamlet, Shakespeare, or both) to Gertrude's earlier negation of the Ghost's presence ('Nothing at all, yet all that is I see'). Hamlet had defined the Ghost as a 'gracious figure' possessed of 'piteous action' calling for mercy and kindness to Gertrude (III.iv.104, 128). Gertrude's denial of the Ghost might then represent a negation of the visible presence of good. Her blindness seems to accord with the traditional Christian view of evil expressed by Thomas Aquinas: 'Evil is the deprivation of good, and a privation is not a nature or real essence, it is a negation in a subject.'[6] (Throughout the play, of course, Gertrude is unable to 'see the Ghost' – to grasp the moral implications of her conduct, to perceive good as distinct from evil – any more than she has been able to 'see' her two husbands – 'Look here, upon this picture, and on this' [III.iv.54].) Thus Hamlet's advice to Gertrude bitterly demonstrates the inversion of moral hierarchy in Claudian Denmark. In a world degraded by regicide and incest, good can be no more than the pale negation of a thriving evil. Hamlet's speech exhibits a despairing consciousness of ineradicable corruption.

Perhaps at some level of awareness Hamlet realises that he is himself part of that corruption, even as in the speech itself he, the naysayer, is damned by what he denies. That is, if the poetic negative endows absence with presence, bringing 'Not This' before us in the act of expressing it, then the naysayer must accept the guilt of his bringings-hither no less than the virtue of his forbiddings. 'Nay, I had not known sin', Saint Paul said, 'but by the law: for I had not known lust, except the law had said, "Thou shalt not covet."'[7] If the fate of the naysaying lawgiver is to forbid crimes into existence, that of the moralist executioner is to become guilty not merely of saying evil to deny it but of doing evil to destroy it. Hamlet is well aware that this paradox has spun a web for his own revengeful actions. Pointing to the dead Polonius, he acknowledges that –

> heaven hath pleased it so,
> To punish me with this, and this with me.
> That I must be their scourge and minister.
> (III.iv.180–2)

The minister punishes sin without sacrificing his own virtue, but the scourge suffers the fate of the dyer's hand, which is subdued to what it works in – and Hamlet's hand is at work in the dark dyes of revenge and a leprous distilment that bathes the world of the court. In various ways he has sought sanctuary from the corruption about him, and increasingly within him, but by this time he has come to know the futility of that. Thrusting blindly through the arras, he has plunged himself most fatally into the contaminating milieu of action. And action, unfortunately, like things in nature, cannot be negated – it simply is.[8] Hamlet can renege on his word, as Polonius warns Ophelia ('Do not believe his vows; for they are brokers' [I.iii.128]), but he cannot withdraw his swordthrust without discovering the blood of Polonius on his blade and the future madness and death of Ophelia on his conscience. From this perspective, Hamlet's advice to Gertrude illustrates the play-long process by which he comes to participate in the evil he seeks to purge.

Finally, perhaps most importantly, we can regard Hamlet's speech as symptomatic of the evaporation of differences and the consequent blurring of individual identities brought on by the acts of Claudius. If poetic negation is positive, then Not This exists on an equal footing with This. The absent is present, the denied affirmed, the forbidden consummated in the verbal act of negation itself. If the most radical demarcation of all, that between Being and Not-Being, is erased, how shall lesser distinctions stand? The discreteness of things cannot be guaranteed. Identities dissolve in a sea of undifferentiation, and the Uncertainty Principle is enthroned.

So it is in Denmark at the opening of the play as we discover Horatio and the guards groping about in darkness in search of identities: 'Who's there? . . . Stand, and unfold yourself . . . Bernardo? . . . Who's there? . . . What, is Horatio there?' Then as they await – not a Ghost, but something quite indefinable, 'this thing' (l. 21) – Bernardo speaks of how

> Last night of all
> When yond same star that's westward from the pole
> Had made his course to illume that part of heaven
> Where now it burns, Marcellus and myself,
> The bell then beating one . . .
>
> (I.i.35–9)

And the Ghost enters, providing a visual predicate for Bernardo's uncompleted sentence and thereby creating a temporal indistinction between 'last night' and this night. The Ghost itself, passing back and forth between otherworld and this-world, breaks down the borders between life and death and between fantasy and reason. Bernardo's casual 'I have seen nothing' (l.22) is literalised by negative personification into 'I have seen Nothing', as what Horatio first calls mere 'fantasy' becomes 'something more than fantasy' (ll.23, 54). Then, in the interim between the two appearances of the Ghost, when Horatio speaks of the impending invasion by Fortinbras, the temporal merger of 'last night' with this night in Bernardo's aborted sentence is reiterated as the incessant work of mobilisation 'does not divide the Sunday from the week' (l.76) and 'doth make the night joint-labourer with the day' (l.78). The time is not merely out of joint, as Hamlet later complains, but appears to have no joint at all.

There is some suggestion here of a reversion to chaos, that vast sickening of enterprise so famously attributed by Ulysses to the 'neglection of degree' (*Troilus*, I.iii,127).[9] Indeed, the confusion of Sunday and the rest of the week, of day and night, of otherworld and this-world, and of life and death suggests an undoing of the creative divisions that God laboured over in Genesis as He gave form to the formless. God, surveying His work, beheld that 'it was very good', but Hamlet, surveying Denmark, concludes that 'It is not nor it cannot come to good' (I.ii.158). God created Eden as Adam's world, but for Hamlet the world is 'an unweeded garden/ That grows to seed' (I.ii.135–6). And God established marriage, wherein a man 'shall cleave unto his wife: and they shall be one flesh' (Genesis 2:24); but Hamlet declaims to Ophelia, 'I say we will have no more marriage' (III.i.149–50), and ridicules Claudius as 'My mother', for as he explains, 'Father and mother is man and wife', man and wife is one flesh, and so, my mother' (IV.iii.55–6).

In these remarks Hamlet seems possessed of the Uncreating Word. But the discreations in Denmark are owing not to Hamlet but to Claudius, who in rising against his brother and sovereign, and overstepping the bounds between brother and sister-in-law, violates the medieval-renaissance concept of 'Degree' by which men situate themselves within society and nature. The differences of Degree as they are ramified throughout life ensure the identities of men and things. Without them, as Ulysses says, 'Each thing meets/ In mere oppugnancy' (*Troilus*, I.iii.110–11). So it is with words too, especially in the unctuous first speech of Claudius:

> Therefore our sometime sister, now our queen,
> The imperial jointress to this warlike state,

Have we, as 'twere with a defeated joy—
With an auspicious and a dropping eye,
With mirth in funeral and with dirge in marriage,
In equal scale weighing delight and dole—
Taken to wife.

(I.ii.8–14)

A funeral marked by mirth, it goes without saying, is not a funeral, nor is a marriage accompanied by dirge a marriage. In deference, if not to true feeling, at least to decorum, which distinguishes between occasions and styles, a deferment of the 'o'erhasty marriage' might have preserved a trace of order and ceremony in what becomes instead a grotesque hybrid, a funeral-marriage.

The running together of funeral and marriage signals a breakdown of the borders between other entities. Hamlet the grieving son of the dead king discovers that he is not merely 'cousin Hamlet' to the new king but 'my son' as well, which is rather more kinship than he cares for: 'A little more than kin, and less than kind' (I.ii.65). Claudius is now his 'uncle-father' and Gertrude his 'aunt-mother' (II.ii.376), a hyphenisation of relations that leads to the total undifferentiation of Hamlet's reference to Claudius as 'My mother' (IV.iii.55). This destruction and merger of identities leaves Hamlet longing in his first soliloquy for a corresponding dissolution of self, for a deliquescence of his corporeal being in a union with nothingness: 'O, that this too too sullied flesh would melt,/ Thaw, and resolve itself into a dew' (I.ii.129–30). All such repellent, hyphenised 'unions' flow poisonously into the cup from which Gertrude drinks in the final scene and which Hamlet forces upon the already dying Claudius with the words, 'Drink off this potion. Is thy union here?' (V.ii.328). Hamlet's killing of Claudius is, in this context, an act of restorative destruction, an undoing of unions that came into existence not through the linking of like to like but through the disintegration of proper differences.

From James L. Calderwood, *To Be and Not To Be: Negation and Metadrama in 'Hamlet'* (New York, 1983), pp. 53–63.

NOTES

[In his reading of *Hamlet* James Calderwood draws upon two ideas from structuralist and deconstructionist criticism. First, structuralism argues that in the end all texts are about the problems of writing, that they are self-reflexive. In the case of plays this self-reflexive quality of texts also has to do with the way a play like *Hamlet* is 'metadramatic', with the way, that is, the play not only draws attention to the idea of acting but how the action itself seems to be about drama. Think, for example, of the play-within-the-play and how it focuses on different styles of acting, on the role of the audience, on playwriting and double plots. But, secondly, deconstruction also argues that there is no final, fixed meaning in a text, that every positive idea is, as it were, shadowed by a negative one.

It is this second idea that Calderwood takes up in the extract printed above, exploring the way in which Hamlet's language is characterised by negation and how the play resists the sort of 'positive' interpretation that Calderwood himself advances in the first part of his book, where he argues that Hamlet can only act once he achieves an identity separate from that of his father whose name he shares. Calderwood goes on to relate the negative quality in Hamlet's language to Claudius's poisoning of Old Hamlet, an act that violates 'Degree' in Denmark and blurs identities. In this context, Calderwood suggests, Hamlet's killing of Claudius restores proper differences to Denmark as well as to the Word. Like most poststructuralist criticism, Calderwood's analysis resists easy paraphrase, partly because it is concerned with the paradoxical nature of language, partly because it is so self-consciously paradoxical in its approach. Again, in common with much poststructuralist criticism, Calderwood's writing occasionally remains bafflingly obscure even after several readings. And yet, despite such difficulties, *To Be and Not To Be* is worth reading and wrestling with both for the many insights it offers into *Hamlet* as well as for the flashes of light it throws on to curious areas of the play that we might be tempted to ignore because of their oddness. All quotations in the extract are from *The Complete Works of Shakespeare*, ed. David Bevington, 3rd edn (Glenview, 1980). Ed.]

1. Maynard Mack, 'The World of *Hamlet*', *The Yale Review*, 41 (1952), 504.

2. Kenneth Burke, *Language as Symbolic Action* (Berkeley and Los Angeles, 1968), p. 419. Bergson and Burke were partly anticipated by Plato in his response to the Sophists. The Sophists argued that if we speak of that which is not we speak of nothing – which is true enough when we say, for instance, 'The furry lizard does not exist' – and then claimed that they themselves could not be convicted of falsehood or error because these involve saying the thing that is not, and what is not is nothing. Plato, on the other hand, held that Not-Being has Being, on the grounds that if we say that A is not B we are not saying that A is nothing but merely that it is something other than B. The difference depends on whether we take the verb 'is' as an existence-claim or merely as a functional copula. See Plato's *Sophist*, especially 257b–258e, in *The Collected Dialogues of Plato*, ed. Edith Hamilton and Huntington Cairns (Princeton, 1961).

3. Kenneth Burke (see note 2 above) p. 430. Joseph Vendryès makes the same point a few years after Bergson: 'To make the reader feel the

contrary of a given impression, it is not enough to bracket the words which convey it with a negative. For that is not the way to suppress the impression one wishes to avoid: one evokes the image, while thinking he is banishing it.' That is, as Maurice Merleau-Ponty sums up, 'There are denials that affirm'. See Vendrès, *Le Langage* (Paris, 1923), pp. 159–60; cited by Merleau-Ponty in *The Prose of the World*, ed. Claude Lefort, trans. John O'Neill (Evanston, 1973), p. 30. In stressing the positive aspects of negation, these writers invert the position of Ferdinand de Saussure, who stresses the negative, differential aspect of apparent positive values in language: 'there are only differences, with no positive terms' (*Course in General Linguistics*, trans. Wade Baskin [New York, 1966], p. 120).

4. Kenneth Burke, *Language as Symbolic Action* (Berkeley and Los Angeles, 1968), p. 420.

5. Plato, *Cratylus*, in *The Collected Dialogues of Plato*, ed. Edith Hamilton and Huntington Cairns (Princeton, 1961); Ferdinand de Saussure, *Course in General Linguistics*, trans. Wade Baskin (New York, 1966).

6. *Saint Thomas Aquinas: Philosophical Texts*, trans. Thomas Gilby (New York, 1960), p. 168, from III *Contra Gentes*, 7. See also Sigurd Burckhardt, *Shakespearean Meanings* (Princeton, 1968), p. 271.

7. Romans 7:7. Also Montaigne quotes Ovid, 'She who does not, because forbidden, really does' (*The Complete Works of Montaigne*, trans. Donald M. Frame [Stanford, 1948], p. 478); and I recall having read, though I cannot find where, that at an early point in Greek or Roman history the incidence of patricide rose sharply after the promulgation of a law against it. More authoritative yet, somewhere in the works of Groucho Marx is the statement, 'I was a teetotaller until Prohibition'.

8. Like picturable things, actions have no negatives. Just as we do not have words like 'un-dog' or 'non-book' (though we have 'nonentity' for an unpicturable abstraction), so we do not have words like 'un-reading' or 'non-walking', presumably because if we are *not* engaged in these actions we *are* engaged in others. As Plato argued, if the dog is not black, it is white or brown or whatever: it is not nothing. The negative form of an action is what we take to be its opposite – 'going' vs. 'coming', 'moving' vs. 'standing', 'working' vs. 'playing', etc. – all of which are positive terms.

9. See René Girard, *Violence and the Sacred*, trans. Patrick Gregory (Baltimore and London, 1977): originally *La Violence et le sacre* (Paris, 1972), pp. 49–51.

6

A Heart Cleft in Twain: The Dilemma of Shakespeare's Gertrude

REBECCA SMITH

Gertrude, in Shakespeare's *Hamlet*, has traditionally been played as a sensual, deceitful woman. Indeed, in a play in which the characters' words, speeches, acts, and motives have been examined and explained in myriad ways, the depiction of Gertrude has been remarkably consistent, as a woman in whom 'compulsive ardure . . . actively doth burn,/ And reason panders will' (III.iv.86–8).[1] Gertrude prompts violent physical and emotional reactions from the men in the play, and most stage and film directors – like Olivier, Kozintsev, and Richardson – have simply taken the men's words and created a Gertrude based on their reactions. But the traditional depiction of Gertrude is a false one, because what *her* words and actions actually create is a soft, obedient, dependent, unimaginative woman who is caught miserably at the centre of a desperate struggle between two 'mighty opposites', her 'heart cleft in twain' (III.iv.156) by divided loyalties to husband and son. She loves both Claudius and Hamlet, and their conflict leaves her bewildered and unhappy.

Three famous film versions of *Hamlet* illustrate the standard presentation, wherein Gertrude is a vain, self-satisfied woman of strong physical and sexual appetites. Thus, Grigori Kozintsev (1964) shows her gazing into a hand mirror and arranging her hair as she chastens Hamlet for the particularity of his grief in the face of the commonness of death. Tony Richardson (1969) repeatedly shows her eating and drinking. Jack Jorgens's description in *Shakespeare on Film* is vividly accurate: 'Richardson's film shows the bed as a "nasty sty" where overweight Claudius and pallid Gertrude drink blood-red wine and feast with their dogs on greasy chicken and fruit.'[2] Gertrude sustains herself throughout the play with frequent goblets of greedily swilled wine.

In the same way, in the Olivier *Hamlet* (1948), the dramatic symbol for Gertrude is a luxurious canopied bed. This bed is one of the first and last images on the screen and emphasises both Gertrude's centrality in the play and Olivier's interpretation of the centrality of sexual appetite in Gertrude's nature. Even her relationship with her son is tinged with sexuality. Olivier's Hamlet brutally hurls Gertrude – the ultimate sexual object – onto her bed, alternating embraces and abuse in the accusatory closet scene. In Richardson's and Kozintsev's film versions, the sexual passion between Claudius and Gertrude receives similarly emphatic treatment. For example, Richardson has Claudius and Gertrude conduct much royal business from their bed; and in one particularly obvious scene, Kozintsev's Gertrude is led by Claudius through the midst of people scantily costumed as satyrs and nymphs and dancing in frenzied celebration. She is then literally pushed into a darkened room, whereupon Claudius moves toward her (and the camera) with a lustfully single-minded expression on his face. The misrepresentations that these film versions of Gertrude perpetuate take their cues from respected critical interpretations of Gertrude,[3] which seem to assume that only a deceitful, highly sexual woman could arouse such strong responses and violent reactions in men, not a nurturant and loving one, as is Shakespeare's Gertrude.

Gertrude, like Hamlet, is a character who undergoes subtle but significant changes between Shakespeare's sources and his play, changes which increase her complexity and ambiguity. In the earliest Amleth/Hamlet stories, Gertrude clearly is culpable. In Saxo Grammaticus's twelfth-century *Historiae Danicae*, Gerutha/Gertrude marries Feng/Claudius, who is the known murderer of her husband. François de Belleforest, in his sixteenth-century retelling of the story in the *Histoires Tragiques*, makes one important addition to the depiction of Gertrude: he states that the Queen committed adultery with her brother-in-law during her marriage to the King.[4] Finally, in the *Ur-Hamlet*, significant actions by Gertrude reinforce the suspicion of her culpability: 'After the death of Corambis (Polonius) she blames herself for Hamlet's madness, and believes that she is thereby punished for her incestuous re-marriage, or else that her marriage, by depriving Hamlet of the crown, has driven him mad from thwarted ambition. Hamlet upbraids her for her crocodile tears, and urges her to assist in his revenge, so that in the King's death her infamy should die.'[5] In this earlier version, Gertrude promises to 'conceale, consent, and doe my best/What stratagem soe're thou shalt deuise', and she sends Hamlet warnings by Horatio, thus taking direct steps to aid Hamlet's revenge and thereby rid herself of guilt.[6]

As Kenneth Muir points out, Shakespeare's play apparently follows the main lines of the Ur-Hamlet (with its secret murder, doubtful ghost, feigned and real madness, play-within-a-play, closet scene, killing of the Polonius/Corambis figure, voyage to England, suicide of Ophelia, and fending match with Laertes – Shakespeare's additions including only the pirates, Fortinbras, and possibly the gravediggers).[7] The changes that Shakespeare does make in the structure and characters of the play demand attention as significant indicators of a redirection that adds subtlety and thematic complexity: melodrama is replaced by tragedy. In Shakespeare's Hamlet, many questions about Gertrude arise that cannot be fully answered: the murder of old Hamlet is not public knowledge, but does Gertrude know, or at least suspect? Is she guilty of past adultery as well as current incest? Does the closet scene demonstrate her acknowledgement of sexual guilt, and does she thereafter align herself with Hamlet in his quest for revenge and thus shun Claudius's touch and bed? Indeed, does Gertrude demonstrate change and development in the course of the play, or is she incapable of change?

Finding answers to these questions about Gertrude is complicated by the fact that in Hamlet one hears a great deal of discussion of Gertrude's personality and actions by other characters. She is a stimulus for and object of violent emotional reactions in the ghost, Hamlet, and Claudius, all of whom offer extreme descriptions of her. The ghost expresses simultaneous outrage, disgust, and protectiveness in his first appearance to Hamlet: 'Let not the royal bed of Denmark be / A couch for luxury and damned incest. / But howsomever thou pursues this act, / Taint not thy mind, nor let thy soul contrive / Against thy mother aught' (I.v.82–6). The ghost first asks Hamlet for revenge, describes his present purgatorial state, spends ten lines sketchily outlining the secret murder, and then begins a vivid sixteen-line attack on the sexual relationship of Claudius and Gertrude (ll. 42–57). He returns to a brief description of the actual murder only because he 'scent[s] the morning air, / Brief let me be' (ll. 58–9). Before he disappears, he returns to the topic of Gertrude's sexual misdeeds, but again admonishes Hamlet to 'leave her to heaven'. The ghost's second appearance to Hamlet is prompted by the need for further defence of Gertrude. Hamlet's resolution when he is preparing to visit his mother's bedchamber after 'The Mouse-trap', to 'be cruel, not unnatural', to 'speak daggers to her, but use none' (III.ii.395–6), seems to be failing. His frenzied attack on Gertrude gains verbal force and violence (which, on stage, is usually accompanied by increasing physical force and violence) until the ghost intervenes. Hamlet shares the ghost's obsession with Gertrude's sexuality, but is dissipating the energy that should be directed toward avenging his father's murder in attacking Gertrude for, he claims, living 'In the rank sweat of an enseamed bed, / Stew'd in corruption, honeying and making love / Over the nasty sty!' (III.iv.93–5). The ghost must intervene to whet Hamlet's 'almost blunted purpose' of revenge and to command Hamlet to protect Gertrude, to 'step between her and her fighting soul', since 'conceit in weakest bodies strongest works' (ll. 111–14).

Hamlet's violent emotions toward his mother are obvious from his first soliloquy, in which twenty-three of the thirty-one lines express his anger and disgust at what he perceives to be Gertrude's weakness, insensitivity, and, most important, bestiality: 'O most wicked speed: to post / With such dexterity to incestious [sic] sheets' (I.ii.156–7). Gertrude's apparent betrayal of his idealised Hyperion father, not the actual death, has given rise to Hamlet's melancholy state at the start of the play. A. C. Bradley's analysis of the cause of Hamlet's sickness of life and longing for death is vividly corroborative: 'It was the moral shock of the sudden ghostly disclosure of his mother's true nature, falling on him when his heart was aching with love, and his body doubtless weakened by sorrow. . . . Is it possible to conceive an experience more desolating to a man such as we have seen Hamlet to be; and is its result anything but perfectly natural? It brings be-wildered horror, then loathing, then despair of human nature.'[8]

Later, when the ghost tells Hamlet that Claudius, Gertrude's second husband, is the murderer of her first, his generalised outrage at women increases and spreads. His sense of betrayal is soon further fed by the unexpected rejection of his love by Ophelia, who obeys the commands of her brother and father that result from their one-dimensional conception of a woman as a sexual 'object'. Laertes advises Ophelia that 'best safety lies in fear' (I.iii.43), and Polonius, in a mean-minded speech, demands her immediate rejection of Hamlet's apparently 'honourable' (l. 111) espousals of love. To all of this, Ophelia replies, 'I shall obey, my lord' (l. 136). Hereafter, Hamlet is described by Ophelia as behaving quite strangely (II.i.74–

97), and he is heard by the audience speaking to Ophelia abusively or coarsely, as he does to his mother. His experiences lead him to attack what he perceives to be the brevity of women's love (I.ii.129–59; III.ii.154), women's wantonness (III.i.145), and the ability that women have to make 'monsters' of the men (III.i.138) over whom they have so much power. Indeed, in the sea of troubles that may lead one to seek an end to life, 'despis'd love' (III.i.71) is fourth in the list of heartaches.

Claudius creates an impression of Gertrude for the audience because she is the object of violent conflicting emotions for him as she is for the ghost and Hamlet. She is, he says, 'My virtue or my plague' (IV.vii.13). He suffers under a 'heavy burthen' (III.i.53) of guilt, but he refuses to give up 'those effects for which I did the murther: / My crown, mine own ambition, and my queen' (III.iii.54–5). He speaks respectfully to Gertrude throughout the play, and tells Laertes that one of the reasons for his toleration of Hamlet's extraordinary behaviour is his love for Gertrude:

> The Queen his mother
> Lives almost by his looks, and for myself—
> My virtue or my plague, be it either which—
> She is so conjunctive to my life and soul,
> That, as the star moves not but in his sphere,
> I could not but by her.
>   (IV.vii.11–16)

In Belleforest's version of the Hamlet story, the Claudius figure kills the King ostensibly to save the life of the Queen, his mistress. In Shakespeare's *Hamlet*, Gertrude's attractiveness for Claudius is one of the causes – and his sexual possession of her one of the results – of the murder of old Hamlet. To possess Gertrude, Claudius is brazenly willing to risk the displeasure of 'the general gender' (IV.vii.18) who bear great love for young Hamlet and does not hesitate to displace him on the throne by marrying Gertrude – 'our sometime sister, now our queen, / Th'imperial jointress to this warlike state' (I.ii.8–9). Claudius is as obsessed by Gertrude as the two Hamlets are, and – although he clearly loves her – he shares the Hamlets' conception of Gertrude as an *object*. She is 'possess'd' as one of the 'effects' of his actions (III.iii.53–4) and is thereafter 'Taken to wife' (I.ii.14). It may then seem contradictory that he does not forcibly stop Gertrude from drinking the poisoned wine, but there are, in the context of the final scene of the play, many strong reasons for his self-restraint. Therefore, one has no reason to assume that his lecture to Laertes on the

ephemerality of love – which 'Dies in his own too much' (IV.vii.118)
– arises out of his experiences with Gertrude.

Although she may have been partially responsible for Claudius's
monstrous act of fratricide and although her marriage to Claudius
may have been indirectly responsible for making a 'monster' of
Hamlet, Gertrude is never seen in the play inducing anyone to do
anything at all monstrous. Jan Kott's assertion notwithstanding –
that Gertrude 'has been through passion, murder, and silence. ...
suppress(ing) everything inside her', so that one senses 'a volcano
under her superficial poise'⁹ – when one closely examines Gertrude's
actual speech and actions in an attempt to understand the character,
one finds little that hints at hypocrisy, suppression, or uncontrolled
passion and their implied complexity.

Gertrude appears in only ten of the twenty scenes that comprise
the play; furthermore, she speaks very little, having less dialogue
than any other major character in *Hamlet* – a mere 157 lines out of
4,042 (3.8 per cent).¹⁰ She speaks plainly, directly, and chastely
when she does speak, using few images except in the longest of her
speeches, which refer to Hamlet's and Ophelia's relationship
(III.i.36–41 and V.i.243–6), to Ophelia's death (IV.vii.166–83), to
her sense of unspecified guilt (IV.v.17–20), and to Hamlet's madness
in the graveyard (V.i.284–8). Gertrude tells Ophelia before the
spying scene that she hopes that the 'happy cause of Hamlet's
wildness' is Ophelia's 'good beauties'. If so, she trusts that Ophelia's
'virtues' can effect a cure (III.i.39–40); and later, when relaying the
news of Ophelia's death, Gertrude characteristically disdains liberality
and creates her bittersweet pictures in the language of the 'cull-cold
maids'. Gertrude's brief speeches include references to honour,
virtue, flowers, and a dove's golden couplets; neither structure nor
content suggests wantonness. Gertrude's only mildly critical comments are in response to the verbosity of Polonius ('More matter
with less art' [II.ii.95]) and that of the Player Queen ('The lady doth
protest too much, methinks' [III.ii.230]).

Gertrude usually asks questions (ten questions in her approximately
forty-five lines of dialogue in the closet scene) or voices solicitude for
the well-being and safety of other characters. She divides her concern
between Claudius and Hamlet; indeed, Claudius observes that she
'lives almost by his [Hamlet's] looks' (IV.vii.12). Her first speeches
are to Hamlet, admonishing an end to his 'particular' grief and
pleading that he stay in Denmark with her: 'Let not thy mother lose
her prayers, Hamlet, / I pray thee stay with us, go not to Wittenberg'

(I.ii.118–19). In her second appearance on stage, she directs Rosencrantz and Guildenstern 'to visit / My too much changed son'
(II.ii.35–6) in an attempt to discover the cause of his change.
However, in the same scene she also demonstrates her perspicuity by
intuitively, and correctly, analysing Hamlet's behaviour: 'I doubt it is
no other but the main, / His father's death and our o'erhasty
marriage' (II.ii.56–7). Gertrude's dialogue gains atypical force when
she must defend both Claudius (IV.v.110–11, 117, 129) and Hamlet
(V.i.264, 273, 284–8) to Laertes, and in her desperate defence of
Hamlet to Claudius when he asks of Hamlet's whereabouts after the
murder of Polonius. Hamlet, she says, killed Polonius because of a
'brainish apprehension' and 'weeps for what is done' (IV.i.11, 27).

Gertrude's actions are as solicitous and unlascivious as her language. She usually enters a scene with the King, and she is alone on
stage only with Hamlet in the closet scene and with mad Ophelia
(both times expressing feelings of some kind of guilt). She repeatedly
leaves scenes after being ordered out by Claudius, which he does
both to protect her from the discovery of his guilt and to confer with
her privately about how to deal with Hamlet. Little proof for the
interpretation of Gertrude as a guileful and carnal woman emerges
from her other textually implicit actions, as, for example, when she
sorrowfully directs the attention of Polonius and Claudius to Hamlet:
'But look where sadly the poor wretch comes reading' (II.ii.168). She
acquiesces in the plan to determine the cause of Hamlet's extraordinary behaviour by spying on him, using Ophelia as a decoy, and leaves
when ordered to, so the plan can be carried out, saying, 'And for
your part, Ophelia, I do wish / That your good beauties be the happy
cause / Of Hamlet's wildness. So shall I hope your virtues / Will bring
him to his wonted way again, / To both your honours' (III.i.36–41).
She later sends messengers to Hamlet to bring him to her after 'The
Mousetrap' and attempts to deal roundly with him, but she is forced
to sit down and to contrast the pictures of her first husband and
Claudius (III.iv.34, 53). Even after her encounter with Hamlet in the
closet scene, she apparently attempts to restrain Laertes physically
when he madly bursts in to accuse Claudius of killing Polonius ('Let
him go, Gertrude, do not fear our person' [IV.v.123]). She accepts a
sprig of rue from Ophelia, to be worn 'with a difference' (IV.v.183),
and later scatters flowers on Ophelia's grave. It also is observable
from the text that she offers Hamlet a napkin with which to wipe his
face during the fencing match and wipes his face for him once.
Finally, and most important, she drinks the poisoned wine and dies

onstage, using her dying words to warn Hamlet of the poison (V.ii.291, 309–10), but not accusing Claudius. Although both the ghost and Hamlet repeatedly speak in vivid language of her gambolling between incestuous sheets (and presumably she does sometimes share a bed with Claudius), the text never states or implies that Gertrude gives or receives the wanton pinches or 'reechy kisses' (III.iv.183–4) that so obsess, enrage, and disgust the imaginations of Hamlet and the ghost.

Her own words and actions compel one to describe Gertrude as merely a quiet, biddable, careful mother and wife. Nonetheless, one can still examine Gertrude's limited actions and reactions to answer the knotty interpretative question of Gertrude's culpability in the murder of her first husband. When speaking to Hamlet, the ghost does not state or suggest Gertrude's guilt in his murder, only in her 'falling-off' from him to Claudius (I.v.47). When Hamlet confronts her after 'The Mousetrap', she asks in apparent innocence, 'What have I done, that thou dar'st wag thy tongue / In noise so rude against me?' (III.iv.39–40). She has not been verbally guileful before, so one has no reason to suspect her of duplicity in this instance. And when Hamlet informs her that old Hamlet was murdered by Claudius, she does not indicate prior knowledge. Instead, she exclaims in horror, 'As kill a King!' (l. 30), and pleads for the third time that Hamlet mitigate his attack. 'No more!' (l. 101). She is not aware of any personal guilt, and she does not want to hear of the guilty deeds of one of the men she loves.

Clearly, Gertrude's innocence of involvement in the murder is most strongly suggested. However, many critics have interpreted the text differently, asserting that at the least Gertrude is guilty of having had a sexual relationship with Claudius before the murder of her husband because the ghost uses the word *adulterate*[11] when describing Claudius and asserts, in reference to Gertrude, that 'lust, though to a radiant angel link'd, / Will sate itself in a celestial bed / And prey on garbage' (I.v.55–7). But if Gertrude had been involved in an adulterous affair with Claudius, she would surely have known that she was 'conjunctive' to his 'life and soul' and that he was ambitious. She might therefore have suspected him to be capable of murder in order to obtain her and the crown (which a marriage to her would assure him), but she has no such suspicions. The ghost does use the past tense to describe Claudius's and Gertrude's sexual liaison. Claudius 'won to his shameful lust' Gertrude's will: 'O Hamlet, what a falling off *was* there' (ll. 45–7, emphasis added). Still, it is not clear if the ghost is referring to a time before his murder or if the past to which he refers is that period since his death, during which Claudius has won and married Gertrude. Hamlet's anger and disgust at Gertrude's hasty marriage and the dexterity with which she moved to 'incestious sheets' – feelings expressed even before he had talked with the ghost or knew of the murder – further support the interpretation that Gertrude was not guilty of a sexual liaison with Claudius before her husband's murder, but that her hasty, apparently careless betrayal of the memory of her first husband is what, in Hamlet's eyes, 'makes marriage vows / As false as dicers' oaths' (III.iv.44–5). Indeed, in the closet scene Hamlet never accuses her of adultery, but abhors her choice of an 'adulterate' second husband: 'Could you on this fair mountain leave to feed, / And batten on this moor? ... what judgment / Would step from this to this?' (ll. 67–71).

Although Gertrude is not an adulterer, she has been 'adulterated' by her contact, even innocently in marriage, with Claudius. Similarly, his crimes and deceit have, in fact, made Gertrude guilty of incest.[12] In order to marry, Claudius and Gertrude would have been required to obtain a dispensation to counteract their canonical consanguinity or affinity. Obviously, if his crime of fratricide were publicly known – as it is by the ghost and Hamlet – Claudius's dispensation to marry his victim's wife, his sister-in-law, certainly would not have been granted. Therefore, one could assert that the relationship between Claudius and Gertrude is incestuous because the dispensation was based on false pretences and would not have been granted if the truth were known. Because they know the truth, the ghost and Hamlet persist in terming the relationship incestuous; but Gertrude has married in innocence and good faith, not as a party to the deception.

Gertrude does readily admit her one self-acknowledged source of guilt – that her marriage was 'o'erhasty', but in all other instances she feels guilt only after Hamlet has insisted that she be ashamed.[13] And it is not ever completely clear to what Gertrude refers in the closet scene when she mentions the black spots on her soul – if it is a newly aroused awareness of her adulterate and incestuous relationship, if it is her marriage to a man whom Hamlet so clearly despises, or if it is merely her already lamented o'erhasty marriage:

> O Hamlet, speak no more!
> Thou turn'st my eyes into my very soul.
> And there I see such black and grained spots
> As will not leave their tinct.

(III.iv.88–9)

Hamlet's violent cajolery in the closet scene has created unaccustomed feelings of guilt in this accommodating woman, who wants primarily to please him. However, she has not pleased Hamlet by acting in a way that pleased Claudius – by marrying him so soon after her husband's death and in spite of their consanguinity. For Hamlet, her act 'roars so loud and thunders in the index' (III.iv.52), and his displeasure has 'cleft' the Queen's heart 'in twain' (l.156) because she obviously loves both Hamlet and Claudius and feels pain and guilt at her inability to please both.

Hamlet is commanded by the ghost to moderate his attack, to 'step between her and her fighting soul' because of Gertrude's 'amazement' and because of the force of imagination in a weak body (III.iv.112–14). It is even possible that Gertrude's 'fighting soul' results not only from an awakened sense of guilt at Hamlet's words but also from the conflict between her persistent, extreme love for her son and her momentary terror of him. After all, in the preceding 115 lines, Hamlet has certainly demonstrated emotional, and probably physical, brutality toward Gertrude; indeed, she has called for help in fear that he will murder her (l.21). Hamlet has stabbed Polonius and shown little remorse, and he continues the extraordinary behaviour that prompts her amazement:

> Alas, how is't with you,
> That you do bend your eye on vacancy,
> And with th' incorporal air do hold discourse?
> Forth at your eyes your spirits wildly peep,
> And as the sleeping soldiers in th' alarm,
> Your bedded hair, like life in excrements,
> Start up and stand an end. O gentle son,
> Upon the heat and flame of thy distemper
> Sprinkle cool patience. Whereon do you look?
> (III.iv.116–24)

Since the beginning of the play, Hamlet has been obsessed with Claudius's and Gertrude's guilt, and it is this which precipitates his distempered behaviour. Indeed, judged without Hamlet's strong predisposition, Gertrude's behaviour at 'The Mousetrap' would lead no one to believe that she has been herself reflected in the Player Queen. However, Hamlet believes that she has – and Hamlet is a powerful first-person force in the play who encourages one to see all events and people from his perspective, nearly compelling one to see Gertrude's one-line response to the play's action as an admission of guilt: 'The lady doth protest too much, methinks' (III.ii.230).

Gertrude's remark at this play-within-the-play can be given another interpretation that may be more accurate, in view of Gertrude's accommodating, dependent personality: her words are not a guileful anticipation and deflection of comparisons between herself and the Player Queen. Instead, being a woman of so few words herself, Gertrude must sincerely be irritated by the Player Queen's verbosity, just as she was earlier by that of Polonius. Obviously, Gertrude believes that quiet women best please men, and pleasing men is Gertrude's main interest. Indeed, Gertrude's concern to maintain a strong relationship with two men is demonstrated by her only other lines at the play — brief lines — asking her 'dear Hamlet' to sit beside her (l.108) and voicing distress for Claudius's obvious consternation at the end of the play: 'How fares my lord?' (l.267). After the play, Gertrude is, according to Guildenstern, 'in most great affliction of spirit' (ll.311–12) and calls Hamlet for a chastening session in her room for two reasons: the conference, with Polonius as spy, had already been planned before the presentation of the play; and more important, she is quite upset because one of the men for whom she cares greatly has 'much offended' (III.iv.9) the other. In no way, by word or act, does she indicate that the play has spontaneously created any sense of guilt in her.

Obviously, this analysis of Gertrude's behaviour does not suggest any changes or clear moral development in her. After the play-within-the-play and the closet scene, Gertrude agrees to Hamlet's request that she not 'ravel all this matter out', since he is 'essentially ... not in madness, / But mad in craft' (III.iv.186–8). She says, 'I have no life to breathe / What thou has said to me' (ll.198–9). And she is true to her word. She does not unravel it to Claudius, whom Hamlet hates and fears. However, she is immediately seen in the next scene telling Claudius of something else — the murder of Polonius — and defending Hamlet in his apparent madness; and although she is true to Hamlet, the scene nonetheless works to undercut her position as an honest woman. That Gertrude does not promise Hamlet to refrain from going to Claudius's bed may possibly suggest an admission of guilt about the relationship. Those who claim that Gertrude does admit to committing adultery and incest cite her one self-revealing aside, four lines in which she directly grieves for her sinful, sick soul and self-destructive, fearful guilt:

> To my sick soul, as sin's true nature is,
> Each toy seems prologue to some great amiss,

> So full of artless jealousy is guilt,
> It spills itself in fearing to be spilt.
> (IV.v.17–20)

But the nature of this lamented guilt remains unclear; it is apparently unfelt until aroused by Hamlet's attack. If it arises out of the conflict between her love for Claudius and her remorse for betraying the memory of her first husband, she obviously chooses, like Claudius, to 'retain th'offence' (III.iii.56), because she soon thereafter tries physically and verbally to protect Claudius from Laertes.

Gertrude has not moved in the play toward independence or a heightened moral stance; only her divided loyalties and her unhappiness intensify. Given the presentation of Gertrude in Shakespeare's text, it is impossible to see the accuracy of Olivier's and Kozintsev's film presentations and of many stage depictions that show Gertrude shrinking after Act III from Claudius's touch because of her newly awakened sense of decency and shame. Nor does the text suggest, as Olivier does in his film, that she is suspicious of the pearl that Claudius drops in Hamlet's wine goblet. Gertrude does not drink the wine to protect Hamlet or to kill herself because of her shame, she drinks it in her usual direct way to toast Hamlet's success in the fencing match, after first briskly and maternally advising him to wipe his face. In fact, Gertrude's death is symbolic of the internal disharmony caused by her divided loyalties. In order to honour Hamlet, she directly disobeys Claudius for the first time:

> Queen   The Queen carouses to thy fortune, Hamlet.
> Hamlet   Good Madam!
> King   Gertrude, do not drink.
> Queen   I will, my lord, I pray you pardon me.
> King   [*Aside*] It is the pois'ned cup, it is too late.
> (V.ii.289–92)

Gertrude dies asserting that she is poisoned and calling out for her 'dear Hamlet', but still not attacking Claudius.

Gertrude's words and actions in Shakespeare's *Hamlet* create not the lusty, lustful, lascivious Gertrude that one generally sees in stage and film productions but a compliant, loving, unimaginative woman whose only concern is pleasing others: a woman who seemed virtuous (I.v.46), and who would, so Hamlet asserts, hang on her first husband, 'As if increase of appetite had grown / By what it fed on' (I.ii.143–5). This same careful woman, soon after her husband's death, 'with remembrance of herself, (I.ii.7), marries his brother –

probably because of her extremely dependent personality – and tries to relieve her much-loved son's melancholy by counselling him in temporality: 'Thou know'st 'tis common, all that lives must die, / Passing through nature to eternity' (ll.72–3). As these and most of her other lines demonstrate, Gertrude may be the object of violent emotions, but she displays no passion, only quietly consistent concern for the well-being of the two other characters: Claudius and, most profoundly, Hamlet. She is easily led, and she makes no decisions for herself except, ironically, the one that precipitates her death. Her personality is, both figuratively and literally, defined by other characters in the play. Because of her malleability and weakness, the distorted image created and reflected by others – not the one created by her own words and actions – has predominated.

In creating Gertrude, Shakespeare clearly diverged from the sources he followed quite closely in other areas, making her of a piece with the rest of the play – that is, problematic. But Gertrude is problematic not because of layers of complexity or a dense texture such as that of Hamlet but because, as with the ghost, Shakespeare does not provide all the 'answers', all the necessary clues that would allow one to put together her character and fully understand her speech, actions, and motivations. Still, Gertrude is not a flat, uninteresting character as a result of her limited range of responses and concerns. Gertrude's words and acts interest the audience because, obviously, she is of extreme interest to the combatants in the play – the ghost, Hamlet and Claudius – all of whom see her literally and in quite heightened terms as a sexual *object*. However, if she were presented on stage and film as only her own words and deeds create her, Gertrude might become another stereotypical character: the nurturing, loving, careful mother and wife – malleable, submissive, totally dependent, and solicitous of others at the expense of herself. This is still a stereotype, but a more positive one than that of the temptress and destroyer – self-indulgent and soulless. And certainly it more accurately reflects the Gertrude that Shakespeare created.

From *The Woman's Part: Feminist Criticism of Shakespeare*, ed. Carolyn Ruth Swift Lenz, Gayle Greene and Carol Thomas Neely (Urbana, 1980), pp. 194–210.

NOTES

[Rebecca Smith's essay is the first of three feminist essays on *Hamlet* in this anthology, each of which comes at the play from a different angle. Smith focuses on the way Gertrude has traditionally been played 'as a sensual, deceitful woman'. She argues, however, that what we have in the text is not this stereotype of the temptress figure but instead another stereotype figure, that of the 'compliant, loving, unimaginative woman'. Smith also takes issue with the standard film presentations of Gertrude and points to the problematic nature of Shakespeare's portrayal of the Queen. Smith's essay itself first appeared in an important early volume of feminist criticism which challenged the separation of the text from author and audience. More recent feminist criticism has gone on from this position to show the ways in which texts are not isolated objects but part of a broader context including history and politics. Ed.]

1. William Shakespeare, *Hamlet*, in *The Riverside Shakespeare*, ed. G. Blakemore Evans *et al.* (Boston, 1974). All further references are to this edition.

2. Jack Jorgens, *Shakespeare on Film* (Bloomington, 1977), p. 27.

3. The 'received' critical opinion of Gertrude is most clearly stated by Ernest Jones, *Hamlet and Oedipus* (Garden City, 1954). He says that the Queen's 'markedly sensual nature . . . is indicated in too many places in the play to need specific reference, and is generally recognized' (p. 91). Other influential critics have interpreted her similarly. A. C. Bradley, *Shakespearean Tragedy* (London, 1956), says that the 'ghastly disclosure' of Gertrude's true nature is a moral shock to Hamlet. She marries Claudius not for state reasons or out of family affection; instead, her marriage shows 'an astounding shallowness of feeling [and] an eruption of coarse sensuality, "rank and gross", speeding posthaste to its horrible delight' (pp. 118–20). H. D. F. Kitto, *Form and Meaning in Drama* (London, 1956), reprinted in part in *Shakespeare Criticism: 1935–60*, ed. Anne Ridler (Oxford, 1970), states that 'a mad passion . . . swept [Gertrude] into the arms of Claudius' (p. 158). Similarly L. C. Knights, *An Approach to 'Hamlet'* (London, 1961), describes the court's qualities as 'coarse pleasures', 'moral obtuseness', 'sycophancy', 'base and treacherous plotting', and 'brainless triviality': 'This is the world that revolves round the middle-aged sensuality of Claudius and Gertrude' (p. 42). Harry Levin, *The Question of Hamlet* (London, 1959), contrasts Ophelia (virginal, 'faithful daughter and sister') to Gertrude (adulterous, corrupted, 'faithless mother and wife') who is 'associated with the artificial enticement of cosmetics' (p. 66). J. Dover Wilson, *What Happens in Hamlet* (Cambridge, 1935), insists that Hamlet knows that Gertrude is 'a criminal, guilty of the filthy sin of incest', and finally comes to see her 'as rotten through and through' (p. 44). And, in the same vein, E. M. W. Tillyard, *Shakespeare's Prob-*

lem Plays (Toronto, 1968), comments on the 'lascivious and incestuous guilt of Gertrude' which has 'made the world ugly' for Hamlet (pp. 21–2).

In contrast, it is interesting to note that some earlier *women* writers have been more generous to Gertrude. Consider the evaluation by Lillie Buffum Chace Wyman in an appendix to *Gertrude of Denmark: An Interpretive Romance* (Boston, 1924), p. 238. Wyman says, 'The critics have generally denounced Gertrude's second marriage as sinful in its very nature. It is rather absurd to echo Hamlet so completely as to this. Such an opinion certainly has been very dominant in some ages and some countries. It is doubtful, however, whether it was ever so universally an accepted belief as to make it certain that Shakespeare intended that such a mountain of odium should be heaped upon her, as writers have been piling up for centuries. In this connection, it may be noted that the Roman Catholic Church upheld the marriage of Katharine to Henry the Eighth. And certainly Shakespeare, however Anglican he may have been personally, did not represent Katharine as a loathsome creature in his drama on that subject, and he did permit Henry's courtiers to jeer at the King's pretence of scruple.' Rosamond Putzel in 'Queen Gertrude's Crime', *Renaissance Papers, 1961*, ed. George Walton Williams (Durham, 1962), pp. 37–46, argues that the evidence in the play does not prove that Gertrude committed adultery and that her characterisation suggests that she did not.

4. Saxo Grammaticus, *Amleth*, and F. de Belleforest, *The Hystorie of Hamblet, Prince of Denmarke*, in *Hamlet*, Norton Critical Edition, ed. Cyrus Hoy (New York, 1963), pp. 123–41.

5. Kenneth Muir, *Shakespeare's Sources* (London, 1961), p. 112. See also Geoffrey Bullough, 'Introduction' to *Hamlet* in *Narrative and Dramatic Sources of Shakespeare*, vol. 7 (London, 1973), pp. 3–59.

6. Kenneth Muir, *Shakespeare's Sources* (London, 1961), p. 112. [Shakespeare's *Hamlet* is probably based on a lost Elizabethan play of the same title. This earlier source-play, possibly by Thomas Kyd, is generally referred to as the *Ur-Hamlet*. Ed.]

7. Ibid., p. 114. See also Frank Kermode, 'Introduction' to *Hamlet*, in *The Riverside Shakespeare* (Boston, 1974), pp. 1136–7.

8. A. C. Bradley, *Shakespearean Tragedy* (London, 1956), pp. 118–19.

9. Jan Kott, *Shakespeare Our Contemporary*, trans. Boleslaw Taborski (Garden City, 1966), p. 61.

10. Line counts and percentage from Marvin Spevack, *A Complete and Systematic Concordance to the Works of Shakespeare*, vol. 3 (Hildesheim, 1968), pp. 828, 751.

11. The adjective *adulterate* denotatively refers to something that makes other things inferior, impure, or corrupted by its addition and need not

be limited to a specific reference to sexual intercourse between a married person and someone who is not that person's spouse. Bertram Joseph, *Conscience and the King* (London, 1953), defines *adulterate* by reference to Renaissance sources, namely, Thomas Wilson, who states in his *Christian Dictionary* (1612) that adultery means 'all manner of uncleanness, about desire of sex, together with occasion, causes, and means thereof, as in the 7th Commandment', and Perkins, who says in *A Golden Chain* (1616) that adultery means 'as much as to do anything, what way so ever', that stains one's own chastity or that of another. Joseph also quotes from the homily 'Against Whoredom and Uncleanness' in *Certain Sermons or Homilies* (1623), which defines adultery as 'all unlawful use of those parts, which be ordained for generation' (p. 17). Clearly, the ghost's use of the word *adulterate* may refer to Claudius's impurity resulting from his lust for Gertrude and the corruption that he spreads to Gertrude when she becomes his wife, not necessarily to a sexual liaison between the two before Old Hamlet's murder.

12. See Jason P. Rosenblatt, 'Aspects of the Incest Problem in *Hamlet*', *Shakespeare Quarterly*, 29 (1978), 349–64, for a thorough analysis of the sixteenth-century religious controversy on consanguineous marriages.

13. It is significant that without Hamlet's guidance, Gertrude herself lacks conscious awareness of guilt. Shakespeare may thus demonstrate in Gertrude the commonplace judgment of his society that women must rely on men for guidance and support. Richard Hooker, for example, speaks of the giving of women in marriage as a customary reminder of 'the very imbecility of their nature and sex' which 'doth bind them to be always directed, guided and ordered by others . . .'; see his *Of the Laws of Ecclesiastical Polity*, V.lxxiii.5 (London, 1954), vol. 2, p. 393. Such conventional assumptions about female 'imbecility' may help to explain both Hamlet's anger at Gertrude and the ghost's charity toward her. However, as Carolyn Heilbrun has pointed out, Gertrude is no imbecile. While Heilbrun accepts the ghost's description of Gertrude as lustful, she urges that the Queen 'is also intelligent, penetrating, and gifted with a remarkable talent for concise and pithy speech'. See 'The Character of Hamlet's Mother', *Shakespeare Quarterly*, 8 (1957), 201–6.

7

Chaste Constancy in 'Hamlet'

MARILYN FRENCH

The play opens in murky light, on a cold battlement, and its first line is a question. Soon, a ghost appears, but he does not speak. He speaks to no one, throughout the play, but Hamlet. By revealing the ghost to eyes others than Hamlet's – indeed to the audience – Shakespeare establishes its objective reality, validates its existence. The presence of the sceptical, rational Horatio emphasises that the ghost is not a figment hallucinated by a fevered mind. The ghost is as real as a ghost can be.

What is ambiguous is the import of the ghost, not just whether it is a 'spirit of health or goblin damn'd', but what its message really means. Maynard Mack and Harry Levin have pointed out that the entire play occurs in an atmosphere of ambiguity, irony, and interrogation.[1] Doubt is the prevailing emotion.[2] All the major characters except Horatio are at some time or in some way acting a part: even Horatio is being careful not to show what he knows or feels.[3] All the other characters manifest inconstancy; they are continually checking up on each other – probing, eavesdropping, spying, even betraying.[4] The world of *Hamlet* is a world of incertitude.[5]

Generally, the incertitude that informs the play is attributed to some split – between seeming and being, appearance and reality; between an ideal good and a real evil; between a false ideal that is really an outmoded traditional code, and a perversion of that code; between intellect and action; between inside and outside.[6] The incertitude is sometimes seen as afflicting Hamlet alone, sometimes as the sickness that is polluting all of Denmark.[7] But the incertitude of the entire drama clusters around, flows out of the ambiguous figure of the ghost who speaks only to Hamlet. It is necessary to examine his message.

The ghost begins by telling Hamlet about purgatorial punishments that sound more like hell. This is odd. Although he was killed without time for 'reck'ning', the terrible torments he implies and describes sound severe for a man who, we are told over and again, was perfection itself – a Hyperion, a Jove, a Mars, a Mercury, a great soldier and a loving faithful husband. One wonders what he can have done to deserve such torture.

The ghost lingers on the horrible nature of the place where he now resides, and then announces, briefly, the horrible truth of the place where he used to reside: man is murderous, woman is unchaste. He dwells rather differently on these two facts, giving each a different amount of attention and a different rhetoric.

First he recounts the overall fact of the murder, and the cover story given out. In this section, he calls Claudius a *serpent*. But quickly, the focus of his attention moves elsewhere – to Claudius as an *incestuous, adulterate beast*. His treachery and 'witchcraft' are damned, not because of the murder, but because of Claudius' seduction of Gertrude. And, within a few lines, the ghost is attacking not Claudius, but his queen – and with considerable self-congratulation: 'what a falling-off was there' (I.v.47). In haste, the speech moves to a passionate climax, as the ghost describes Gertrude as lewd and lustful, sated in a 'celestial' bed, and declining from it to 'prey on garbage' (I.v.56, 57). This is strong language indeed. What on earth could make a bed *celestial*? And the Claudius we have seen does not seem to be garbage, nor Gertrude, a predator.

The ghost returns to his tale for five and a half lines. The remainder of this section focuses on the horrible sensation of being poisoned, and the ugly look of a poisoned body. This is the longest segment of all the ghost's speeches. In this segment, Claudius is referred to as 'thy uncle', and 'a brother'. Nothing more. Then the ghost returns to his present condition of torment and rises to his second climax: 'O horrible!' (I.v.80).

At the opening of the ghost's dialogue with Hamlet, after his first description of hell pains, the ghost several times commands Hamlet to revenge his murder. Nevertheless, in the rest of the speech, Claudius and his act are given negligible attention. After his outburst – 'O horrible!' – the ghost returns to the sexual element – *luxury* and *damned incest*. Then he forbids Hamlet to take action against Gertrude, and in moments, he departs.

This is a strange speech for a man who was deprived of life in his full vigour and power. He does order revenge against Claudius, but his real fury is directed against Gertrude and his outrage at the 'pollution' of his bed, that is, the royal bed of Denmark. Although we must accept that the ghost speaks the truth, since it is confirmed in the course of the play – that Claudius seduced Gertrude and killed King Hamlet, and strongly suggested that Gertrude had an affair with Claudius while her husband was alive – it is still difficult to decipher precisely what the ghost is saying. It is difficult because his priorities are contradictory to his explicit orders. His orders are: revenge my murder: leave your mother to heaven. The priorities of his speech are: (1) and first in attention – his own sensations in the torments he is now undergoing, the ugly and unpleasant sensation and appearance of being poisoned: (2) and first in fury – Gertrude's lustful inconstancy; (3) and first in outrage – Gertrude and Claudius enjoying themselves in 'his' bed. Then, more or less equal in importance or attention – the recounting of his murder, the orders of revenge and restraint, and self-praise of a rather high order.

In fact, the ghost's major priorities are identical to Hamlet's, both in his immediate response to the spirit and throughout the play. Hamlet's highest value, his primary response to experience, is to 'feel' it – through sensation, emotion, or reflective thought. His response to life, then, is 'feminine' – to experience it, and to articulate it (which would be masculine [a structuring] if it were expressed to others and thus became a form of action). As it is, he articulates his feeling-thoughts mainly to the audience – himself. Thus, after the ghost leaves, Hamlet devotes thirteen lines to expression of his feelings. His second priority is hatred for his mother; and he moves immediately from his own feelings to 'O most pernicious woman!' (I.v.105). Only finally does he arrive at Claudius, and calls him *villain*. Under the circumstances, it seems a weak word, and its etymology suggests the view of him Hamlet will take throughout the play: he damns Claudius not because he is evil or wicked or hateful, but because he is a diminishment of an ideal (explicitly a diminishment from his predecessor). Claudius is damned because he is illegitimate.

Hamlet has already given us a similar set of priorities in the first soliloquy, in I.ii. He spends ten lines describing his own emotional/ intellectual state, which is extremely depressed, even despairing. It is not his father's death that has shaken him: he grants that only a phrase – 'But two months dead' (I.ii.138). He spends only a phrase considering the difference between Claudius and his father. He then moves to the real object of his outrage: Gertrude. He cannot bear his mother's remarriage, but it is the speed, rather than the deed itself – remarriage – that he harps on. Haste in remarriage might, in an ordinary way, bother a person who is very conscious of social forms, of ceremony and ritual. But Hamlet is not elsewhere shown to be such a person: it is Laertes who cares about ceremony, and protests his father's and sister's scant burials.[8] The speed of Gertrude's remarriage violates Hamlet's sensibilities because of what it betrays: sexual desire in Gertrude, desire great enough to lead *her* to ignore standard social forms. The horror and shock he feels at the fact that she can feel desire at all is evident later, in his speech to her in her chamber, but it underlies all earlier references to the marriage. For Hamlet, sexual desire in a woman is a posting 'with ... dexterity to incestious sheets' (I.ii.157). The phrases he uses here and elsewhere to describe sexual acts have the same ugly fascination of the abomination, the same fastidious revulsion, found in Iago's description of sex between Desdemona and Othello, Desdemona and Cassio. The haste of the marriage suggests Gertrude's desire existed before King Hamlet's death. Any remarriage by Gertrude shows her inconstant; hasty remarriage suggests she may also be unchaste.

And for Hamlet, there is no mean between chastity – pure, cold, and holy – and depravity in women. In addition, for Hamlet as for his ghost-father, men are divided into gods, the celestial, falling off into garbage, the ideal and the perversion.[9] Hyperion lacking, the satyr appears: men and women are gods or they are beasts. For Hamlet, there is no realm of the human, no masculine principle. There is the superhuman and the subhuman, and his categories apply to both genders. Hamlet's values are thus absolutist: one must have very fixed, firm standards so to categorise human behaviour. Hamlet's thinking is very *young* thinking. And the young man has suddenly been thrust by events into a situation that is not easily understandable, and not at all manageable by absolute thinking. He, like the rest of us, lives in a world where the ideal exists, but only at moments, and only in certain areas of people's behaviour. Like us, Hamlet has 'declined' into an ambivalent and ambiguous world.

The second scene of the play presents the earthly dimension of the cosmic ambiguity which the ghost will later present. Claudius opens it with mixed grief for death and joy for marriage, an 'auspicious and a dropping eye'. He proceeds to state business with authority, intelligence, and benevolence of manner. He is not a king debilitated by lack of assurance, intelligence, or corrupted by egoism. He is concerned with the welfare of his country, seeking peaceful means to secure it. He is generous to Laertes and kind to Hamlet. He maintains his equanimity even after Hamlet's surly response to him: 'Why, 'tis a loving and a fair reply' (I.ii.121).

In general, the world that surrounds Hamlet is as morally ambiguous as the actual world. Claudius is a good ruler; he loves his wife and is patient and kind with her difficult son. He is also a murderer and an adulterer, according to the ghost. Gertrude is a loving concerned mother, a compassionate queen, a loving wife (to Claudius, so far as we see her), who is also able to comment with force and intelligence on Polonius' tediousness and the Player Queen's protestations. She is also inconstant.

Polonius is a more complex figure than either the King or the Queen. He seems to love his children; he seems to have the welfare of the kingdom in mind. His means of action, however, are totally corrupt. In I.iii. both Polonius and Laertes tell Ophelia that the words and actions of Hamlet that she has taken as 'holy' are mere seemings. The nature of the male is lustful and deceitful, they inform her: she must not honour her love lest she dishonour her father. She must guard her chastity closely, for men are inconstant, their blazes 'giving more light than heat, extinct in both, / Even in their promise' (I.iii.117–19). Nature itself is dangerous: 'the chariest maid is prodigal enough / If she unmask her beauty to the moon' (I.iii.36–7).

The assumptions of Ophelia's 'guardians' are that females are responsible for human sexuality, but that the world is full of aggressive lecherous men out to destroy utterly desirable, utterly helpless women. Female virtue is identical with chastity; thus, Polonius, who has carefully trained his daughter to be obedient and chaste, is able to use her as a piece of bait for his spying without any sense that he has compromised her – after all, her hymen is still intact.

The viciousness that both Polonius and Laertes attribute to men underlies another scene, in which Polonius gives orders for his son to be spied upon and even slandered, sure that Laertes is engaged in some vice, and willing to defame him in order to discover a truth he believes he already knows. And Laertes, who rushes home like an obedient son to avenge his father's murder, is willing to resort to treacherous and underhanded means to accomplish it.

In a sense, *Hamlet* is a fulfilment of the Old Testament verdict that the imagination of man's heart is evil from his youth. A sense of human nature as incorrigibly vicious leads to a code enjoining self-control and assumed virtue as necessary if humankind is to live together in society. But the irrationality of paradox underlying such a set is emphasised in the family scene. In the very middle of that scene, and juxtaposed with the two men's warnings to Ophelia, occurs Polonius' sermon to his son advising proper male behaviour – moderation, self-control, and calculation for effect. Yet the old man ends: 'To thine own self be true.' To which self? The moral schizophrenia which is the real disease of this play is capsulised in this scene.

The eavesdropping, setting of traps, and spying which are Polonius' notions of statecraft come in time, because of Hamlet's odd behaviour, to characterise the entire Danish court. Rosencrantz and Guildenstern are really awed by the King and Queen, and are, like Ophelia, obedient to the proper authority. They thus sacrifice the bond of human friendship to a social propriety. So too Laertes, later, obeys Claudius' suggestions as to how to revenge the murder, and in suggesting the poisoned rapier, sacrifices the code of honour he has been trained in. Obedience to constituted authority has sometimes been seen as one of Shakespeare's articles of belief, but in this play as well as the other problem plays, such obedience leads inevitably to corruption.[10] Hamlet's sense of Claudius as illegitimate can lead us to believe that it is Claudius personally who is to blame for this, but surely the play has a more universal significance than that. It is difficult to find in Shakespeare (outside of some rather cardboard figures in the history plays) a man who is both legitimate and powerful. Except (perhaps) for Henry V, the fully legitimate figures in Shakespeare are invariably dead and haloed by memory.

And to repeat: the Claudius who opens scene ii appears as legitimate as it is possible to be. Indeed, Hamlet's response to the courteous, patient, cordial King could lead a newcomer to the play to decide that Hamlet is a sullen resentful young man hugging his own untested virtue while accusing his parents of hypocrisy, and the soliloquy which follows it could reinforce our sense of Hamlet's priggish self-righteousness. But it does not. This is not because at this point in the play we believe Hamlet's feelings or judgments to be correct, but because of the power of his outrage. It overwhelms us, we are impelled into sympathy with him because the dramatist has so magnificently articulated his anguish and his hate. G. Wilson Knight has remarked that we see Denmark largely through Hamlet's eyes, yet they may not be trustworthy.[11] It does not matter, however:

Hamlet's feelings are the most powerful things in the play, and they sweep us up.

The Prince has several responses to what he sees around him. His intellectual response is to question the whole notion of legitimacy – as his creator did in the first tetralogy. At first, he questions only the legitimacy of his world, and finds everywhere hypocrisy, mere seemings. Lacking chaste constancy to guarantee male transcendence, the world falls back into mere nature, is an 'unweeded garden' possessed by 'things rank and gross in nature' (I.ii.135, 136). The masculine principle, based on control and transcendence of nature, becomes a mockery in the face of an amoral, engulfing, animal nature. Since the masculine principle is the pole that attempts to deduce or impose significance on human life, the undermining of legitimacy also undermines whatever significance an age has attributed to *bios*. Without the guarantee of female chaste constancy, life loses all meaning.

The young idealist is thrown into despair by this perception. He has believed what he was taught too (like Ophelia and Laertes), that women were chaste and constant, males legitimate and noble, that both genders bent to the support and protection of the other in the face of the rough winds of heaven.

But the truth he discovers is other: no man should 'scape whipping. Thus, quickly, Hamlet's questioning of male legitimacy extends to his own. The 'vicious mole of nature' infects him as well as other humans. His own flesh is – perhaps – sullied; he is rogue, slave, peasant, whore, drab, an arrant knave crawling between earth and heaven, a sinner who now believes that all humans are depraved. And this belief, conveyed to Hamlet by the ghost's information, becomes a self-fulfilling prophecy.

Hamlet harps on his major concerns throughout the play. His dialogue with Polonius in II.ii contains three main themes: an attack on the fragility of female chaste constancy; mockery of the counsellor, who, as he is old and foolish, is illegitimate and not deserving of respect; and his desire to die. Immediately afterwards he tells Rosencrantz and Guildenstern that Denmark is a prison – a cage full of illegitimates – and moves to the theme of illegitimacy. He announces, almost with surprise, that 'then are our beggars bodies, and our monarchs and outstretch'd heroes the beggars' shadows' (II.ii.263–4). Soon afterwards, he refers to himself as a beggar.

Loss of faith in the inlaw feminine principle leads to loss of faith in male legitimacy, and thus to suspicion of male pretensions. But

Hamlet's whole world is built on male pretensions. Seeing male prerogatives as pretensions, however, leads to his sense of Claudius as a diminished thing, his abuse of the old counsellor who was his father's adviser as well, and his disrespectful treatment of his mother. It leads also to his sense of himself as being weak as a peasant, wordy as a whore, as helpless as an infant to put the times in joint.

Hamlet's real hate for Claudius is not for the fact of the murder, but for his illegitimacy: Claudius is, he claims, a slave, a cutpurse, a 'king of shreds and patches' (II.iv.102). In this way, the seemingly digressive scenes with the players are central to the play. In a world where everyone is vicious, everyone is a player. What is important in such a world is *how* you play the game; Hamlet's instructions to the players are a parallel to Polonius' directions to Laertes, and to Hamlet's own orders to his mother to assume a virtue she does not possess.

The appearance of the actors is preceded by a discussion of the inconstancy and low standards of a city audience willing to take children in place of men (which Hamlet compares with the willingness of the Danes – and implicitly of his mother – to take his uncle in place of the real thing). Hamlet asks the players to perform an esoteric piece, a passage describing a situation somewhat like Hamlet's own: a man avenges his father's killing by killing the father of the man who killed him. The language, however, describes the destruction of the feminine principle – Priam is old and physically powerless; he is reverent, his head is milky; at his fall, the heavens should cry milky tears; Hecuba is constant, worn out by childbearing – by a 'painted tyrant', who is momentarily paralysed in his slaughter by an accident that 'takes prisoner Pyrrhus' ear' (II.ii.480, 477), an allusion that reminds us of the 'leprous distilment' poured into the ear of Hamlet's father, paralysing him by posseting his blood; and the poison poured in Hamlet's ear by the ghost, paralysing him.

The relations between appearance and reality are not simple in this play – or elsewhere in Shakespeare. For the players' expressions, offering an acted despair, seem realer than Hamlet's expression of his real despair. He mistrusts everyone around him (except Horatio), but some of what occurs around him is real in some way. Ophelia is part of a trap, but she is innocent; Claudius feels guilty despite his assurance. Hamlet's 'mad' seemings are as real as, or perhaps more genuine than his calmer behaviour. Certitude resides only with legitimacy, which seems to have vanished from the earth.

Challenge of the very notion of legitimacy informs Hamlet's confrontation with Claudius after his murder of Polonius, as he derisively tells the King 'your fat king . . . may go a progress through the guts of a beggar' (IV.iii.23; 30–1). And challenge of legitimacy reaches its climax in the graveyard scene, when Hamlet traces the transformation of the most legitimate of legitimates, the world's greatest conquerors, through to the loam used to stuff bungholes. He does not, in this scene, come to terms with his mortality, as much as he discards finally the entire notion of legitimacy.[12]

Nevertheless, he claims it on occasion. He uses his father's ring to seal the substituted letter Rosencrantz and Guildenstern bear with them to England; he challenges Laertes in Ophelia's grave, crying 'It is I, Hamlet the Dane!' And his final act, his request that Horatio remain alive to tell his story, is another motion toward legitimacy: he cares about his name, fame, honour, immortality.[13]

This split in attitudes towards male legitimacy is of a piece with many other of Hamlet's attitudes. His language is alternately lofty or vulgar – or at least, slangy – if always eloquent.[14] His behaviour alternates between rash cruelty, savage action, and gentle, melancholy reflection.[15] He vacillates between thinking he must avenge his father by killing Claudius, and wanting to avenge himself by injuring Gertrude. He frequently exhorts himself to anger against the King; but he must exhort himself to control his anger against his mother.

For, if Hamlet's primary intellectual response to the information given him by the ghost is to question legitimacy, his primary emotional response is outrage at his mother's failure in chaste constancy.[16] Hamlet passes Claudius in the chapel, missing his chance and rationalising this with a religious 'reason'. But Hamlet would surely know that repentance for sins like Claudius' requires penance more substantial than prayer. He does have bloody thoughts, but they are not directed at the King. They are directed at Gertrude, and despite his attempts at control, he does physically assault her to the degree that she thinks he is about to kill her. Within moments, he stabs Polonius, taking him for the King, although he has just seen Claudius in the chapel. It is unclear whether Hamlet is being illogical or simply unthinking: what is clear is that in his mother's closet he is emotionally fevered enough to act, furious enough to kill, and could have killed Claudius – *there*.

The central act of the play opens with a court scene involving plotting to discover Hamlet's problem by setting Ophelia out as a trap. In their encounter, Hamlet savagely attacks Ophelia. At the end of the act, he savagely attacks his mother. The central act of the play is thus framed by Hamlet's attacks on women, underscoring the centrality – and failure – of chaste constancy in Hamlet's moral universe.

Hamlet begins to attack Ophelia by suggesting that she may be chaste, but will not be for long because even his mother is not – 'the time gives it proof' (III.i.114).[17] He moves immediately to a satiric estimation of his own illegitimacy and viciousness. He ends with a scathing attack on Ophelia, and all women, as false, wanton, and able to turn men into monsters. As we have seen before, failure in one woman is projected to failure in all in Shakespeare's work. Hamlet's words and rhythms in these speeches are powerful; there is nothing in the play that can compare to these speeches in hatred except those uttered to his mother.

He attacks Gertrude more directly. Her act, he says,

> blurs the grace and blush of modesty,
> Calls virtue hypocrite, takes off the rose
> From the fair forehead of an innocent love
> And sets a blister there, makes marriage vows
> As false as dicers' oaths, O, such a deed
> As from the body of contraction plucks
> The very soul, and sweet religion makes
> A rhapsody of words. Heaven's face does glow
> O'er this solidity and compound mass
> With heated visage, as against the doom;
> Is thought-sick at the act.
>
> (III.iv.41–51)

Hamlet is outraged that Gertrude should feel desire at all:

> O shame, where is thy blush? Rebellious hell,
> If thou canst mutine in a matron's bones,
> To flaming youth let virtue be as wax
> And melt in her own fire. Proclaim no shame
> When the compulsive ardure gives the charge,
> Since frost itself as actively doth burn,
> And reason panders will....
>   Nay, but to live
> In the rank sweat of an enseamed bed,
> Stew'd in corruption, honeying and making love
> Over the nasty sty!...
> Let the bloat king tempt you again to bed,
> Pinch wanton on your cheek, call you his mouse,
> And let him, for a pair of reechy kisses,
> Or paddling in your neck with his damn'd fingers,
> Make you to ravel all this matter out.
>
> (III.iv.81–8; 91–4; 182–6)

Like his ghost-father, Hamlet barely mentions Claudius in this scene, and his references are diminishing rather than angry or hating: Gertrude, Hamlet says, has stepped from a man who combined the qualities of the gods, to a 'mildewed ear' (III.iv.64).

The scene with Gertrude is, on one level of the play, the climax. After Hamlet has persuaded his mother to refrain from Claudius' bed, he becomes a somewhat different person. He is openly flip and derisive to Claudius, which he has not been before. He seems to feel he has accomplished his real task, as indeed, if the ghost's words at the beginning of the play are examined carefully, he has. He accepts without demur the decision to send him to England. And upon his return, knowing Claudius sent him abroad to be killed, he goes back to the court easily, without pressure, seemingly without anxiety.

Whatever Hamlet may say to himself (and to us), there is no escaping the conclusion that Hamlet does not want to kill Claudius: Claudius the King is not important to him. Claudius the King is man dressed in a little brief authority, mere shreds and patches on a stick whose head will someday be a skull lying in the ground beside Yorick's. Like Pyrrhus, Claudius is a 'painted tyrant'. Hamlet is not interested in power-in-the-world. He knows legitimacy is a delusion, a pretension.

Claudius, Gertrude's husband, is another matter. The root of Hamlet's feeling about his mother's sexuality may perhaps be Oedipal jealousy, but it has been transformed into something very different. The play is full of clues to the source of his outrage as Hamlet feels it: it lies in a sense of humankind as vicious, and of sex as disgusting, loathsome, and bestial, as a giving up of the control necessary to distinguish man from animal. Woman, the link between these two realms, must therefore renounce sexuality, and this act is *absolutely necessary* to purify, sanctify any human claims to humanness, to difference from, transcendence of the beast. A chaste constant woman would not feel desire, would do 'but duty', and would firmly corset her man, and guarantee a line of legitimate males.

The placing of so much moral weight on the state of a vagina is rationally absurd, and charges of insufficient objective correlatives to Hamlet's emotional state are understandable. But chaste constancy is the cornerstone of Shakespeare's moral universe throughout his work. Hamlet's feelings are understandable only in the context of this fact, understandable perhaps only through immersion in the entire canon. For Shakespeare, without chaste constancy, nothing is real except death, because only death endures when women are not constant, and in a world of appearances, only what endures is real.

The central segment of *Hamlet* opens with the plot and the attack on Ophelia, closes with the attack on Gertrude. Between these is the visit of the players and the performance of 'The Mousetrap'. The entire spoken portion of the play-within-a-play concerns constancy, and is implicitly a reproach to inconstant women. The King insists constancy is difficult and perhaps impossible; the Queen insists it is possible and swears herself to it. Hamlet comments: 'If she should break it now!' (III.ii.224). He arranges for the play to catch the conscience of the King, he says; but that conscience, which is moved to prayer (or its attempt), seems of little interest to him once it is caught. It is rather the conscience of the Queen that Hamlet is fishing for.

The two crimes that have been committed in Denmark are murder and 'incest'. Both acts are permissible if performed with licence – with ceremonial purification by the state operating under what are claimed to be divine sanctions (Henry VIII married his brother's legal wife). The state (or its military or judicial agents) may kill those called enemies or criminals, and may even praise its own acts. Copulation is permitted in marriage (and tolerated in men who use women who have been isolated and segregated in a special class designed precisely for this purpose – demimondaines and prostitutes). Murder is the extreme of the masculine principle; copulation is the foundation of giving birth, the extreme of the feminine principle. Of the two, copulation without sanctification, by a woman, is the worse crime. This is suggested in *Much Ado*, and is explicit in both the design and the plot of *Hamlet*. In *Measure for Measure*, the subject is debated by Angelo and Isabel. They disagree on most things, but agree on this.

Because of the importance of chaste constancy in *Hamlet*, the intellectual level (plot) of the play conflicts with the emotional level (design). The split apparent in Hamlet's sensibility and behaviour is built into the very structure of the play. The linear plot – Hamlet's bond to avenge his father – is irrelevant to his real priorities. Thus, his path *is* blocked, his paralysis is real – he is uninterested in doing what he thinks he should do, and wants to do what he knows he should not do. And nothing can repair the situation. The Queen's failure in chaste constancy cannot be altered; it can be remedied, and is, although early in the play Hamlet does not conceive of ordering his mother to refrain from sex. But even so, its fatal work has been done: Gertrude's failure has inspired Claudius to kill his brother: God is dead, a creature of shreds and patches sits on the throne. And indeed, when Hamlet does finally kill Claudius, he does not kill a king, he kills an 'incestious, murd'rous' man (V.ii.325), the man who 'whor'd' his mother (V.ii.64).

On the mythic level, *Hamlet* is about a young man growing into adulthood. His memories of the past are idyllic – his father is full of both power and 'divine' virtues, is a perfect synthesis of masculine and feminine principles. He is the full incarnation of the ideal and legitimate male: God, King, Father. And, like the ideal Henry V, and the ideal fathers who follow him in haunting the first tetralogy, he is dead. He exists as memory, tradition, and above all, certitude. He haunts, with knowledge of a prelapsarian virtue and certitude, the imagination of an idealist unlucky enough to stumble on sexuality in his mother and murder in his father.

Claudius and King Hamlet have performed the same acts. Both are devoted to Gertrude and have made love to her, one after ceremonial purification, the other without it. Both have killed, one in a cere-monially purified way (war), the other independently and for himself (murder). On the mythic level, the dead King and his loving wife are the idyllic creations of childhood; the murderous King and his ardent wife are the parents the young man returns to discover after years spent away at school. The disguise convention that permits Hero to die and be resurrected is here internalised and reversed: the play opens after both funeral and wedding. The old King and his wife have died and have been resurrected in Claudius and Gertrude.

Hamlet's primary response in action to the discovery or realisation that all human experience is bounded by its two most profound acts – killing and giving birth (with the implicit corollary that birth requires sexual intercourse) – is to meditate upon and feel its implications. It is because of this tendency that Hamlet is seen as sensitive, intellectual, and feminine.[18] Actually, his actions are more violent, and rasher than those of any other character. He is as malicious (to Rosencrantz and Guildenstern) as Claudius, as savage as Laertes, as given to plots (the play-within-the-play) as Polonius. And like Hamlet, the play is formally and in content divided between the gender principles.

To meditate on and consciously feel experience is 'feminine'. Such behaviour never moves in a linear way, but occurs in clusters which may be static and are essentially associative rather than logical. Thus, the structure of *Hamlet* is at times 'feminine', comedic, and seems digressive for a tragedy. There are loose connections, many delays, and full stops during the soliloquies which are devoted to Hamlet's sensations/emotions/thoughts.[19] The rigorous causal logic of action-oriented plays is lacking, as Tillyard complains.[20] Rather, the play 'creates so marvellous a sense of the actual improvisation of life that we can find no simple logic in its sprawling action'.[21]

In addition, the play has a more multiple focus than most of the tragedies, and resembles comedy in this. It casts attention on Polonius, his family, and servant; on Claudius with a series of characters; on Gertrude and Ophelia, as well as the protagonist. And it shows the effect, not just in behaviour, action, but in feeling and thought, of a thought pattern or set that is rooted in a belief in the inherent viciousness of humankind. The series of son-father vengeances that appears in the larger play and the play within demonstrate the impossibility of right action in an illegitimate world. G. Wilson Knight suggests that 'the question of the relative morality of Hamlet and Claudius reflects the ultimate problem of this play'.[22] But that relativity embraces others too – Laertes, Fortinbras, and the female figures as well. *Hamlet*, along with *King Lear*, directly confronts the void in which we live if we permit ourselves to penetrate the carefully erected curtain of significance that normally obscures it. Incertitude about the purpose of life leads to incertitude about any code of behaviour.

From Marilyn French, *Shakespeare's Division of Experience* (London, 1982), pp. 145–58.

NOTES

[Marilyn French begins her book *Shakespeare's Division of Experience* by examining what she calls the gender principles in traditional Western attitudes and values. The masculine principle, she suggests, 'is predicated on the ability to kill', and is associated with 'prowess and ownership, with physical courage, assertiveness, authority ... and legitimacy' (p. 21). But it also 'values action over feeling' (p. 22). The feminine principle, predicated on the ability to give birth, is split in two. Its 'outlaw' aspects associate woman with 'darkness, chaos, flesh, the sinister, magic and above all, sexuality' (p. 23), whereas its 'inlaw' aspects associate her with feeling, mercy, with the divine. Thus, French continues, 'females may be saints and goddesses, or they may be whores and bitches' (p. 26). They have little power in the world or in Shakespeare's plays except when they disguise themselves as men; again, in the plays they do not change or develop and are 'either utterly good or utterly evil' (p. 29).

These ideas provide the basis for French's discussion of *Hamlet* above. Hamlet's intellectual response to the Ghost's story, French suggests, is to question male legitimacy in Claudius, but 'his primary emotional response is outrage at his mother's failure in chaste constancy', outrage that she can feel sexual desire at all. This split in attitudes, French argues, is reflected in the play's structure as a whole, as well as in Hamlet's language and in his paralysis – 'he is uninterested in doing what he thinks he should do, and wants to do what he knows he should not do'. Lively and provocative, French's analysis not only offers new insights into new aspects of *Hamlet*, but also reveals how far modern criticism has moved away from Aristotelian notions of tragedy, with its stress on character and tragic flaw, towards seeing tragedy instead in terms of the destructive and limiting codes that shape people – towards seeing tragedy, that is, as a construct of ideology. All quotations in the extract are from *The Riverside Shakespeare*, ed. G. Blakemore Evans (Boston, 1974). Ed.]

1. Maynard Mack, 'The World of *Hamlet*', *Yale Review*, 41 (1952), 502–23; Harry Levin, *The Question of 'Hamlet'* (New York, 1959).

2. See Maynard Mack (above).

3. Mack (above) points out that all the major persons of the drama are players. This notion is developed by Ann Righter, *Shakespeare and the Idea of the Play* (London, 1964).

4. That the characters are continually checking up on each other is pointed out by Robert Heilman, 'The Lear World', *English Institute Essays: 1948*, ed. D. A. Robertson, Jr. (New York, 1949).

5. Many critics have suggested this or something like it. Dover Wilson was probably the first to suggest it in *What Happens in 'Hamlet'* (Cambridge, 1935).

6. These are suggested, in order, by: Theodore Spencer, *Shakespeare and the Nature of Man* (New York, 1942); Theodore Spencer (as above) and H. B. Charlton, *Shakespearian Tragedy* (Cambridge, 1948); Norman Council, *When Honour's at the Stake* (London, 1973) and E. K. Chambers, *Shakespeare* (London, 1925), as well as Patrick Cruttwell, *The Shakespearian Moment* (New York, 1955), who speaks of lost ideals; E. K. Chambers (as above); and Erich Heller, *The Artist's Journey Into the Interior* (New York, 1976), among others.

7. A. P. Rossiter, *Angel with Horns*, ed. Graham Storey (London, 1961), p. 179, writes that Hamlet is inclined to believe in absolute good and evil but is placed in circumstances which cause him to act as if there were no absolutes. H. D. F. Kitto sees the entire play-world as polluted: 'A Classical Scholar looks at Shakespeare', in *More Talking of Shakespeare*, ed. John Garrett (London, 1959). Alice Shalvi, *The Relationship of Renaissance Concepts of Honour to Shakespeare's Problem Plays* (Salzburg, 1972), and Norman Council, *When Honour's at the Stake*

(London, 1973), both see Hamlet as attempting to act genuinely in the face of a society riddled with outworn and conventional moral precepts. It was Caroline Spurgeon, of course, who first pointed to the images of sickness, disease, and disfigurement. See her *Shakespeare's Imagery* (Boston, 1961), p. 316.

8. This is discussed by Alice Shalvi (above), p. 132.

9. James Joyce has not been taken seriously as a Shakespeare critic, despite the importance of Shakespeare the man and his creations to *Ulysses*. But, although Joyce seized on only those elements of Shakespeare that were useful to him, he was an incisive reader of the poet. The character of Stephen Dedalus is to some degree modelled on Hamlet. Stephen is paralysed, fearing the consequences both of action and inaction; he desires above all certitude, a rational explanation of the cosmos that would provide him with a clear basis for right action. He also wants undying love, love for him alone. He sees Shakespeare's obsession with cuckoldry and money as a need to possess, to pin down; he associates Shakespeare with Shylock and with Othello. Stephen's fiction about Shakespeare is as much about himself as the playwright, but it has relevance to Shakespeare's work, particularly *Hamlet*. The young man describes Shakespeare thus: 'Lover of an ideal or a perversion, like José he kills the real Carmen.' Stephen too is filled with disgust for sexuality, and sees fornication as a clasping and sundering, doing 'the coupler's will', and conception and gestation as being 'wombed in sin darkness' (James Joyce, *Ulysses* [New York, 1966], pp. 212, 38).

10. Norman Council, *When Honour's at the Stake* (London, 1973), p. 110, discusses conventional virtue as being untrustworthy as a guide to action.

11. G. Wilson Knight, *The Wheel of Fire* (New York, 1947), p. 43.

12. Maynard Mack, 'The World of *Hamlet*', *Yale Review*, 41 (1952), 502–23, claims that in the graveyard, Hamlet finally accepts his mortality.

13. Patrick Cruttwell, *The Shakespearian Moment* (New York, 1955), p. 85, points out that at the end of their lives, both Hamlet and Othello show concern with their reputations on earth.

14. Wolfgang Clemen, *The Development of Shakespeare's Imagery* (Cambridge, 1951), p. 109.

15. Robert Ornstein, *The Moral Vision of Jacobean Tragedy* (Madison, 1960), p. 235, analyses the way the point of view of the drama allows us to accept Hamlet's brutality and cruelty without questioning it.

16. Many critics, from Boas on, have pointed out that it is 'the queen's frailty' that moves Hamlet rather than the King's 'villainy' (Frederick Boas, *Shakspere and His Predecessors*, New York, 1986, p. 403). Tillyard discusses this situation at length in *Shakespeare's Problem*

Plays (Toronto, 1949), pp. 22–6, as does Dover Wilson in *The Essential Shakespeare* (Cambridge, 1932), p. 119.

17. Numerous critics have suggested a connection between Hamlet's feelings about his mother and his treatment of Ophelia. Reuben Brower, *Hero and Saint* (New York, 1971), p. 263, writes of Troilus that he, 'like Hamlet ... feels that if his love is false all "womankind", all "mothers", must be so too'. O. J. Campbell, however, sees in Hamlet's tirade to Ophelia (III.i) 'little importance for the plot of the play', since it is 'merely a familiar satiric interlude' (*Shakespeare's Satire* [New York, 1943], p. 153).

18. G. Wilson Knight, *The Wheel of Fire* (New York, 1947), p. 307, sees Hamlet's mind as set between extremes of 'extraversion and introversion, of masculine and feminine'.

19. Frederick Boas, *Shakspere and His Predecessors* (New York, 1986), p. 389, writes that the soliloquies have little relation to the 'actual progress of events' in the play. Wolfgang Clemen, *Shakespeare's Dramatic Art* (London, 1972), p. 65, finds the structure full of retarding episodes and digressions and concludes that the play is 'loosely constructed'.

20. E. M. W. Tillyard, *Shakespeare's Problem Plays* (Toronto, 1949), p. 29.

21. Robert Ornstein, *The Moral Vision of Jacobean Tragedy* (Madison, 1960), p. 234.

22. G. Wilson Knight, *The Wheel of Fire* (New York, 1947), p. 28.

8

Representing Ophelia: Women, Madness and the Responsibilities of Feminist Criticism

ELAINE SHOWALTER

'As sort of a come-on, I announced that I would speak today about that piece of bait named Ophelia, and I'll be as good as my word.' These are the words which begin the psychoanalytic seminar on *Hamlet* presented in Paris in 1959 by Jacques Lacan. But despite his promising come-on, Lacan was *not* as good as his word. He goes on for some 41 pages to speak about Hamlet, and when he does mention Ophelia, she is merely what Lacan calls 'the object Ophelia' – that is, the object of Hamlet's male desire. The etymology of Ophelia, Lacan asserts, is 'O-phallus', and her role in the drama can only be to function as the exteriorised figuration of what Lacan predictably and, in view of his own early work with psychotic women, disappointingly suggests is the phallus as transcendental signifier.[1] To play such a part obviously makes Ophelia 'essential', as Lacan admits; but only because, in his words, 'she is linked forever, for centuries, to the figure of Hamlet'.

The bait-and-switch game that Lacan plays with Ophelia is a cynical but not unusual instance of her deployment in psychiatric and critical texts. For most critics of Shakespeare, Ophelia has been an insignificant minor character in the play, touching in her weakness and madness but chiefly interesting, of course, in what she tells us about Hamlet. And while female readers of Shakespeare have often attempted to champion Ophelia, even feminist critics have done so with a certain embarrassment. As Annette Kolodny ruefully admits: 'it is after all, an imposition of high order to ask the viewer to attend to Ophelia's sufferings in a scene where, before, he's always so comfortably kept his eye fixed on Hamlet'.[2]

Yet when feminist criticism allows Ophelia to upstage Hamlet, it also brings to the foreground the issues in an ongoing theoretical debate about the cultural links between femininity, female sexuality, insanity, and representation. Though she is neglected in criticism, Ophelia is probably the most frequently illustrated and cited of Shakespeare's heroines. Her visibility as a subject in literature, popular culture, and painting, from Redon who paints her drowning, to Bob Dylan, who places her on Desolation Row, to Cannon Mills, which has named a flowery sheet pattern after her, is in inverse relation to her invisibility in Shakespearean critical texts. Why has she been such a potent and obsessive figure in our cultural mythology? In so far as Hamlet names Ophelia as 'woman' and 'frailty', substituting an ideological view of femininity for a personal one, is she indeed representative of Woman, and does her madness stand for the oppression of women in society as well as in tragedy? Furthermore, since Laertes calls Ophelia a 'document in madness', does she represent the textual archetype of woman *as* madness or madness *as* woman? And finally, how should feminist criticism represent Ophelia in its own discourse? What is our responsibility towards her as character and as woman?

Feminist critics have offered a variety of responses to these questions. Some have maintained that we should represent Ophelia as a lawyer represents a client, that we should become her Horatia, in this harsh world reporting her and her cause aright to the unsatisfied. Carol Neely, for example, describes advocacy – speaking *for* Ophelia – as our proper role: 'As a feminist critic', she writes, 'I must "tell" Ophelia's story.'[3] But what can we mean by Ophelia's story? The story of her life? The story of her betrayal at the hands of her father, brother, lover, court, society? The story of her rejection and marginalisation by male critics of Shakespeare? Shakespeare gives us very little information from which to imagine a past for Ophelia. She appears in only five of the play's twenty scenes; the pre-play course of her love story with Hamlet is known only by a few ambiguous flashbacks. Her tragedy is subordinated in the play; unlike Hamlet, she does not struggle with moral choices or alternatives. Thus another feminist critic, Lee Edwards, concludes that it is impossible to reconstruct Ophelia's biography from the text: 'We can imagine Hamlet's story without Ophelia, but Ophelia literally has no story without Hamlet.'[4]

If we turn from American to French feminist theory, Ophelia might confirm the impossibility of representing the feminine in patriarchal discourse as other than madness, incoherence, fluidity, or silence. In French theoretical criticism, the feminine or 'Woman' is that which escapes representation in patriarchal language and symbolism; it remains on the side of negativity, absence, and lack. In comparison to Hamlet, Ophelia is certainly a creature of lack. 'I think nothing, my lord', she tells him in the Mousetrap scene, and he cruelly twists her words:

> Hamlet   That's a fair thought to lie between maids' legs.
> Ophelia   What is, my lord?
> Hamlet   Nothing.
>
> (III.ii.117–19)

In Elizabethan slang, 'nothing' was a term for the female genitalia, as in *Much Ado About Nothing*. To Hamlet, then, 'nothing' is what lies between maids' legs, for, in the male visual system of representation and desire, women's sexual organs, in the words of the French psychoanalyst Luce Irigaray, 'represent the horror of having nothing to see'.[5] When Ophelia is mad, Gertrude says that 'Her speech is nothing', mere 'unshaped use'. Ophelia's speech thus represents the horror of having nothing to say in the public terms defined by the court. Deprived of thought, sexuality, language, Ophelia's story becomes the Story of O— the zero, the empty circle or mystery of feminine difference, the cipher of female sexuality to be deciphered by feminist interpretation.[6]

A third approach would be to read Ophelia's story as the female subtext of the tragedy, the repressed story of Hamlet. In this reading, Ophelia represents the strong emotions that the Elizabethans as well as the Freudians thought womanish and unmanly. When Laertes weeps for his dead sister he says of his tears that 'When these are gone, / The woman will be out' – that is to say, that the feminine and shameful part of his nature will be purged. According to David Leverenz, in an important essay called 'The Woman in Hamlet', Hamlet's disgust at the feminine passivity in himself is translated into violent revulsion against women, and into his brutal behaviour towards Ophelia. Ophelia's suicide, Leverenz argues, then becomes 'a microcosm of the male world's banishment of the female, because "woman" represents everything denied by reasonable men'.[7]

It is perhaps because Hamlet's emotional vulnerability can so readily be conceptualised as feminine that this is the only heroic male role in Shakespeare which has been regularly acted by women, in a tradition from Sarah Bernhardt to, most recently, Diane Venora, in a production directed by Joseph Papp. Leopold Bloom speculates on this tradition in *Ulysses*, musing on the Hamlet of the actress Mrs Bandman Palmer: 'Male impersonator. Perhaps he was a woman? Why Ophelia committed suicide?'[8]

While all of these approaches have much to recommend them, each also presents critical problems. To liberate Ophelia from the text, or to make her its tragic centre, is to re-appropriate her for our own ends; to dissolve her into a female symbolism of absence is to endorse our own marginality; to make her Hamlet's anima is to reduce her to a metaphor of male experience. I would like to propose instead that Ophelia *does* have a story of her own that feminist criticism can tell; it is neither her life story, nor her love story, nor Lacan's story, but rather the *history* of her representation. This essay tries to bring together some of the categories of French feminist thought about the 'feminine' with the empirical energies of American historical and critical research: to yoke French theory and Yankee knowhow.

Tracing the iconography of Ophelia in English and French painting, photography, psychiatry, and literature, as well as in theatrical production, I will be showing first of all the representational bonds between female insanity and female sexuality. Secondly, I want to demonstrate the two-way transaction between psychiatric theory and cultural representation. As one medical historian has observed, we could provide a manual of female insanity by chronicling the illustrations of Ophelia; this is so because the illustrations of Ophelia have played a major role in the theoretical construction of female insanity.[9] Finally, I want to suggest that the feminist revision of Ophelia comes as much from the actress's freedom as from the critic's interpretation.[10] When Shakespeare's heroines began to be played by women instead of boys, the presence of the female body and female voice, quite apart from details of interpretation, created new meanings and subversive tensions in these roles, and perhaps most importantly with Ophelia. Looking at Ophelia's history on and off the stage, I will point out the contest between male and female representations of Ophelia, cycles of critical repression and feminist reclamation of which contemporary feminist criticism is only the most recent phase. By beginning with these data from cultural history, instead of moving from the grid of literary theory, I hope to conclude with a fuller sense of the responsibilities of feminist criticism, as well as a new perspective on Ophelia.

*

'Of all the characters in *Hamlet*', Bridget Lyons has pointed out, 'Ophelia is most persistently presented in terms of symbolic meanings'.[11] Her behaviour, her appearance, her gestures, her costume, her props, are freighted with emblematic significance, and for many generations of Shakespearean critics her part in the play has seemed to be primarily iconographic. Ophelia's symbolic meanings, moreover, are specifically feminine. Whereas for Hamlet madness is metaphysical, linked with culture, for Ophelia it is a product of the female body and female nature, perhaps that nature's purest form. On the Elizabethan stage, the conventions of female insanity were sharply defined. Ophelia dresses in white, decks herself with 'fantastical garlands' of wild flowers, and enters, according to the stage directions of the 'Bad' Quarto, 'distracted' playing on a lute with her 'hair down singing'. Her speeches are marked by extravagant metaphors, lyrical free associations, and 'explosive sexual imagery'.[12] She sings wistful and bawdy ballads, and ends her life by drowning.

All of these conventions carry specific messages about femininity and sexuality. Ophelia's virginal and vacant white is contrasted with Hamlet's scholar's garb, his 'suits of solemn black'. Her flowers suggest the discordant double images of female sexuality as both innocent blossoming and whorish contamination; she is the 'green girl' of pastoral, the virginal 'Rose of May' and the sexually explicit madwoman who, in giving away her wild flowers and herbs, is symbolically deflowering herself. The 'weedy trophies' and phallic 'long purples' which she wears to her death intimate an improper and discordant sexuality that Gertrude's lovely elegy cannot quite obscure.[13] In Elizabethan and Jacobean drama, the stage direction that a woman enters with dishevelled hair indicates that she might either be mad or the victim of a rape; the disordered hair, her offence against decorum, suggests sensuality in each case.[14] The mad Ophelia's bawdy songs and verbal licence, while they give her access to 'an entirely different range of experience' from what she is allowed as the dutiful daughter, seem to be her one sanctioned form of self-assertion as a woman, quickly followed, as if in retribution, by her death.[15]

Drowning too was associated with the feminine, with female

fluidity as opposed to masculine aridity. In his discussion of the 'Ophelia complex', the phenomenologist Gaston Bachelard traces the symbolic connections between women, water, and death. Drowning, he suggests, becomes the truly feminine death in the dramas of literature and life, one which is a beautiful immersion and submersion in the female element. Water is the profound and organic symbol of the liquid woman whose eyes are so easily drowned in tears, as her body is the repository of blood, amniotic fluid, and milk. A man contemplating this feminine suicide understands it by reaching for what is feminine in himself, like Laertes, by a temporary surrender to his own fluidity – that is, his tears; and he becomes a man again in becoming once more dry – when his tears are stopped.[16]

Clinically speaking, Ophelia's behaviour and appearance are characteristic of the malady the Elizabethans would have diagnosed as female love-melancholy, or erotomania. From about 1580, melancholy had become a fashionable disease among young men, especially in London, and Hamlet himself is a prototype of the melancholy hero. Yet the epidemic of melancholy associated with intellectual and imaginative genius 'curiously bypassed women'. Women's melancholy was seen instead as biological, and emotional in origins.[17]

On the stage, Ophelia's madness was presented as the predictable outcome of erotomania. From 1660, when women first appeared on the public stage, to the beginnings of the eighteenth century, the most celebrated of the actresses who played Ophelia were those whom rumour credited with disappointments in love. The greatest triumph was reserved for Susan Mountfort, a former actress at Lincoln's Inn Fields who had gone mad after her lover's betrayal. One night in 1720 she escaped from her keeper, rushed to the theatre, and just as the Ophelia of the evening was to enter for her mad scene, 'sprang forward in her place . . . with wild eyes and wavering motion'.[18] As a contemporary reported, 'she was in truth *Ophelia herself*, to the amazement of the performers as well as of the audience – nature having made this last effort, her vital powers failed her and she died soon after'.[19] These theatrical legends reinforced the belief of the age that female madness was a part of female nature, less to be imitated by an actress than demonstrated by a deranged woman in a performance of her emotions.

The subversive or violent possibilities of the mad scene were nearly eliminated, however, on the eighteenth-century stage. Late Augustan stereotypes of female love-melancholy were sentimantalised versions which minimised the force of female sexuality, and made female insanity a pretty stimulant to male sensibility. Actresses such as Mrs Lessingham in 1772, and Mary Bolton in 1811, played Ophelia in this decorous style, relying on the familiar images of the white dress, loose hair, and wild flowers to convey a polite feminine distraction, highly suitable for pictorial reproduction, and appropriate for Samuel Johnson's description of Ophelia as young, beautiful, harmless, and pious. Even Mrs Siddons in 1785 played the mad scene with stately and classical dignity. For much of the period, in fact, Augustan objections to the levity and indecency of Ophelia's language and behaviour led to censorship of the part. Her lines were frequently cut, and the role was often assigned to a singer instead of an actress, making the mode of representation musical rather than visual or verbal.

But whereas the Augustan response to madness was a denial, the romantic response was an embrace.[20] The figure of the madwoman permeates romantic literature, from the gothic novelists to Wordsworth and Scott in such texts as 'The Thorn' and *The Heart of Midlothian*, where she stands for sexual victimisation, bereavement, and thrilling emotional extremity. Romantic artists such as Thomas Barker and George Shepheard painted pathetically abandoned Crazy Kates and Crazy Anns, while Henry Fuseli's 'Mad Kate' is almost demonically possessed, an orphan of the romantic storm.

In the Shakespearean theatre, Ophelia's romantic revival began in France rather than England. When Charles Kemble made his Paris debut as Hamlet with an English troupe in 1827, his Ophelia was a young Irish ingénue named Harriet Smithson. Smithson used 'her extensive command of mime to depict in precise gesture the state of Ophelia's confused mind'.[21] In the mad scene, she entered in a long black veil, suggesting the standard imagery of female sexual mystery in the gothic novel, with scattered bedlamish wisps of straw in her hair. Spreading the veil on the ground as she sang, she spread flowers upon it in the shape of a cross, as if to make her father's grave, and mimed a burial, a piece of stage business which remained in vogue for the rest of the century.

The French audiences were stunned. Dumas recalled that 'it was the first time I saw in the theatre real passions, giving life to men and women of flesh and blood'.[22] The 23-year-old Hector Berlioz, who was in the audience on the first night, fell madly in love, and eventually married Harriet Smithson despite his family's frantic opposition. Her image as the mad Ophelia was represented in popular lithographs and exhibited in bookshop and printshop windows. Her costume was imitated by the fashionable, and a coiffure 'à la folle', consisting of a 'black veil with wisps of straw tastefully interwoven' in the hair, was widely copied by the Parisian beau monde, always on the lookout for something new.[23]

Although Smithson never acted Ophelia on the English stage, her intensely visual performance quickly influenced English productions as well; and indeed the romantic Ophelia – a young girl passionately and visibly driven to picturesque madness – became the dominant international acting style for the next 150 years, from Helena Modjeska in Poland in 1871, to the 18-year-old Jean Simmons in the Laurence Olivier film of 1948.

Whereas the romantic Hamlet, in Coleridge's famous dictum, thinks too much, has an 'overbalance of the contemplative faculty' and an overactive intellect, the romantic Ophelia is a girl who *feels* too much, who drowns in feeling. The romantic critics seem to have felt that the less said about Ophelia the better; the point was to *look* at her. Hazlitt, for one, is speechless before her, calling her 'a character almost too exquisitely touching to be dwelt upon'.[24] While the Augustans represent Ophelia as music, the romantics transform her into an *objet d'art*, as if to take literally Claudius's lament, 'poor Ophelia / Divided from herself and her fair judgment, / Without the which we are pictures'.

Smithson's performance is best recaptured in a series of pictures done by Delacroix from 1830 to 1850, which show a strong romantic interest in the relation of female sexuality and insanity.[25] The most innovative and influential of Delacroix's lithographs is *La Mort d'Ophélie* of 1843, the first of three studies. Its sensual languor, with Ophelia half-suspended in the stream as her dress slips from her body, anticipated the fascination with the erotic trance of the hysteric as it would be studied by Jean-Martin Charcot and his students, including Janet and Freud. Delacroix's interest in the drowning Ophelia is also reproduced to the point of obsession in later nineteenth-century painting. The English Pre-Raphaelites painted her again and again, choosing the drowning which is only described in the play, and where no actress's image had preceded them or interfered with their imaginative supremacy.

In the Royal Academy show of 1852, Arthur Hughes's entry shows a tiny waif-like creature – a sort of Tinker Bell Ophelia – in a filmy white gown, perched on a tree trunk by the stream. The overall effect is softened, sexless, and hazy, although the straw in her hair resembles a crown of thorns. Hughes's juxtaposition of childlike femininity and Christian martyrdom was overpowered, however, by John Everett Millais's great painting of Ophelia in the same show. While Millais's Ophelia is sensous siren as well as victim, the artist rather than the subject domintes the scene. The division of space between Ophelia and the natural details Millais had so painstakingly pursued reduces her to one more visual object; and the painting has such a hard surface, strangely flattened perspective, and brilliant light that it seems cruelly indifferent to the woman's death.

*

These Pre-Raphaelite images were part of a new and intricate traffic between images of women and madness in late nineteenth-century literature, psychiatry, drama, and art. First of all, superintendents of Victorian lunatic asylums were also enthusiasts of Shakespeare, who turned to his dramas for models of mental aberration that could be applied to their clinical practice. The case study of Ophelia was one that seemed particularly useful as an account of hysteria or mental breakdown in adolescence, a period of sexual instability which the Victorians regarded as risky for women's mental health. As Dr John Charles Bucknill, president of the Medico-Psychological Association, remarked in 1859, 'Ophelia is the very type of a class of cases by no means uncommon. Every mental physician of moderately extensive experience must have seen many Ophelias. It is a copy from nature, after the fashion of the Pre-Raphaelite school.'[26] Dr John Conolly, the celebrated superintendent of the Hanwell Asylum, and founder of the committee to make Stratford a national trust, concurred. In his *Study of Hamlet* in 1863 he noted that even casual visitors to mental institutions could recognise an Ophelia in the wards: 'the same young years, the same faded beauty, the same fantastic dress and interrupted song.'[27] Medical textbooks illustrated their discussions of female patients with sketches of Ophelia-like maidens.

But Conolly also pointed out that the graceful Ophelias who dominated the Victorian stage were quite unlike the women who had become the majority of the inmate population in Victorian public asylums. 'It seems to be supposed', he protested, 'that it is an easy task to play the part of a crazy girl, and that it is chiefly composed of singing and prettiness. The habitual courtesy, the partial rudeness of mental disorder, are things to be witnessed. . . . An actress, ambitious of something beyond cold imitation, might find the contemplation of such cases a not unprofitable study.'[28]

Yet when Ellen Terry took up Conolly's challenge, and went to an asylum to observe real madwomen, she found them 'too *theatrical*' to teach her anything.[29] This was because the iconography of the romantic Ophelia had begun to infiltrate reality, to define a style for mad young women seeking to express and communicate their distress. And where the women themselves did not willingly throw themselves into Ophelia-like postures, asylum superintendents, armed with the new technology of photography, imposed the costume, gesture, props, and expression of Ophelia upon them. In England, the camera was introduced to asylum work in the 1850s by Dr Hugh Welch Diamond, who photographed his female patients at the Surrey Asylum and at Bethlem. Diamond was heavily influenced by literary and visual models in his posing of the female subjects. His pictures of madwomen, posed in prayer, or decked with Ophelia-like garlands, were copied for Victorian consumption as touched-up lithographs in professional journals.[30]

Reality, psychiatry, and representational convention were even more confused in the photographic records of hysteria produced in the 1870s by Jean-Martin Charcot. Charcot was the first clinician to install a fully-equipped photographic atelier in his Paris hospital, La Salpêtrière, to record the performances of his hysterical stars. Charcot's clinic became, as he said, a 'living theatre' of female pathology; his women patients were coached in their performances for the camera, and, under hypnosis, were sometimes instructed to play heroines from Shakespeare. Among them, a 15-year-old girl named Augustine was featured in the published volumes called *Iconographies* in every posture of *la grande hystérie*. With her white hospital gown and flowing locks, Augustine frequently resembles the reproductions of Ophelia as icon and actress which had been in wide circulation.[31]

But if the Victorian madwoman looks mutely out from men's pictures, and acts a part men had staged and directed, she is very differently represented in the feminist revision of Ophelia initiated by newly powerful and respectable Victorian actresses, and by women critics of Shakespeare. In their efforts to defend Ophelia, they invent a story for her drawn from their own experiences, grievances, and desires.

*

Probably the most famous of the Victorian feminist revisions of the Ophelia story was Mary Cowden Clarke's *The Girlhood of Shake-*

speare's Heroines, published in 1852. Unlike other Victorian moral-
ising and didactic studies of the female characters of Shakespeare's
plays, Clarke's was specifically addressed to the wrongs of women,
and especially to the sexual double standard. In a chapter on Ophelia
called 'The rose of Elsinore', Clarke tells how the child Ophelia was
left behind in the care of a peasant couple when Polonius was called
to the court at Paris, and raised in a cottage with a foster-sister and
brother, Jutha and Ulf. Jutha is seduced and betrayed by a deceitful
knight, and Ophelia discovers the bodies of Jutha and her still-born
child, lying 'white, rigid, and still' in the deserted parlour of the
cottage in the middle of the night. Ulf, a 'hairy loutish boy', likes to
torture flies, to eat songbirds, and to rip the petals off roses, and he is
also very eager to give little Ophelia what he calls a bear-hug. Both
repelled and masochistically attracted by Ulf, Ophelia is repeatedly
cornered by him as she grows up; once she escapes the hug by hitting
him with a branch of wild roses; another time, he sneaks into her
bedroom 'in his brutish pertinacity to obtain the hug he had
promised himself', but just as he bends over her trembling body,
Ophelia is saved by the reappearance of her real mother.

A few years later, back at the court, she discovers the hanged body
of another friend, who has killed herself after being 'victimised and
deserted by the same evil seducer'. Not surprisingly, Ophelia breaks
down with brain fever – a staple mental illness of Victorian fiction –
and has prophetic hallucinations of a brook beneath willow trees
where something bad will happen to her. The warnings of Polonius
and Laertes have little to add to this history of female sexual
trauma.[32]

On the Victorian stage, it was Ellen Terry, daring and unconven-
tional in her own life, who led the way in acting Ophelia in feminist
terms as a consistent psychological study in sexual intimidation, a
girl terrified of her father, of her lover, and of life itself. Terry's debut
as Ophelia in Henry Irving's production in 1878 was a landmark.
According to one reviewer, her Ophelia was 'the terrible spectacle of
a normal girl becoming hopelessly imbecile as the result of overwhelming mental agony. Hers was an insanity without wrath or rage,
without exaltation or paroxysms.'[33] Her 'poetic and intellectual
performance' also inspired other actresses to rebel against the
conventions of invisibility and negation associated with the part.

Terry was the first to challenge the tradition of Ophelia's dressing
in emblematic white. For the French poets, such as Rimbaud, Hugo,
Musset, Mallarmé and Laforgue, whiteness was part of Ophelia's

essential feminine symbolism; they call her 'blanche Ophélia' and compare her to a lily, a cloud, or snow. Yet whiteness also made her a transparency, an absence that took on the colours of Hamlet's moods, and that, for the symbolists like Mallarmé, made her a blank page to be written over or on by the male imagination. Although Irving was able to prevent Terry from wearing black in the mad scene, exclaiming 'My God, Madam, there must be only *one* black figure in this play, and that's Hamlet!' (Irving, of course, was playing Hamlet), nonetheless actresses such as Gertrude Eliot, Helen Maude, Nora de Silva, and in Russia Vera Komisarjevskaya, gradually won the right to intensify Ophelia's presence by clothing her in Hamlet's black.[34]

By the turn of the century, there was both a male and a female discourse on Ophelia. A. C. Bradley spoke for the Victorian male tradition when he noted in *Shakespearean Tragedy* (1904) that 'a large number of readers feel a kind of personal irritation against Ophelia; they seem unable to forgive her for not having been a heroine'.[35] The feminist counterview was represented by actresses in such works as Helena Faucit's study of Shakespeare's female characters, and *The True Ophelia*, written by an anonymous actress in 1914, which protested against the 'insipid little creature' of criticism, and advocated a strong and intelligent woman destroyed by the heartlessness of men.[36] In women's paintings of the *fin de siècle* as well, Ophelia is depicted as an inspiring, even sanctified emblem of righteousness.[37]

While the widely read and influential essays of Mary Cowden Clarke are now mocked as the epitome of naïve criticism, these Victorian studies of the girlhood of Shakespeare's heroines are of course alive and well as psychoanalytic criticism, which has imagined its own prehistories of oedipal conflict and neurotic fixation; and I say this not to mock psychoanalytic criticism, but to suggest that Clarke's musings on Ophelia are a pre-Freudian speculation on the traumatic sources of a female sexual identity. The Freudian interpretation of *Hamlet* concentrated on the hero, but also had much to do with the re-sexualisation of Ophelia. As early as 1900, Freud had traced Hamlet's irresolution to an Oedipus complex, and Ernest Jones, his leading British disciple, developed this view, influencing the performances of John Gielgud and Alec Guinness in the 1930s. In his final version of the study, *Hamlet and Oedipus*, published in 1949, Jones argued that 'Ophelia should be unmistakably sensual, as she seldom is on stage. She may be "innocent" and docile, but she is very aware of her body'.[38]

In the theatre and in criticism, this Freudian edict has produced such extreme readings as that Shakespeare intends us to see Ophelia as a loose woman, and that she has been sleeping with Hamlet. Rebecca West has argued that Ophelia was not 'a correct and timid virgin of exquisite sensibilities', a view she attributes to the popularity of the Millais painting; but rather 'a disreputable young woman'.[39] In his delightful autobiography, Laurence Olivier, who made a special pilgrimage to Ernest Jones when he was preparing his *Hamlet* in the 1930s, recalls that one of his predecessors as actor-manager had said in response to the earnest question, 'Did Hamlet sleep with Ophelia?' – 'In my company, always.'[40]

The most extreme Freudian interpretation reads *Hamlet* as two parallel male and female psychodramas, the counterpointed stories of the incestuous attachments of Hamlet and Ophelia. As Theodor Lidz presents this view, while Hamlet is neurotically attached to his mother, Ophelia has an unresolved oedipal attachment to her father. She has fantasies of a lover who will abduct her from or even kill her father, and when this actually happens, her reason is destroyed by guilt as well as by lingering incestuous feelings. According to Lidz, Ophelia breaks down because she fails in the female developmental task of shifting her sexual attachment from her father 'to a man who can bring her fulfilment as a woman'.[41] We see the effects of this Freudian Ophelia on stage productions since the 1950s, where directors have hinted at an incestuous link between Ophelia and her father, or more recently, because this staging conflicts with the usual ironic treatment of Polonius, between Ophelia and Laertes. Trevor Nunn's production with Helen Mirren in 1970, for example, made Ophelia and Laertes flirtatious doubles, almost twins in their matching fur-trimmed doublets, playing duets on the lute with Polonius looking on, like Peter, Paul, and Mary. In other productions of the same period, Marianne Faithfull was a haggard Ophelia equally attracted to Hamlet and Laertes, and, in one of the few performances directed by a woman, Yvonne Nicholson sat on Laertes' lap in the advice scene, and played the part with 'rough sexual bravado'.[42]

Since the 1960s, the Freudian representation of Ophelia has been supplemented by an antipsychiatry that represents Ophelia's madness in more contemporary terms. In contrast to the psychoanalytic representation of Ophelia's sexual unconscious that connected her essential femininity to Freud's essays on female sexuality and hysteria, her madness is now seen in medical and biochemical terms, as schizophrenia. This is so in part because the schizophrenic woman has become the cultural icon of dualistic femininity in the mid-twentieth century as the erotomaniac was in the seventeenth and the hysteric in the nineteenth. It might also be traced to the work of R. D. Laing on female schizophrenia in the 1960s. Laing argued that schizophrenia was an intelligible response to the experience of invalidation within the family network, especially to the conflicting emotional messages and mystifying double binds experienced by daughters. Ophelia, he noted in *The Divided Self*, is an empty space. 'In her madness there is no one there. . . . There is no integral self-hood expressed through her actions or utterances. Incomprehensible statements are said by nothing. She has already died. There is now only a vacuum where there was once a person.'[43]

Despite his sympathy for Ophelia, Laing's readings silence her, equate her with 'nothing', more completely than any since the Augustans; and they have been translated into performances which only make Ophelia a graphic study of mental pathology. The sickest Ophelias on the contemporary stage have been those in the productions of the pathologist-director Jonathan Miller. In 1974 at the Greenwich Theatre his Ophelia sucked her thumb; by 1981, at the Warehouse in London, she was played by an actress much taller and heavier than the Hamlet (perhaps punningly cast as the young actor Anton Lesser). She began the play with a set of nervous tics and tuggings of hair which by the mad scene had become a full set of schizophrenic routines – head banging, twitching, wincing, grimacing, and drooling.[44]

But since the 1970s too we have had a feminist discourse which has offered a new perspective on Ophelia's madness as protest and rebellion. For many feminist theorists, the madwoman is a heroine, a powerful figure who rebels against the family and the social order; and the hysteric who refuses to speak the language of the patriarchal order, who speaks otherwise, is a sister.[45] In terms of effect on the theatre, the most radical application of these ideas was probably realised in Melissa Murray's agitprop play *Ophelia*, written in 1979 for the English women's theatre group 'Hormone Imbalance'. In this blank verse retelling of the Hamlet story, Ophelia becomes a lesbian and runs off with a woman servant to join a guerrilla commune.[46]

While I've always regretted that I missed this production, I can't proclaim that this defiant ideological gesture, however effective politically or theatrically, is all that feminist criticism desires, or all to which it should aspire. When feminist criticism chooses to deal with representation, rather than with women's writing, it must aim for a maximum interdisciplinary contextualism, in which the complexity of attitudes towards the feminine can be analysed in their fullest cultural and historical frame. The alternation of strong and weak Ophelias on the stage, virginal and seductive Ophelias in art, inadequate or oppressed Ophelias in criticism, tells us how these representations have overflowed the text, and how they have reflected the ideological character of their times, erupting as debates between dominant and feminist views in periods of gender crisis and redefinition. The representation of Ophelia changes independently of theories of the meaning of the play or the Prince, for it depends on attitudes towards women and madness. The decorous and pious Ophelia of the Augustan age and the postmodern schizophrenic heroine who might have stepped from the pages of Laing can be derived from the same figure; they are both contradictory and complementary images of female sexuality in which madness seems to act as the 'switching-point, the concept which allows the co-existence of both sides of the representation'.[47] There is no 'true' Ophelia for whom feminist criticism must unambiguously speak, but perhaps only a Cubist Ophelia of multiple perspectives, more than the sum of all her parts.

But in exposing the ideology of representation, feminist critics have also the responsibility to acknowledge and to examine the boundaries of our own ideological positions as products of our gender and our time. A degree of humility in an age of critical hubris can be our greatest strength, for it is by occupying this position of historical self-consciousness in both feminism and criticism that we maintain our credibility in representing Ophelia, and that, unlike Lacan, when we promise to speak about her, we make good our word.

From *Shakespeare and the Question of Theory*, ed. Patricia Parker and Geoffrey Hartman (London, 1985), pp. 77–94.

NOTES

[Elaine Showalter is one of America's most influential feminist critics. In the essay printed above she takes up the critical problem of Ophelia and how feminists should respond to her presentation. Part of the difficulty of discussing Ophelia, as Showalter notes, is that she appears in only five of the play's scenes, and yet she has been constantly represented in painting, photography and literature. Much of Showalter's essay is taken up with examining these presentations of Ophelia and how they depend not on the meaning of *Hamlet* but rather on attitudes towards women and madness.

What emerges is not only a series of contradictory Ophelias alternating between strong and weak, virginal and seductive, inadequate and oppressed, but a very powerful sense of how such views of Ophelia reflect the ideological assumptions of the times that produced them. Showalter's conclusion, that there is no 'true', unambiguous Ophelia separate from the values we bring to the text, is a challenging ending to a stimulating essay that shows just why feminist criticism has had such a major effect on recent Shakespeare studies.

Showalter begins her essay by referring to Jacques Lacan, the French philosopher and psychoanalyst who has had an enormous influence on poststructuralism generally. For Lacan, *Hamlet* is a tragedy of desire, a type of the Oedipus story in which Claudius has already acted the part of Oedipus by murdering Old Hamlet, so confronting Hamlet with a dilemma: even if he were to kill Claudius, that would not enable him to fulfil his desire, because death does not destroy the (father) phallus now represented by Claudius. Lacan's analysis is not easy to follow, but underlying it is his reinterpretation of Freud in linguistic terms. Lacan argues that the unconscious is structured, in fact, like a language, and it is this idea which has been taken up by recent feminists in their analysis of the place of women in culture, often stressing with Lacan how language is patriarchal and inadequate in its accounts of female sexuality. In many ways Showalter's essay parallels this argument, but with striking originality. Ed.]

1. Jacques Lacan, 'Desire and the interpretation of desire in *Hamlet*', in *Literature and Psychoanalysis: The Question of Reading: Otherwise*, ed. Shoshana Felman (Baltimore, 1982), pp. 11, 20, 23. Lacan is also wrong about the etymology of Ophelia, which probably derives from the Greek for 'help' or 'succour'. Charlotte M. Yonge suggested a derivation from 'ophis', 'serpent'. See her *History of Christian Names* (1884, republished Chicago, 1966), pp. 346–7. I am indebted to Walter Jackson Bate for this reference.

2. Annette Kolodny, 'Dancing through the minefield: some observations on the theory, practice, and politics of feminist literary criticism', *Feminist Studies*, 6 (1980), 7.

3. Carol Neely, 'Feminist modes of Shakespearean criticism', *Women's Studies*, 9 (1981), 11.

4. Lee Edwards, 'The labors of Pysche', *Critical Inquiry*, 6 (1979), 36.

5. Luce Irigaray: see *New French Feminisms*, ed. Elaine Marks and Isabelle de Courtivron (New York, 1982), p. 101. The quotation above, from III.ii, is taken from the Arden Shakespeare, *Hamlet*, ed. Harold Jenkins (London and New York, 1982), p. 295. All quotations from *Hamlet* are from this text.

6. On images of negation and feminine enclosure, see David Wilbern, 'Shakespeare's "nothing"', in *Representing Shakespeare: New*

Psychoanalytic Essays, ed. Murray M. Schwarz and Coppélia Kahn (Baltimore, 1981).

7. David Leverenz, 'The woman in Hamlet: an interpersonal view', *Signs*, 4 (1978), 303. [Reprinted in this volume – see p. 132 Ed.]

8. James Joyce, *Ulysses* (New York, 1961), p. 76.

9. Sander L. Gilman, *Seeing the Insane* (New York, 1981), p. 126.

10. See Michael Goldman, *The Actor's Freedom: Toward a Theory of Drama* (New York, 1975), for a stimulating discussion of the interpretative interaction between actor and audience.

11. Bridget Lyons, 'The iconography of Ophelia', *English Literary History*, 44 (1977), 61.

12. See Maurice and Hanna Charney, 'The language of Shakespeare's madwomen', *Signs*, 3 (1977), 451, 457; and Carroll Camden, 'On Ophelia's madness', *Shakespeare Quarterly*, 15 (1964), 254.

13. See Margery Garber, *Coming of Age in Shakespeare* (London, 1981), pp. 155–7; and Bridget Lyons, 'The iconography of Ophelia', *English Literary History*, 44 (1977), 65, 70–2.

14. On dishevelled hair as a signifier of madness or rape, see Maurice and Hanna Charney, 'The language of Shakespeare's madwomen', *Signs*, 3 (1977), 452–3, 457; and Allen Dessen, *Elizabethan Stage Conventions and Modern Interpreters* (Cambridge, 1984), pp. 36–8. Thanks to Allan Dessen for letting me see advance proofs of his book.

15. Maurice and Hanna Charney, 'The language of Shakespeare's madwomen', *Signs*, 3 (1977), 456.

16. Gaston Bachelard, *L'eau et les rêves* (Paris, 1942), pp. 109–25. See also Brigitte Peucker, 'Dröste-Hulshof's Ophelia and the recovery of voice', *The Journal of English and Germanic Philology*, 82 (1983), 374–91.

17. Vieda Skultans, *English Madness: Ideas on Insanity 1580–1890* (London, 1977), pp. 79–81. On historical cases of love-melancholy, see Michael MacDonald, *Mystical Bedlam* (Cambridge, 1982).

18. C. E. L. Wingate, *Shakespeare's Heroines on the Stage* (New York, 1895), pp. 283–4, 288–9.

19. Charles Hiatt, *Ellen Terry* (London, 1898), p. 11.

20. Max Byrd, *Visits to Bedlam: Madness and Literature in the Eighteenth Century* (Columbia, 1974), p. xiv.

21. Peter Raby, *Fair Ophelia: Harriet Smithson Berlioz* (Cambridge, 1982), p. 63.

22. Ibid., p. 68.

23. Ibid., pp. 72, 75.

24. Quoted in Carroll Camden, 'On Ophelia's madness', *Shakespeare Quarterly*, 15 (1964), 247.

25. Peter Raby, *Fair Ophelia: Harriet Smithson Berlioz* (Cambridge, 1982), p. 182.

26. J. C. Bucknill, *The Psychology of Shakespeare* (London, 1859, reprinted New York, 1970), p. 110. For more extensive discussions of Victorian psychiatry and Ophelia figures, see Elaine Showalter, *The Female Malady: Women, Madness and English Culture* (New York, 1985).

27. John Conolly, *Study of Hamlet* (London, 1863), p. 177.

28. Ibid., pp. 177–8, 180.

29. Ellen Terry, *The Story of My Life* (London, 1908), p. 154.

30. Diamond's photographs are reproduced in Sander L. Gilman, *The Face of Madness: Hugh W. Diamond and the Origin of Psychiatric Photography* (New York, 1976).

31. See Georges Didi-Huberman, *L'Invention de l'hystérie* (Paris, 1982), and Stephen Heath, *The Sexual Fix* (London, 1983), p. 36.

32. Mary Cowden Clarke, *The Girlhood of Shakespeare's Heroines* (London, 1852). See also George C. Gross, 'Mary Cowden Clarke, *The Girlhood of Shakespeare's Heroines*, and the sex education of Victorian women', *Victorian Studies*, 16 (1972), 37–58, and Nina Auerbach, *Women and the Demon* (Cambridge, 1983), pp. 210–15.

33. Charles Hiatt, *Ellen Terry* (London, 1898), p. 114. See also C. E. L. Wingate, *Shakespeare's Heroines on the Stage* (New York, 1895), pp. 304–5.

34. Ellen Terry, *The Story of My Life* (London, 1908), pp. 155–6.

35. A. C. Bradley, *Shakespearean Tragedy* (London, 1904), p. 160.

36. Helena Faucit Martin, *On Some of Shakespeare's Female Characters* (Edinburgh and London, 1891), pp. 4, 18; and *The True Ophelia* (New York, 1914), p. 15.

37. Among these paintings are the Ophelias of Henrietta Rae and Mrs F. Littler. Sarah Bernhardt sculpted a bas relief of Ophelia for the Women's Pavilion at the Chicago World's Fair in 1893.

38. Ernest Jones, *Hamlet and Oedipus* (New York, 1949), p. 139.

39. Rebecca West, *The Court and the Castle* (New Haven, 1958), p. 18.

40. Laurence Olivier, *Confessions of an Actor* (Harmondsworth, 1982), pp. 102, 152.

41. Theodor Lidz, *Hamlet's Enemy: Madness and Myth in Hamlet* (New York, 1975), pp. 88, 113.

42. Richard David, *Shakespeare in the Theatre* (Cambridge, 1978), p. 75. This was the production directed by Buzz Goodbody, a brilliant young feminist radical who killed herself that year. See Colin Chambers, *Other Spaces: New Theatre and the RSC* (London, 1980), especially pp. 63–7.

43. R. D. Laing, *The Divided Self* (Harmondsworth, 1965), p. 195n.

44. Richard David, *Shakespeare in the Theatre* (Cambridge, 1978), pp. 82–3; thanks to Marianne DeKoven, Rutgers University, for the description of the 1981 Warehouse production.

45. See, for example, Hélène Cixous and Catherine Clément, *La Jeune Née* (Paris, 1975).

46. For an account of this production, see Micheline Wandor, *Understudies: Theatre and Sexual Politics* (London, 1981), p. 47.

47. I am indebted for this formulation to a critique of my earlier draft of this paper by Carl Friedman, at the Wesleyan Center for the Humanities, April 1984.

9

The Woman in Hamlet: An Interpersonal View

DAVID LEVERENZ

'John, I guess there are some people around here who think you have some little old lady in you.'

(John Dean, *Blind Ambition*)

'Who's there?' Bernardo's anxious shout, which begins Shakespeare's most problematic play, raises the fundamental question of Hamlet's identity. Various male authority figures advance simple answers. For the Ghost, Hamlet is a dutiful son who should sweep to his revenge and forget about his mother. For Claudius, Hamlet is a possible rebel who should be either made tractable or banished and killed. For Polonius, Hamlet is the heir gone mad through frustrated love of Ophelia, whom Polonius has denied him partly for reasons of state. But for Hamlet, the roles of dutiful son, ambitious rebel, or mad lovesick heir are just that: roles, to be played for others but not felt for himself. The 'Who' remains unsettled within and without, 'the heart of my mystery' (III.ii.351).[1]

The mixed and contradictory expectations of these father figures reflect their own divided image of dutiful reason and bestial lust. At times their power seems to be defined by their ability to order women and children around. Hamlet sees Gertrude give way to Claudius, Ophelia give way to Polonius, and himself at last yield to the Ghost. But Hamlet also sees duplicity and falseness in all the fathers, except perhaps his own, and even there his famous delay may well indicate unconscious perception, rather than the unconscious guilt ascribed to him by a strict Freudian interpretation. Hamlet resists his father's commands to obey. Despite his illusory idealisation of the senior Hamlet as pure and angelic, he senses the Ghost's complicity in the paternal double-speak that bends Gertrude and Ophelia, indeed bends feelings and the body itself, to self-falsifying Reason and filial loyalty. Hamlet is part hysteric, as Freud said, and part Puritan in his disgust at contamination and his idealisation of his absent father. But he is also, as Goethe was the first to say, part woman. Goethe was wrong, as Freud was wrong, to assume that 'woman' means weakness. To equate women with weak and tainted bodies, words, and feelings while men possess noble reason and ambitious purpose is to participate in Denmark's disease dividing mind from body, act from feeling, man from woman.

Hamlet's tragedy is the forced triumph of filial duty over sensitivity to his own heart. To fulfil various fathers' commands, he has to deny his self-awareness, just as Gertrude and Ophelia have done. That denial is equivalent to suicide, as the language of the last act shows. His puritanical cries about whoredom in himself and others, his hysterical outbursts to Ophelia about nunneries and painted women, are the outer shell of a horror at what the nurtured, loving, and well-loved soul has been corrupted to. From a more modern perspective than the play allows, we can sense that the destruction of good mothering is the real issue, at least from Hamlet's point of view.

Freudians, too many of whom have their own paternal answers to 'Who's there', see Hamlet as an unconscious Claudius-Oedipus, or as a man baffled by pre-Oedipal ambivalences about his weak-willed, passionate, fickle mother.[2] While acknowledging Hamlet's parricidal and matricidal impulses, we should see these inchoate feelings as responses, not innate drives. Interpersonal expectations, more than self-contained desires, are what divide Hamlet from himself and conscript him to false social purposes. In this perspective, taken from Harry Stack Sullivan, R. D. Laing, and D. W. Winnicott, Hamlet's supposed delay is a natural reaction to overwhelming interpersonal confusion.[3] His self-preoccupation is paradoxically grounded not so much in himself as in the extraordinary and unremitting array of 'mixed signals' that separate role from self, reason from feeling, duty from love.

Hamlet has no way of unambiguously understanding what anyone says to him. The girl who supposedly loves him inexplicably refuses his attentions. His grieving mother suddenly marries. His dead father, suddenly alive, twice tells him to deny his anger at his mother's shocking change of heart. Two of his best friends 'make love to this employment' of snooping against him (V.ii.57). Polonius, Claudius, and the Ghost all manifest themselves as loving fathers, yet expect the worst from their sons and spy on their children, either directly or through messengers. Who is this 'uncle-father' and 'aunt-mother' (II.ii.366), or this courtier-father, who preach the unity of being true to oneself and others yet are false to everyone, who can 'smile, smile, and be a villain' (I.v.108)? Gertrude's inconstancy not only brings on disgust and incestuous feelings, it is also the sign of diseased doubleness in everyone who has accommodated to his or her social role. Usurping Claudius is the symbol of all those 'pre-tenders', who are now trying to bring Hamlet into line. No wonder Hamlet weeps at the sight of a genuine actor – the irony reveals the problem – playing Hecuba's grief. The male expressing a woman's constancy once again mirrors Hamlet's need. And the role, though feigned, at least is openly played. The actor's tears are the play's one unambiguous reflection of the grief Hamlet thought his mother shared with him before the onset of so many multitudinous double-dealings.

To kill or not to kill cannot be entertained when one is not even sure of existing with any integrity. Being, not desiring or revenging, is the question. Freudians assume that everyone has strong desires blocked by stronger repressions, but contemporary work with schizophrenics reveals the tragic variety of people whose voices are only amalgams of other people's voices, with caustic self-observation or a still more terrifying vacuum as their incessant inward reality. This is Hamlet to a degree, as it is Ophelia completely. As Laing says of her in *The Divided Self*, 'in her madness, there is no one there. She is not a person. There is no integral selfhood expressed through her actions or utterances. Incomprehensible statements are said by nothing. She has already died. There is now only a vacuum where there was once a person.'[4] Laing misrepresents her state only because there are many voices in Ophelia's madness speaking through her, all making sense, and none of them her own. She becomes the mirror for a madness-inducing world. Hamlet resists these pressures at the cost of a terrifying isolation. Once he thinks his mother has abandoned him, there is nothing and no one to 'mirror' his feelings, as Winnicott puts it.[5] Hamlet is utterly alone, beyond the loving semi-understanding of reasonable Horatio or obedient Ophelia.

A world of fathers and sons, ambition and lust, considers grief 'unmanly', as Claudius preaches (I.ii.94). Hamlet seems to agree, at least to himself, citing his 'whorish' doubts as the cause of his inability to take manly filial action. This female imagery, which reflects the play's male-centred world view, represents a covert homosexual fantasy, according to Freudian interpretation.[8] Certainly Hamlet's idealisations of his father and of Horatio's friendship show a hunger for male closeness. Poisoning in the ear may unconsciously evoke anal intercourse. And the climactic swordplay with Laertes does lead to a brotherly understanding. But these instances of covert homosexual desire are responses to a lack. Poisoning in the ear evokes conscious and unconscious perversity to intimate the perversion of communication, especially between men. The woman in Hamlet is the source of his most acute perceptions about the diseased, disordered patriarchal society that tries to 'play upon this pipe' of Hamlet's soul (III.ii.336), even as a ghost returning from the dead.

*

The separation of role from self is clear in the opening scene. Anxiety precipitates a genuine question, 'Who's there?' It is answered not with 'Francisco', the natural rejoinder, but with 'Nay, answer me. Stand and unfold yourself' (I.i.2). Francisco restores public ritual by the prescribed challenge of a guard, not the response of a friend. To private uneasiness he responds with public norms. Bernardo's answer to the command to 'unfold yourself' is equally self-avoiding. 'Long live the king!' he cries (I.i.3). His identity, in the prescribed convention, is equivalent to respect for the king. Yet the not-so-long-lived king has just died, and the new king, who was to have been Hamlet the younger, has been displaced by the old king's brother. Who *is* the rightful king? Who is there? The question returns, under the formulaic phrase that denies any problems of loyalty or succession.

Francisco departs with an odd and disconcerting addition to a conventional farewell: 'For this relief much thanks. 'Tis bitter cold, / And I am sick at heart' (I.i.8–9). Tensions between the head and the heart, noble reason and diseased emotion, centre the play. Yet this first expression of heart-sick feelings has no explanation. The watch has been 'quiet' – 'Not a mouse stirring', Francisco gratuitously adds (I.i.10). By Act III Hamlet will be devising a play he calls 'The Mousetrap', which would make the new king a mouse and suggest that royal stability is corroded at its base. But for now these jagged interchanges, like the half-lines staggered on the page and the roles confused by the guards, seem simply 'out of joint', with no clear perspective on who has been guarding what, why Bernardo seems scared, and why Francisco feels sick at heart. The darker questions recede into the comfortable self-definitions of Horatio and Marcellus, who respond to the next 'Who is there?' with 'Friends to this ground' (Horatio) 'And liegemen to the Dane' (Marcellus, I.i.15). Horatio, whose first word is 'Friends', is the only one of this group to define himself both within and beyond conventional public deference. As yet we cannot sense the incompatibility between being friends and being liegemen. By Act V the gap is so wide that Horatio declares himself 'more an antique Roman than a Dane' (V.ii.330) and tries to drink from the poisoned cup to follow his friend both from and to a poisoned state. All we know now, though, is that more seems afoot than simply the changing of a guard.[7]

Identity, in the first scene, is defined as role, specifically as loyalty among functionaries of a state. But feelings have been partly voiced that are curiously disconnected from roles. There is no coherent voice for more private feelings, in this case fear; rote is the norm. The polarity between mind and passions reflects larger polarities in the social order, or rather in a society pretending to be ordered along the father's lines. These polarities become more apparent in the contrast between Claudius's opening speech and Hamlet's first soliloquy. Claudius speaks in the language of public command, with phrases tailored and balanced, the royal 'we' firmly affixed to his crown. Oxymorons prescribe a unity of opposites, and his balanced phrasing is only twice disrupted with the reality of seized power: 'Taken to wife', and 'So much for him' (I.ii.14, 25). For Claudius, reason, nature, and submission are rejoined in a facile unity.

> Fie, 'tis a fault to heaven,
> A fault against the dead, a fault to nature,
> To reason most absurd, whose common theme
> Is death of fathers, and who still hath cried,
> From the first corse till he that died to-day,
> 'This must be so.'
>
> (I.ii.101–6)

To personify an abstraction, reason, is characteristic of Claudius's perspective, in which abstract states are more real than persons. Unfortunately reality intrudes; in the rush of his logic he misrepresents 'the first corse', who was obviously Abel, not a father but a brother killed by brother, as in Claudius's crime. The heart will intrude its guilt, no matter how speech tries to deny fact and feeling.

The rhetoric of formal obedience avoids, while suggesting, the simple stark reality of a father's murder, a son's grief, and a murderer's guilt.

Claudius's speech reveals a second assumption already sensed in the personification of reason. When he speaks of 'our whole kingdom ... contracted in one brow of woe' (I.ii.3–4), he presents his kingdom as a single person. He further connects the language of personal love with the language of public war, since making war among states has the same unity of opposites that he wants to prescribe for individuals, even for his wife. Gertrude, whom he defines only in her disjointed roles as 'our sometime sister, now our queen', is thus 'Th' imperial jointress to this warlike state' (I.ii.9). Marriage is simply the prelude to aggression. The only arena for 'joining' is the ordering of the state for war, not the expressing of desire in the marriage bed. Polonius continues the inversion of love and war more explicitly in his advice to Ophelia: 'Set your entreatments at a higher rate / Than a command to parley' (I.iii.122–3). Laertes also echoes the language of war in speaking of love to her: 'keep you in the rear of your affection, / Out of the shot and danger of desire' (I.ii.34–5). In this collusion of ambitious functionaries, the state is the only real person, whose war with other person-states can be told as love, while the loves and fears of persons can be expressed only as warlike obedience to the purpose of states.[8]

Hamlet's first private discourse opposes the dehumanising unities of the king's public preaching point for point. Where Claudius assumes the oneness of reason and nature in filial subjection, Hamlet piles contrary on rebellious contrary, especially of mind and body. Indeed, Hamlet's soliloquy is obsessed with language of the body – sullied (or solid) flesh, appetite, feeding, father's dead body, tears, incestuous sheets, 'galled eyes' (I.ii.155), and finally the heart and tongue: 'But break my heart, for I must hold my tongue' (I.ii.159), an intuition that precisely describes his fate. Parts of the body, rank, gross, and unweeded, overwhelm any pretence at understanding.

Elsewhere Hamlet attempts to recast the language of public ritual as personal feeling. When his friends say farewell with the conventional 'Our duty to your honour', Hamlet responds with a half-ironic inversion: 'Your loves, as mine to you' (I.ii.253–4). Duty and love still have something in common, he hopes. But his language in the first Act more broadly participates in the most pervasive assumption of Claudius, that reason is what makes a man. Hamlet is disgusted at the thought of 'some complexion ... breaking down the pales and forts of reason' (I.iv.27–8). Those 'pales and forts' echo Claudius's equation between war and love. Here is the inward castle of the mind on which, metaphorically, Bernardo and Francisco stand guard, though against what is still uncertain. 'Nobility' connotes the mind's royalty, as befits a prince's role. 'Nature', on the other hand, is associated with the rabble, revelling in the bestial dregs of 'swinish phrase' and scandal, 'some vicious mole of nature in them' (I.iv.19, 24) that cannot help but get out. Just as Claudius falsely conjoins nature and obedience into the smooth illusory primacy of reason, so Hamlet, searching for truth at the other extreme, lumps nature, feelings, beasts, and body together, all as negatives.

Hamlet is 'unsocialised', a psychiatrist might say, hearing reports of his hostile puns, asides, and soliloquies. Unfortunately he is far more socialised than he can perceive. He still takes refuge in the shared assumptions of those around him, who locate the self in the mind's obedience to patriarchal order, the body's obedience to abstractions. Whether speaking as Polonius, who can talk so glibly of 'wit' as having 'soul' and 'limbs' (II.ii.90–1) and swear that 'I hold my duty as I hold my soul' (II.ii.44), or as Rosencrantz, who expounds so eloquently on how the 'single and peculiar life' is only part of the 'massy wheel' of majesty (III.iii.11–23), or as Laertes, who takes such pains to instruct Ophelia that Hamlet is 'circumscribed / Unto the voice and yielding of that body / Whereof he is the head' (I.iii.22–4), this common public voice denies private feeling and private identity, while asserting the false union of all the parts of the social body in subjection to majesty. As Rosencrantz declares (III.iii.12–13), this power is 'much more' than 'the strength and armour of the mind' itself. Again the warlike image is symptomatic.

The Ghost seems to be the one father who speaks straight, and Hamlet's encounter with him precipitates clarity about what has happened and what he must do. But while confirming Hamlet's perception of external wickedness, the Ghost invalidates Hamlet's feelings. He speaks to the mind's suspicions of Claudius while denying Hamlet's more profound heartsickness over Gertrude. Claudius's villainy is clear, and clearly stated. But many other aspects of the Ghost's account are mixed signals denying simple feeling. After hearing of the 'sulph'rous and tormenting flames' awaiting his father, Hamlet cries 'Alas, poor ghost!' – a Gertrude-like response (I.v.4). 'Pity me not', the Ghost rejoins (I.v.5), rejecting the empathy he has just solicited. He wants only 'serious hearing' and revenge. Yet the Ghost then gratuitously describes 'my prison house' and forces its horrors on Hamlet by suggesting that knowledge of the truth would shatter his son's body. This is already a Laingian 'knot',[9] designed to exaggerate the father's strength and the son's weakness. Feelings are frivolous; manly endurance is true fortitude. As he will do with Gertrude, the Ghost implies that his son is too frail to hear; so is anyone with 'ears of flesh and blood' (I.v.22). Don't pity me, runs the message – but boy, what you *would* feel ... Yet why is father in Purgatory? Not because of his heroic or virtuous strength but because of 'the foul crimes done in my days of nature' (I.v.12). So in these first few lines the father has: (1) told his son not to pity, yet encouraged him to pity, (2) accentuated his son's earthy weakness and his own immortal strength, yet told Hamlet of 'foul crimes', and (3) equated pity with frivolity and dutiful hearing with seriousness, while picturing Hamlet's feelings in language that dismembers the body in its exaggerated seriousness.

The mixed signals persist. We never learn what the 'foul crimes' consist of, though they are apparently extensive enough to have the Ghost cry out 'O, horrible! O, horrible! most horrible!' at the thought of his 'account' for 'my imperfections' (I.v.78–9). Yet the major burden of his discourse is to contrast his 'dignity' and 'virtue' with Claudius's crimes. We have already heard from others, notably Horatio, about King Hamlet's warlike 'frown' and armour (I.i.60–2). There is very little in the Ghost's own speech, however, to support a sense of virtuous integrity. His surprisingly weak affirmation of his love's 'dignity' states simply 'That it went hand in hand even with the vow / I made to her in marriage', presumably to remain faithful (I.v.48–50). Even his love can be fully summarised not by feeling but by 'vow' or public ritual. And as a king, his peacetime behaviour seems to have been primarily sleeping on the job. Otherwise he would not have been killed as he was 'Sleeping within my orchard, / My custom always of the afternoon' (I.v.59–60). He is also viciously uncharitable to his queen, while at the same time forbidding his son from having that same feeling.[10] Throughout his speech the Ghost is preoccupied with the body, and as with Hamlet, Gertrude is the focus for that concern. Her change from 'seeming-virtuous' behaviour to 'lust' puts the Ghost into a paroxysm of disgust, not so much at the vile seducer as at the woman who could move from 'a radiant angel' to a beast who preys 'on garbage' (I.v.46, 55–7). The king of 'foul crimes' presents himself as an angel now.

Hamlet's idealisation of his father and disgust with Claudius reveals, as Freudians have rightly argued, a splitting of the son's ambivalence toward the father. But the various mixed signals in the Ghost's speech show how the father's communication, not the son's intrapsychic repressions, fosters ambivalence. Father is, in fact, more like Claudius than the Ghost can dare admit. They both speak with the arrogant abstractedness of majesty – 'So the whole ear of Denmark / Is . . . / Rankly abused' (I.v.36–8) – yet they both show their particular bodies, in word or deed, subverting the false nobility of royal role. And the Ghost is particularly ambivalent about 'nature' itself. Though he invokes his own 'foul crimes done in my days of nature' (I.v.12), he concludes, 'If thou hast nature in thee, bear it not' (I.v.81). From 'Pity me not' to 'Bear it not', the Ghost's commands falsify both the father's reality and the son's 'nature'. They exaggerate father's virtues, demean Hamlet's responses, and establish a confusing set of connections between nature, lust, feeling, and Gertrude, all of which must be resolutely disowned to follow the father's directives toward filial revenge, a 'natural feeling' unnatural to Hamlet. [11] Even the minor father figures, like old Priam and Yorick, are vivid in their infirm bodies, not in their dignified precepts. Yet precepts are the 'me' that Hamlet has to remember.

Through her impossible attempt to obey contradictory voices, Ophelia mirrors in her madness the tensions that Hamlet perceives. As in Laing's *Sanity, Madness and the Family*, Ophelia's 'madness' is a natural response to the unacknowledged interpersonal falsities of the group. [12] Her history is another instance of how someone can be driven mad by having her inner feelings misrepresented, not responded to, or acknowledged only through chastisement and repression. From her entrance on, Ophelia must continually respond to commands which imply distrust even as they compel obedience. 'Do you doubt that?' she opens, after Laertes has told her, 'do not sleep, / But let me hear from you' (I.iii.3–4). The body's natural desire to sleep must yield to the role of always-attentive sister. Without responding, perhaps not even hearing her rejoinder to his demand, Laertes immediately tries to plunge her into a more severe doubt of Hamlet's affection, and therefore of her own. It is simply toying with lust, he says, 'a fashion and a toy in blood' (I.iii.6). Reflecting the division between mind and body forced on children by fathers themselves divided, Laertes speaks magisterially of how 'nature crescent' in Hamlet must be 'circumscribed' to the larger 'body' of the state 'Whereof he is the head' (I.iii.11, 22–4). Hamlet's voice can go 'no further / Than the main voice of Denmark goes withal' (I.iii.27–8). A prince can express no feeling except as it furthers his social role; the rest is transient sensuality, 'The perfume and sup-pliance of a minute, / No more.' 'No more but so?' Ophelia responds, questioning but trusting, and Laertes rejoins ambiguously, 'Think it no more' (I.iii.9–10). So the Ghost speaks to Hamlet and of Gertrude, emphasising their weakness and his strength.

Ophelia accepts Laertes's commands as a 'lesson' to 'keep / As watchman to my heart . . .' (I.iii.45–6). Yet her advice to him shows her awareness of his possible double self, the pastor and the libertine, the very division he used in describing Hamlet. Punning on 'recks' and 'reckless', she displays an independent wit, much like Hamlet's more constricted opening puns. But her sense of the necessity for a 'watchman' over probable evils of the heart is as unquestioned as her acceptance of the military terminology. The fortress of the female heart needs its Bernardoes. She *will* doubt her feelings henceforth. When Polonius reinterprets what she calls Hamlet's 'tenders / Of his affection to me' (I.iii.99–100) as monetary transactions leading only to her father's exposure as 'a fool', Ophelia hesitantly asserts the 'honourable fashion' of Hamlet's loving speech to her (I.iii.111). Yet she mutely accepts her father's assumption that to 'Tender yourself more dearly' is essential for protecting father's self-image (I.iii.107). Polonius is deliberately unconcerned with what his daughter feels. His command to refuse Hamlet any 'words or talk' flies in the face of everything Ophelia has said (I.iii.134). Yet she has no choice but to say, 'I shall obey, my lord' (I.iii.136).

For his part, Polonius is preoccupied only with how he looks. Always the fawning courtier, the man who can say 'I hold my duty as I hold my soul' in return for being called 'the father of good news' by his new king (II.ii.42–4), his response to Claudius's questions about his daughter flagrantly reveals his unconcern for anything but his own position. 'But how hath she / Received his love?' Claudius inquires. 'What do you think of me?' is her father's answer; 'What might you think?' he anxiously repeats (II.ii.128–30, 139). For Polonius, his daughter is an animal whom he can 'loose' (II.ii.162) to catch Hamlet's motive. He cares for Claudius, for his role as 'assistant for a state' (II.ii.166), not for his daughter's feelings. The subplot makes clear what the main plot obfuscates: fathers perceive children as they do their wives and bodies, as beasts to be controlled for the magnification of their self-images, or rather, for the expression of their divided selves, their reason and their lust. These divisions grow from their complicity in playing a leading role in a corrupt state. Polonius, putting the issue squarely, says to Ophelia, 'You do not understand yourself so clearly / As it behooves my daughter and your honour' (I.iii.96–7). Ophelia must accept the role of honourable possession and deny her love for Hamlet. This is not a question of repressed sexual desire, though certainly her anxieties, like Hamlet's, have to do with feelings denied. It is a question of what it means to understand oneself when the price is falseness to others.

Hamlet himself fosters Ophelia's crisis, to be sure. He sends her an ambiguous poem which can be read as 'Never doubt that I love' or 'Never suspect that I love' (II.ii.119). He tells her he loved her; then, 'I loved you not' (III.i.119). He seems to confirm Laertes's suspicions by warning her of his lust and ordering her to a nunnery, which of course – another mixed signal – could also be a whorehouse. His crude jokes about 'country matters' (III.ii.111) as he lies in her lap at the play toy with her role as honourable daughter, confirm his lust, yet contradict the piteous picture he makes of himself in her room, wordless, his clothes in disarray. His oscillating acts of need and aggression are Hamlet's nasty mirroring of what he perceives to be her mixed signals to him: her loving talks, then her inexplicable denial and silence. First he mirrors her silence, then he mirrors the self that Polonius and Laertes have warned her against. More profoundly, her behaviour to him – since he has no knowledge of her obedience to Polonius's command – so evokes Gertrude's inconstancy that Hamlet's double messages to Ophelia take on a frenzied condemnation of all women. His soliloquies extend that condemnation to the woman in himself. This Laingian knot of miscommunications compounded, of false selves intensified, leads finally to self-mistrust, even to madness.

Not allowed to love and unable to be false, Ophelia breaks. She goes mad rather than gets mad. Even in her madness she has no voice of her own, only a discord of other voices and expectations, customs gone awry. Most obviously, she does what Hamlet preaches, or at least what he feigns, in going mad. Thinking she is not loved by him, she becomes him, or at least what she conceives to be his 'noble mind . . . o'erthrown' (II.i.150). Just as his absence in Act IV is reflected in the absence of her reason, so her suicide embodies what Hamlet ponders in his soliloquies. After all, Polonius has instructed her that love denied leads to madness (II.i.119–19), and Ophelia is forever faithful to her contradictory directives. She herself is a play within a play, or a player trying to respond to several imperious directors at once. Everyone has used her: Polonius, to gain favour; Laertes, to belittle Hamlet; Claudius, to spy on Hamlet; Hamlet, to express rage at Gertrude; and Hamlet again, to express his feigned madness with her as a decoy. She is only valued for the roles that further other people's plots. Treated as a helpless child, she finally becomes one, veiling her perceptions of falsehood and manipulation in her seemingly innocent ballads.

Ophelia's songs give back the contradictory voices lodged within her and expose the contradictions. 'Where is the beauteous majesty of Denmark?' she asks of Gertrude as she enters (IV.v.21) – a question Hamlet has often asked of the state, as well as of his mother. She then shifts to her first interchange with Polonius, expressed as his question and her answer:

> How should I your true-love know
> From another one?
> By his cockle hat and staff
> And his sandal shoon.
> (IV.v.23–6)

Polonius has told her that men are all alike, and Ophelia replies that Hamlet has the constancy of a pilgrim. The first verse also expresses Hamlet's query to Gertrude about her switch in lovers, while the second says good-bye to all faithful true-loves, whether brothers, lovers, or fathers. 'He is dead and gone, lady' could refer to Polonius, Prince Hamlet, Laertes, Hamlet the king, or the mythical pilgrim. Her next songs replace this faithful male with lusting lovers who deflower young maids, then depart without fulfilling their vows of marriage. 'Young men will do't if they come to't. By Cock, they are to blame' (IV.v.60–1). Most readings take this song for Ophelia's own sensual desires under her dutiful exterior – 'For bonny sweet Robin is all my joy' (IV.v.185), where Robin is a colloquial Elizabethan term for penis.[13] But 'all' implies it is the only joy allowed her. The speaker is Gertrude's helpless, manipulated lust, veering suddenly to Polonius and Laertes telling her about the dangers of male desire, and back again to Hamlet's sense of loss. The songs mirror every level of the play, even Polonius's 'flowery' speech: yet they do not express what Ophelia feels, except as sadness. Laertes is right to say, 'Thought and affliction, passion, hell itself, / She turns to favour and to prettiness' (IV.v.186–7). Merging with everyone, she speaks in a collage of voices about present sensuality and absent faithfulness, yet dies, as Gertrude says so empathetically, 'incapable of her own distress' (IV.vii.177).

Ophelia's suicide becomes a little microcosm of the male world's banishment of the female, because 'woman' represents everything denied by reasonable men. In responding to Ophelia's death, Laertes, patently the norm for filial behaviour, is embarrassed by his womanly tears. He forbids himself to cry, 'but yet / It is our trick; nature her custom holds, / Let shame say what it will'. To be manly is to be ashamed of emotion and nature. Saying farewell to her, he says farewell to that part of himself: 'When these [tears] are gone, / The woman will be out' (IV.vii.185–8). His genuine feeling cannot be told except as a wish to get rid of the feeling. Even Hamlet, so much more sensitive than others to 'nature' and 'heart', equates woman with 'frailty' (I.ii.146) or worse. 'Whore' is his word for changeable feelings, whether those of Gertrude, of 'strumpet' Fortune (II.ii.233), or even of himself. Hamlet echoes his stepfather's association of painted woman and painted word (III.i.51–3) as he rails against himself for not being the dutiful son:

> Why, what an ass am I! This is most brave,
> That I, the son of a dear father murthered,
> Prompted to my revenge by heaven and hell,
> Must like a whore unpack my heart with words
> And fall a-cursing like a very drab,
> A stallion!
>
> (II.ii.568–73)

Words, feelings, beasts, and whoredom are as interchangeable as reason and obedience. That women, grief, words, and the heart should be confused with nature, guilt, and the body, while filial obedience is equated with noble reason in opposition, is what is rotten in Denmark. Linguistic disorders express social disorders. Ophelia's drowning signifies the necessity of drowning both words and feelings if Hamlet is to act the role prescribed for him. That he does so is the real tragedy in the play.

*

Hamlet's focus on ears that are abused stands as a metaphor for the violation of female receptivity. By that token, Hamlet in the end becomes his own violator. Far from being a catharsis or a resolute confrontation, or an integration of the underlying issues, the play's end is a study in frustration and failure.[14] Hamlet retreats to filial duty, allowing the 'machine' of his body (II.ii.124) to accomplish the acts required of him. Coming back to a world of fathers and usurpers where ambition and lust have been defined as the only valid motives, he can speak that language without a qualm. 'It is as easy as lying', he has told Rosencrantz and Guildenstern before (III.ii.343). Surrounded by 'Examples gross as earth' of sons 'with divine ambition puffed', like Fortinbras, who can breezily risk everything 'Even for an eggshell' (IV.iv.46, 49, 53), Hamlet at last resolves himself into a Do by obeying the dictates of his father and of 'providence', an abstracted and semi-idealised father. 'I shall win at the odds', he tells Horatio (V.ii.200). It is a world where winning is the only thing; all else is 'foolery' for women. 'But thou wouldst not think how ill all's here about my heart', he tells uncomprehending Horatio. 'But it is no matter . . . it is but foolery, but it is such a kind of gaingiving as would perhaps trouble a woman' (V.ii.201–5). To Hamlet's four times repeated 'but', Horatio lets the woman drop and responds only, 'If your mind dislike anything, obey it'. Concerns for mind and obedience are part of the male world, to which Hamlet's stifled heart now responds not with whorish 'unpacking' but with silence.

Silence is really the theme of the last act, not the almost farcical excess of deeds and rhetoric. The graveyard scene shows the last perversion of reason, as clowns chop logic over the dead. These mini-Claudiuses at least have the merit of not pretending grief, and their wit calls a spade a spade by asserting the absoluteness of law and power, and of class distinctions even in death. Their jokes have to do with the strong and the weak: the gallows-maker or the grave-maker 'builds stronger' (V.i.40, 55), because their social roles abet the permanence of death. 'Has this fellow no feeling of his business, that 'a sings at grave-making?' Hamlet inquires (V.i.62–3). 'Custom hath made it in him a property of easiness', Horatio replies (V.i.64). Feeling and custom, as ever opposed but now with greater clarity, cannot be reconciled. Those who are most at home with 'wit' are also most at ease with custom, reasoning, and playing their roles. Words come as glibly to them as to Osric, in proportion as feelings are denied.

It is clear to Hamlet now that words are of no use. 'Nay, an thou'lt mouth, / I'll rant as well as thou', he throws back at Laertes (V.i.270–1). This is the posturing of animals, nothing more:

> Let Hercules himself do what he may,
> The cat will mew, and dog will have his day.
> (V.i.278–9)

Like Ophelia, Hamlet can mirror how others talk, though with a savage irony that emphasises the distance between his inward feelings and outward rhetoric. He mocks the foppish Osric, who 'did comply, sir, with his dug before 'a sucked it' (V.ii.179). He seems calm, controlled, at arm's length from what he says. Only Gertrude senses the truth:

> This is mere madness;
> And thus a while the fit will work on him.
> Anon, as patient as the female dove
> When that her golden couplets are disclosed,
> His silence will sit drooping.
>   (V.i.271–5)

What seems like a manic-depressive 'fit' to Gertrude (a better diagnosis than Freud's 'hysteria') is actually Hamlet's response to 'the fit' of a senseless society. He mouths its language and assumes its stance of male combat, while 'the female dove' in him prepares for a final silence. Earlier he had berated himself for his dovelike gentleness: 'But I am pigeon-livered and lack gall / To make oppression bitter' (II.ii.562–3). Now, while he puts on the necessary gall, the unspoken woman in him outwardly obeys paternal commands ('my purposes ... follow the king's pleasure', V.ii.190–1), whether of Claudius, the Ghost, or Providence. Inwardly he has already left the world of fathers, roles, and mixed messages to rejoin Ophelia and Gertrude in death's constancy. Not until Gertrude dies does Hamlet, dying, fulfil the Ghost's instructions. To kill Claudius as an afterthought to the Queen's death is his last little 'dig' at the 'old mole' (I.v.162).

So much for Hamlet's 'golden couplets', the fledgling poetry of the self he has tried to 'disclose'. Ending his drama as he begins it, with a play on words, he expires with 'The rest is silence' (V.ii.347). That gnomic phrase could mean that there is no afterlife, despite Hamlet's earlier scruples; that 'rest' is equivalent to silence: that *my* rest is silence; or that the rest of my story is untold. All of these ambiguities are true, or at least more true in their ambiguity than the interpretations that so quickly falsify Hamlet's story. Horatio immediately invalidates the connection between rest and silence by invoking singing angels: 'And flights of angels sing thee to thy rest.' The noise of war, the 'warlike volley' of drums and guns, drives out the silence utterly. We are back in the male world of ambitious sons advancing to their fathers' footsteps.

The play ends in a mindless sequence of ritual male duties, roles without meaning. The Ambassador informs the court that the king's 'commandment is fulfilled / That Rosencrantz and Guildenstern are dead'. Staring at the dead bodies of the King, Queen, Hamlet, and Laertes, he can think only of saying, 'Where should we have our thanks?' (V.ii.359–61). Horatio responds not with the story of Hamlet's struggle to keep the integrity of his 'noble heart' (V.ii.348) but with the narrative of Claudius's villainy, and perhaps of Hamlet's as well:

> So shall you hear
> Of carnal, bloody, and unnatural acts,
> Of accidental judgments, casual slaughters,
> Of deaths put on by cunning and forced cause.
> And, in this upshot, purposes mistook
> Fall'n on th'inventors' heads. All this can I
> Truly deliver.
>
> (V.ii.369–75)

This is the public story of an unnatural world, not the private record of a heart unspoken. It is a tale of deeds, not feelings. Yet it may be the story Hamlet knows will be told. After all, Horatio himself, 'As th'art a man' (V.ii.331), is manfully following his duty to Hamlet's command, sacrificing his wish for suicide. A story born of duty must be a man's story.

All the women are dead, and there are no more womanly tears. Young 'Strong-in-arm', who inherits an irrevocably corrupted world, is the arrogant, stupid, blundering finale to the theme of filial duty, to which both the Ghost and Claudius had demanded Hamlet's conformity. His tribute to Hamlet is cast in the rhetoric of a military command: 'Let four captains / Bear Hamlet like a soldier to the stage' (V.ii.384–5). Here Hamlet is finally 'fit' to the alien mould of soldier in the stage world of the 'captains'. At the play's close, Fortinbras ludicrously undercuts Hamlet's final words:

> For he was likely, had he been put on,
> To have proved most royal; and for his passage
> The soldiers' music and the rites of war
> Speak loudly for him.
>
> (V.ii.386–9)

How right for this man without a touch of the female in him to have such confidence in 'the rites of war' as confirmation of Hamlet's identity! We are back in the world of the first act, with a more ironic consciousness of what it means for Fortinbras to say, 'had he been put on'. A body politic cannot take off its clothes and venture, like Hamlet, 'naked' and 'alone' (IV.vii.50–1); it can only 'put on' more roles. From the first anxious question of the guards to the last pointless order to 'Go, bid the soldiers shoot', the military atmosphere pervades the language of the play.

Having learned how cruel one must be to be 'kind' (1.ii.65), Hamlet puts on a 'most royal' corruptedness (V.ii.387). He acts as the world does, speaks as the world speaks. Yet what a mockery it is, a self-mockery, to say of Fortinbras, 'He has my dying voice' (V.ii.345). The illegitimate succession instituted by Claudius concludes with the triumph of the son against whom these fathers were at war. It is final proof of the interchangeability, in language and body, of all those in authority, whether enemy or friend. It is also the concluding irony of Hamlet's struggle for speech. His last soliloquy is a voice dying into accord with the senseless ambition and mindless 'honour' of Fortinbras: 'O, from this time forth, / My thoughts be bloody, or be nothing worth!' (IV.iv.65–6). But now that the guns 'Speak loudly for him' (V.ii.389), Fortinbras pompously distinguishes between carnage in field and in court, as if Hamlet's death in battle would have been eminently acceptable. 'Such a sight as this / Becomes the field, but here shows much amiss' (V.ii.390–1). Hamlet is right; Fortinbras does inherit his 'dying voice', while the rest *is* silence. Just as the hawkish voices of blood, honour, and ambition inherit the world of the fathers, with its false roles and false proprieties, so Hamlet the dove joins Gertrude and Ophelia as a much too ravished bride of quietness.

*

Hamlet is not so much a full-throated tragedy as an ironic stifling of a hero's identity by structures of rule that no longer have legitimacy. It is the most frustrating of Shakespeare's plays precisely because it is the one most specifically about frustration. Shakespeare uses the opposition between male and female to denote the impossibility of speaking truly in a public role without violating or being violated. Too aware of paternal duplicity, Hamlet remains wordlessly modern in his excess of words, unable to centre himself in a society whose 'offence is rank' (III.iii.36) in every sense, and where the quest for self-knowledge is womanishly at odds with the manly roles he must put on. Even Ophelia only loved his mind. Hamlet's final assumption of a swordsman's identity is not a healthy solution to Oedipal conflicts but a mute submission to his father's command to 'whet thy almost blunted purpose' (III.iv.112). The manly identity is imposed, not grown into. Hamlet delays revenging his father's death because his real struggle is to restore his mother's validation of his feelings, though 'whore' is the only word available to him for his heartsick disgust. For Freudians to call Hamlet a mini-Claudius, to accept his male world's perspectives of ambition and lust as sufficient motives, is to do what all the fathers want to do: explain Hamlet by their own divided selves. Perhaps even incest fantasies, as Laing tells us, may be defences against the dread of being alone.[15]

What T. S. Eliot took for *Hamlet*'s failure, Shakespeare took for theme, as I have tried to show.[16] It *is* a play 'dealing with the effects of a mother's guilt upon her son', not as sexuality but as identity itself. Hamlet's self-doubt is joined to Gertrude's insufficiency. Her 'negative and insignificant' character 'arouses in Hamlet the feeling which she is incapable of representing', Eliot rightly says, while the demand of his father for revenge calls Hamlet to a clear though false role.[17] But these are not flaws in the drama. They are flaws in the patriarchal order, which has cracked all the mirrors for self-confirmation. *Hamlet* succeeds so well, and has lasted so long, because it speaks so keenly to the dissociation of sensibility Eliot elsewhere describes.[18] Whether we call it role and self, reason and nature, mind and body, manly and womanly, or the language of power and the language of feeling, we recognise these dichotomies in our world and in ourselves. How poisonous rule o'ercrows every person's spirit (V.ii.342) is indeed the fundamental answer to 'Who's there', as Eliot's critique implies. To pursue the question, Hamlet learns much too well, is not only to fail, but to participate in the collusion.

From *Signs*, 4 (1978), 291–308.

NOTES

[David Leverenz's interesting essay, as its title suggests, is very much concerned with the psychology of the play. Leverenz sees Hamlet's tragedy as that of 'the forced triumph of filial duty over sensitivity to his own heart', and goes on to explore the tension in the play between Hamlet's private sense of identity and the dehumanising public world of the court and Claudius. This tension, Leverenz observes, is deepened by the Ghost's account of Old Hamlet's murder, with its contradictory language of action and feeling. It is not only Hamlet, however, who is caught in the play's divisions. As Leverenz shows, the tensions Hamlet perceives are mirrored in Ophelia's madness. Her drowning, he suggests, symbolises the way in which the male world of the play banishes or suppresses the 'female', suppresses everything that opposes reason and obedience. The real tragedy of the play, Leverenz concludes, is that Hamlet also drowns his feelings to act the part of revenger, that he retreats in the last act into the world of filial duty, the public world of deeds and ritual male roles of patriarchal society. To a great extent Leverenz's analysis complements those of Marilyn French and Elaine Showalter above, and, as with their essays, reveals the very different way in which modern criticism has begun to think about tragedy as a radical form of drama which questions the social, historical and political values that inform it. A slightly revised version of Leverenz's essay can be found in *Representing Shakespeare: New Psychoanalytic Essays*, ed. Murray M. Schwartz and Coppélia Kahn (Baltimore and London, 1980), pp. 110–28. Ed.]

1. I am using the Pelican edition of *Hamlet*, ed. Willard Farnham (New York, 1957). The 1605 edition's title is *The Tragicall Historie of Hamlet, Prince of Denmarke*. The epigraph is taken from John Dean, *Blind Ambition: The White House Years* (New York, 1976), p. 47.

2. See Norman N. Holland, *Psychoanalysis and Shakespeare*, revised edn (1964; reprinted New York, 1976), pp. 163–206, for various parricidal and matricidal interpretations. Erik Erikson discusses Hamlet's identity as delayed adolescent in 'Youth: Fidelity and Diversity', *Daedalus*, 91 (Winter 1962), 5–27; and Neil Friedman and Richard M. Jones develop further psychosocial perspectives, to which my essay is indebted, in 'On the Mutuality of the Oedipus Complex: Notes on the Hamlet Case', *American Imago*, 20 (Summer 1963), 107–31. More recent psycho-analytic studies include Theodore Lidz, *Hamlet's Enemy: Madness and Myth in Hamlet* (London, 1976); and Norman N. Holland, 'Hamlet – My Greatest Creation', *Journal of the American Academy of Psychoanalysis*, 3 (1975), 419–27. Avi Erlich's *Hamlet's Absent Father* (Princeton, 1977) came to my attention after this essay was first drafted. It argues that Hamlet unconsciously fears his mother and needs his father, a conclusion directly opposed to mine. Though Erlich's book has many useful insights, psychoanalytic theory leads him to mistake a wishful male fantasy for interpersonal reality.

3. See Harry Stack Sullivan, *The Interpersonal Theory of Psychiatry* (New York, 1953); R. D. Laing, *The Divided Self: An Existential Study in Sanity and Madness* (London, 1960); D. W. Winnicott, 'Mirror-Role of Mother and Family in Child Development', in *The Predicament of the Family: A Psychoanalytic Symposium*, ed. P. Lomas (London, 1967), pp. 26–33; also D. W. Winnicott, *The Maturational Processes and the Facilitating Environment* (New York, 1965). I recognise that the interpersonal approach is in some ways tangential to the major post-

Freudian development in psychoanalysis, the British object-relations school. Nevertheless, I believe it is more useful for literary criticism. A quasi-Laingian study of Shakespeare is Terence Eagleton's *Shakespeare and Society: Critical Essays on Shakespearean Drama* (New York, 1971).

4. R. D. Laing, *The Divided Self: An Existential Study in Sanity and Madness* (London, 1960), p. 95. Laing's dismissal of Ophelia's statement as 'incomprehensible' is odd, given his extraordinary sensitivity to the meanings in schizophrenic voices.

5. See D. W. Winnicott, 'Mirror-Role of Mother and Family in Child Development', in *The Predicament of the Family: A Psychoanalytic Symposium*, ed. P. Lomas (London, 1967), pp. 26–33.

6. Ernest Jones, *Hamlet and Oedipus* (London, 1949), pp. 86–7, sees 'repulsion against woman' as coming from repressed sexual feelings and 'splitting of the mother image'; he connects Hamlet's diatribes against women to unconscious fear of incest wishes. Avi Erlich, in *Hamlet's Absent Father* (Princeton, 1977), explores pre-Oedipal dynamics more thoroughly.

7. See Roy Walker, '*Hamlet*: The Opening Scene', in *The Time is Out of Joint* (Folcroft, 1948), reprinted in *Shakespeare: Modern Essays in Criticism*, ed. Leonard F. Dean (New York, 1961), pp. 216–21. For broader commentaries on the play's 'interrogative mood', see also Maynard Mack, 'The World of Hamlet', *Yale Review*, 41 (June 1952), 502–23, widely reprinted; Harry Levin, *The Question of Hamlet* (New York, 1959); and Bernard McElroy, *Shakespeare's Mature Tragedies* (Princeton, 1973), pp. 29–88.

8. Laing defines 'collusion' as a process by which members of an intimate group, such as the family, conspire knowingly or unknowingly to validate one member's 'false self', that self which conforms to other people's expectations. Eagleton's *Shakespeare and Society* (New York, 1971) analyses how various false unities in *Hamlet* force the hero's subjectivity into being manipulated as an object.

9. See R. D. Laing, *Knots* (London, 1970). This is an extension of Gregory Bateson's 'double bind' theory; see G. Bateson, D. D. Jackson, J. Haley, and J. H. Weakland, 'Toward a Theory of Schizophrenia', *Behavioural Science*, 1 (October 1956), 251–64.

10. Harold C. Goddard, in *The Meaning of Shakespeare*, vol. 1 (Chicago, 1951), develops an interpretation along parallel lines, with the Ghost as devil imposing a 'divided mind' on Hamlet. Goddard's reading is finally a Christian one, arguing that Art, or the play within the play, could have converted Claudius to repentance if Hamlet's uncontrollable vengefulness had not intervened. Another Christian reader sensitive to the Ghost's duplicity is Eleanor Prosser, in *Hamlet and Revenge* (Stanford,

1967). Christian readings, like too many Freudian readings, tend to substitute the false answer of duty for the real question of identity.

11. The Ghost has occasioned immense controversy. Of those who see the Ghost as other than benign, see above, and also Richard Flatter, *Hamlet's Father* (New Haven, 1949); G. Wilson Knight, *The Wheel of Fire*, 2nd edn (London, 1965); and J. Dover Wilson, *What Happens in Hamlet* (Cambridge, 1967). Most critics see the Ghost as the good father to whom Hamlet should submit. In *Fools of Time: Studies in Shakespearean Tragedy* (Toronto, 1967), p. 80, Northrop Frye concludes that 'God's main interest, in Elizabethan tragedy, is in promoting the revenge, and in making it as bloody as possible'. For a Jungian view, which superficially resembles my own in its prescription for men to encounter the woman in themselves, see Alex Aronson, *Psyche and Symbol in Shakespeare* (Bloomington, 1972). In Aronson's view the Ghost is Hamlet's dramatised unconsciousness, as Hamlet tries to free himself from 'his entanglement with a Hecate-like Magna Mater' (p. 235).

12. R. D. Laing and Aaron Esterson, *Sanity, Madness and the Family* (London, 1964). Esterson expanded one chapter into *The Leaves of Spring: A Study in the Dialectics of Madness* (London, 1970).

13. See Harry Morris, 'Ophelia's "Bonny Sweet Robin"', *PMLA*, 73 (December 1958), 601–3; also see Carroll Camden, 'On Ophelia's Madness', *Shakespeare Quarterly*, 15 (Spring 1964), 247–55; and Maurice Charney, *Style in Hamlet* (Princeton, 1969), pp. 107–12.

14. There is near-unanimous critical agreement, except for Goddard, that the last act promotes integration. See Maynard Mack, 'The World of Hamlet', *Yale Review*, 41 (June 1952), 502–23: Bernard McElroy, *Shakespeare's Mature Tragedies* (Princeton, 1973), pp. 29–88; Harold Fisch, *Hamlet and the Word: The Covenant Pattern in Shakespeare* (New York, 1971); Irving Ribner, *Patterns in Shakespearian Tragedy* (London, 1960); J. Dover Wilson, *What Happens in Hamlet* (Cambridge, 1967); and Michael Goldman, *Shakespeare and the Energies of Drama* (Princeton, 1972). Goldman goes so far as to say, 'The play ends with a final unambiguous discharge of energy', and the gunshots prove that 'The air has been cleared' (p. 90). Reuben Brower's more sensitive reading, in *Hero and Saint: Shakespeare and the Graeco-Roman Heroic Tradition* (New York and Oxford, 1971), finds the tension between soldier hero and moral hero reduced to soldier in the end. For a stronger dissent from the consensus, see L. C. Knights, *Some Shakespearean Themes and an Approach to 'Hamlet'* (Stanford, 1966), who finds Hamlet engulfed by evil and the cause of further evil. T. McAlindon, in *Shakespeare and Decorum* (New York, 1973), p. 67, notes that Fortinbras is just 'a crude strong-arm', and Frye (*Fools of Time: Studies in Shakespearean Tragedy*, Toronto, 1967, pp. 29–30) sees Hamlet as selfish to the end. Lidz's *Hamlet's Enemy: Madness and Myth in Hamlet*

(London, 1976) reflects the characteristic adaptive bias of lesser Freudians by discussing the play as a ritual re-establishing appropriate social defences; he sees Fortinbras as a 'direct and uncomplicated hero' who 'brings hope for the rebirth of the nation' (p. 112).

15. R. D. Laing, *The Divided Self: An Existential Study in Sanity and Madness* (London, 1960), p. 57. Laing's system suffers from its romanticisation of 'true self' as aloneness rather than the positive interdependence taught by Winnicott. For a psychoanalytic critique of Laing, see David Holbrook, 'R. D. Laing and the Death Circuit', *Encounter*, 31 (July 1968), 35–45. In *Shakespeare and Society* (New York, 1971) Eagleton offers a similar critique of Hamlet himself: 'Hamlet's insistence on not being a puppet leads, finally, to a delight in resisting any kind of definition; it becomes, in fact, socially irresponsible, a merely negative response' (p. 61). My own sense is that Hamlet looks to women rather than to men for self-definition and that structures of male rule induce his negation.

16. T. S. Eliot, 'Hamlet' (1919), reprinted in *Selected Essays*, 3rd edn (London, 1951), pp. 141–6. In *The Tiger's Heart: Eight Essays on Shakespeare* (New York, 1970), p. 76, Herbert Howarth finds Eliot mistaken because the play is about 'the helplessness of what is gentle before the onrush of what is rank', a nice formulation. Richard A. Lanham's *The Motives of Eloquence: Literary Rhetoric in the Renaissance* (New Haven, 1976) concludes that *Hamlet* is two plays with 'two kinds of self', revenger and self-conscious actor looking for the 'big scene' (pp. 129–43). Maurice Charney's *Style in Hamlet* (Princeton, 1969) says Hamlet responds to his world with four styles: self-consciously parodic, witty, passionate, and simple. In my interpretation the clash Lanham sees between the role-playing 'rhetoric' self and the 'serious' revenger self mirrors Hamlet's role-inducing world, with no mirror for the real self. In some respects Eliot is right to question Gertrude as an 'objective correlative'; she is so much more constant in Hamlet's hopes than in her weak, sensual actuality that she raises the question of whether the woman in *Hamlet* is only in Hamlet.

17. T. S. Eliot, 'Hamlet' (1919), reprinted in *Selected Essays*, 3rd edn (London, 1951), p. 146.

18. T. S. Eliot, 'The Metaphysical Poets' (1921), reprinted in *Selected Essays* (London, 1951), pp. 281–91.

10

Revenge in 'Hamlet'

CATHERINE BELSEY

In the revenge plays in the half-century before the civil war it is the sovereign's failure to administer justice which inaugurates the subject's quest for vengeance. Hieronimo rips the bowels of the earth with his dagger, calling for 'justice, O justice, justice, gentle king' (*The Spanish Tragedy*, III.xii.63). Titus Andronicus urges his kinsmen to dig a passage to Pluto's region, with a petition 'for justice and for aid' (*Titus Andronicus*, IV.iii.15). The Duchess Rosaura appeals direct to the monarch:

> Let me have swift and such exemplar justice
> As shall become this great assassinate.
> You will take off our faith else, and if here
> Such innocence must bleed and you look on,
> Poor men that call you gods on earth will doubt
> To obey your laws.
> (*The Cardinal*, III.ii.104–9)

In each case, however, the sovereign fails to enforce the law. Indeed, in *Antonio's Revenge* (*c*.1600) *The Revenger's Tragedy* and *Hamlet* the ruler is the criminal. In the absence of justice the doubt Rosaura defines propels the revenger to take in the interests of justice action which is itself unjust.

Revenge is not justice. Titus is a man 'so just that he will not revenge' (*Titus Andronicus*, IV.i.129). Acting outside the legal institution and in defiance of legitimate authority, individuals have no right to arrogate to themselves the role of the state in the administration of justice: 'never private cause / Should take on it the

154

part of public laws' (*The Revenge of Bussy d'Ambois*, III.ii.115–16). Conscience, which permits passive disobedience, forbids murder, and thus makes cowards of some revengers (*Hamlet*, III.i.83–5).[1] Others, more resolute, like Laertes are deaf to its promptings:

> To hell, allegiance! Vows to the blackest devil!
> Conscience and grace to the profoundest pit!
> I dare damnation. To this point I stand,
> That both the worlds I give to negligence.
> Let come what comes: only I'll be reveng'd
> Most throughly for my father.
>   (*Hamlet*, IV.v.128–33)

When Hamlet differentiates revenge from hire and salary (III.iii.79), he specifies the gap between vengeance and justice. Revenge is always in excess of justice. Its execution calls for a 'stratagem of . . . horror' (*Antonio's Revenge*, III.i.48–50). Titus serves the heads of Chiron and Demetrius to their mother and the Emperor in a pastry coffin. Antonio massacres the innocent Julio and offers him in a dish to his father, after cutting out the tyrant's tongue. Vindice prepares for the Duke a liaison with the skull of the murdered Gloriana, and the 'bony lady' poisons him with a kiss (*The Revenger's Tragedy*, III.v.121). Hippolito holds down his tongue and compels him to witness his wife's adultery while he dies.

The discourse of revenge reproduces the violence and the excess of its practice: 'Look how I smoke in blood, reeking the steam / Of foaming vengeance' (*Antonio's Revenge*, III.v.17–18): 'Then will I rent and tear them thus and thus. / Shivering their limbs in pieces with my teeth' (*The Spanish Tragedy*, III.xiii.122–3): 'Now could I drink hot blood, / And do such bitter business as the day / Would quake to look on' (*Hamlet*, III.ii.380–2): 'I should 'a fatted all the region kites / With this slave's offal' (*Hamlet*, II.ii.574–5). As Claudius assures Laertes, it is in the nature of revenge to 'have no bounds' (*Hamlet*, IV.vii.128). The rugged Pyrrhus – avenging *his* father's death, 'roasted in wrath and fire. / And thus o'er-sized with coagulate gore' (*Hamlet*, II.ii.455–6) – is not, after all, entirely a caricature of the stage revenger.

And yet the act of vengeance, in excess of justice, a repudiation of conscience, hellish in its mode of operation, seems to the revenger (and to the audience?) an overriding imperative. Not to act is to leave crime unpunished, murder triumphant or tyranny in unfettered control. The orthodox Christian remedy is patience: 'Vengeance is mine:

I will repay, saith the Lord' (Rom. 12:19). *The Spanish Tragedy*
offers two contrasting models, dramatises, in effect, two antithetical
worlds, one authoritarian, divinely ordered and controlled, and the
other disordered, unjust, incipiently secular and humanist. In Portu-
gal Alexandro is accused of the murder of Balthazar. Alexandro is
not permitted to speak (I.iii.88), but patience and heaven are invoked
in his defence (III.i.31–5). As he is bound to the stake, insisting that
his death will be avenged on his accuser, Villuppo, an ambassador
arrives with letters for the King which show that Balthazar is alive.
Heaven is evidently ordinant in Alexandro's providential last-minute
release, and in the consequent execution of Villuppo. In Spain the
murder of Horatio initially elicits a parallel response: 'The heavens
are just, murder cannot be hid' (II.v.57): 'Ay, heaven will be reveng'd
of every ill' (III.xiii.2). But when Hieronimo appeals to heaven for
justice a letter 'falleth' (III.ii.23 S.D.). Its auspices are uncertain: it is
addressed to the subject and not to the sovereign; it reveals the
identity of the murderers, and thus inaugurates Hieronimo's quest
for justice, which becomes an act of revenge. The place of heaven –
or hell – in this process is unclear.

Whatever the requirements of Christian patience, the imperatives
of fiction demand that heaven delays the execution of justice, and in
the interim crime continues. Belimperia is imprisoned, Pedringano is
suborned, Serberine murdered. In *Hamlet* Claudius is still in possession of the crown and Gertrude, and is planning the death of the hero
in addition. Vindice has waited nine years and meanwhile crime at
court is met with a travesty of justice. In these circumstances revenge
is a political as well as a moral issue. Thus Hamlet asks,

> Does it not, think thee, stand me now upon –
> He that hath kill'd my king and whor'd my mother;
> Popp'd in between th' election and my hopes;
> Thrown out his angle for my proper life,
> And with such coz'nage – is't not perfect conscience
> To quit him with this arm? And is't not to be damn'd
> To let this canker of our nature come
> In further evil?
>
> (V.ii.63–70)

The question, like most of the questions raised in *Hamlet*, is not
answered. But even Clermont d'Ambois, model of Stoic virtue, is
persuaded by Bussy's Ghost that he has a moral obligation to punish
the murder the king leaves unpunished, and so to do in this world
'deeds that fit eternity':

> And those deeds are the perfecting that justice
> That makes the world last, which proportion is
> Of punishment and wreak for every wrong,
> As well as for right a reward as strong.
> Away, then! Use the means thou hast to right
> The wrong I suffer'd. What corrupted law
> Leaves unperform'd in kings do thou supply.
> (*The Revenge of Bussy d'Ambois*, V.i.91–8)

And in consequence, the Ghost concludes, 'be above them all in dignity' (l.99). The bloody masques and Thyestean banquets are hellish, but they have the effect, none the less, of purging a corrupt social body, and in the process installing the subject as autonomous agent of retribution.

Revenge exists in the margin between justice and crime. An act of injustice on behalf of justice, it deconstructs the antithesis which fixes the meanings of good and evil, right and wrong. Hamlet invokes the conventional polarities in addressing the Ghost, only to abandon them as inadequate or irrelevant:

> Be thou a spirit of health or goblin damn'd,
> Bring with thee airs from heaven or blasts from hell,
> Be thy intents wicked or charitable,
> Thou com'st in such a questionable shape
> That I will speak to thee.
>
> (I.iv.40–4)

The Ghosts in revenge plays consistently resist unequivocal identifications, are always 'questionable' in one of the senses of that word. Dead and yet living, visitants at midnight (the marginal hour) from a prison-house which is neither heaven nor hell, visible to some figures on the stage but not to others, and so neither real nor unreal, they inaugurate a course of action which is both mad and sane, correct and criminal. To uphold the law revengers are compelled to break it. The moral uncertainty persists to the end. Vindice's execution by Antonio either punishes or perpetuates injustice: 'You that would murder him would murder me' (*The Revenger's Tragedy*, V.iii.105). Hamlet dies a revenger, a poisoner, but also a soldier and a prince (*Hamlet*, V.ii.387–95). Clermont d'Ambois survives the duel with Montsurry but kills himself thereafter. Antonio, to his (and the audience's?) 'amazement' (*Antonio's Revenge*, V.vi.28), is greeted by the Senate as a hero, but the play ends with his retirement to a monastery.

CATHERINE BELSEY

The question whether it is nobler to suffer in Christian patience or to take arms against secular injustice is not resolved in the plays. It is ultimately a question about authority – God's, the sovereign's or the subject's. To the extent that the plays condemn revenge, they stay within an orthodoxy which permits only passive disobedience and prescribes no remedy for the subject when the sovereign breaks the law. But in order to be revenge plays at all, they are compelled to throw into relief the social and political weaknesses of this ethical and political position. To the extent that they consequently endorse revenge, they participate in the installation of the sovereign subject, entitled to take action in accordance with conscience and on behalf of law.

From Catherine Belsey, *The Subject of Tragedy: Identity and Difference in Renaissance Drama* (London, 1985), pp. 111–16.

NOTES

[This brief extract from Catherine Belsey's book *The Subject of Tragedy* focuses on some of the contradictions that surround revenge in Renaissance drama and how those contradictions bear upon the political problem of the subject's (individual's) authority to act. 'Revenge', Belsey notes, 'is always in excess of justice', and yet seems 'to the revenger (and to the audience?) an overriding imperative' – to be, that is, both morally and politically necessary. The traditional answer to this dilemma is 'to suffer in Christian patience', but that leaves the social body in the hands of murderers like Claudius. Belsey's overall thesis is that Renaissance drama is part of the political crisis of the seventeenth century which saw the change from an essentially medieval world – ruled by God – to a modern world in which the individual subject feels able to challenge the authority of the king, and take action on his/her own behalf and also on that of the law. What Belsey thus points to is the extent to which revenge in *Hamlet* is not simply a moral problem but rather a political problem of the utmost significance to a century that, in 1649, was to see the execution of Charles I. Though difficult in places, Belsey's book, which embraces both Marxist and feminist ideas, throws a great deal of light on the conflicts and contradictions that inform Renaissance drama.

It is perhaps worth adding that the term 'subject' is a key word in poststructuralist criticism. Literally a subject is one who speaks (I), but in poststructuralism its use is heavily influenced by the writings of the French philosopher and psychoanalyst Jacques Lacan. Lacan argues that the major force which structures the human subject is language. The 'subject', however, is not only the speaker of a speech, but also the 'I' who is grammatically present in the speech. To speak about myself I use the word 'I'. Lacan argues that there is a gap between I and 'I', a gap which opens up in times of social or political or, indeed, psychological crisis when values are shifting or changing, as in the Renaissance or our own age. Revenge is the sign of such a crisis in *Hamlet*, not simply because it plunges the state into chaos but because, as Belsey notes, revenge 'deconstructs the antithesis which fixes the meanings of good and evil, right and wrong' – that is, it undoes the opposition between meanings so that we, like Hamlet, are unsure whether or not he should kill the king. All quotations in the extract are from *William Shakespeare: The Complete Works*, ed. Peter Alexander (London and Glasgow, 1951). Ed.]

1. For an argument to substantiate in detail this reading of the 'To be or not to be' speech, see Catherine Belsey, 'The case of Hamlet's conscience', *Studies in Philology*, 76 (1979), 127–48.

11

Power in 'Hamlet'

LEONARD TENNENHOUSE

Hamlet rehearses [the] dilemma of a state torn between two competitors, neither of whom can embody the mystical power of blood and land associated with the natural body. Hamlet's claim to power derives from his position as son in a patrilinear system as well as from 'popular support'. It is this support which Claudius consistently lacks and which, at the same time, prevents him from moving openly against Hamlet. Following the murder of Polonius, for example, Claudius says of Hamlet, 'Yet must not we put the strong law on him. / He's lov'd of the distracted multitude . . .' (IV.iii.3–4). But this alone does not guarantee authority. Hamlet is not by nature capable of exercising force. To signal this lack, Shakespeare has given him the speech of Stoical writing, which shifts all action onto a mental plane where any show of force becomes self-inflicted aggression. We find this identification of force with self-assault made explicit in Hamlet's speeches on suicide as well as those in which he berates himself for his inability to act.

In contrast with Hamlet, Claudius's authority comes by way of his marriage to Gertrude. Where he would be second to Hamlet and Hamlet's line in a patrilineal system, the queen's husband and uncle of the king's son occupies the privileged male position in a matrilineal system. Like one of the successful figures from a history play, Claudius overthrew the reigning patriarch. Like one of the successful courtiers in a romantic comedy, he married into the aristocratic community. What is perhaps more important, he has taken the position through the effective use of force. Thus Shakespeare sets in opposition the two claims to authority – the exercise of force and the magic of blood – by means of these two members of the royal family. Because each has a claim, neither Hamlet nor Claudius achieves legitimate control over Denmark. Each one consequently assaults the aristocratic body in attempting to acquire the crown. It is to be expected that Claudius could not legally possess the crown, the matrilinear succession having the weaker claim on British political thinking. Thus the tragedy resides not in his failure but in the impossibility of Hamlet's rising according to Elizabethan strategies of state. This calls the relationship between the metaphysics of patriarchy and the force of law into question.

Claudius's criminality is never the problem. What more heinous crime could be committed against the aristocratic body than a fratricide that is also a regicide? Add to this that both Hamlet and his father's ghost consider this crime incestuous in that it allows one member of the king's family to marry another. But even when they acquired state power under the most questionable means, and even when the magic of blood seemed to locate power elsewhere, the monarchs of the chronicle histories could authorise force and sanction their blood by certain displays of power. Thus we see them incorporating popular energy in the processions of state. In particular, we find them including alienated members of the aristocracy. We may observe this in rituals of forgiveness as Bullingbroke uses to forgive Aumerle [in *Richard II*], for example, or Henry's vow [in *2 Henry IV*] to banish Falstaff while promising to those that do reform themselves, 'We will, according to your strengths and qualities, / Give you advancement' (V.v.69–70). *Henry V* concludes in comic fashion with courtship and promises of marriage, much as *Richard III* ends with Richmond's prayer, 'O now let Richmond and Elizabeth, / The true succeeders of each royal house, / By God's fair ordinance conjoin together' (V.v.29–31). All these gestures stress the patron's generosity rather than his power to subordinate. It is important, then, that Claudius cannot seize hold of these signs and symbols of power that would authorise his reign. If Hamlet cannot translate the claims of blood into the exercise of force, it is also true that Claudius cannot command the symbolic elements of his culture which testify to the magic of blood. This is especially apparent in the contrast Shakespeare draws between the patron's feast and the revels Claudius attempts to stage. Significantly, Hamlet must explain to a startled Horatio that the sudden noises of trumpet and cannon do not signal a military invasion but rather announce Claudius's revels:

> The King doth wake to-night and takes his rouse,
> Keeps wassail, and the swagg'ring up-spring reels;
> And as he drains his draughts of Rhenish down,
> The kettle-drum and trumpet thus bray out
> The triumph of his pledge.
>
> (I.iv.8–12)

Add to this the fact that Shakespeare has Hamlet describe Claudius to Gertrude in terms that specifically invoke the figure of misrule:

> A murtherer and a villain!
> A slave that is not twentieth part the tithe
> Of your precedent lord; a vice of kings,
> A cutpurse of the empire and the rule,
> That from a shelf the precious diadem stole,
> And put it in his pocket . . .
> A king of shreds and patches . . .
>
> (III.iv.95–102)

As he leaves, Hamlet urges his mother not to let 'The bloat king tempt you again to bed . . .' (l.182). To call Claudius a 'bloat king', a 'lecherous' man, 'a cutpurse of the empire', 'a vice of kings', is for Shakespeare to cut this usurper out of the same cloth he used in fabricating Falstaff. Thus Claudius acquires the features of illicit power which the history plays subordinate, if not purge, in sanctifying power.

Rather than authorising the state, then, Shakespeare lines up the benign image of carnival – a populist support – in opposition to Claudius. When Laertes returns to demand justice for the murder of his father, he exhibits the same features of popular authority which Shakespeare gave the heroes of his chronicle history plays and attributed to Hamlet as well:

> young Laertes, in a riotous head,
> O'erbears your officers. The rabble call him lord,
> And as the world were now but to begin,
> Antiquity forgot, custom not known,
> The ratifiers and props of every word,
> They cry, 'Choose we, Laertes shall be king!'
>
> (IV.v.102–7)

In light of the power these features have to authorise force in the history plays, then, we must sit up and take note when the figure of popular energy is caught up in Claudius's conspiracy to turn the banquet table into the scene of Hamlet's death. Transformed, these materials testify to the hierarchising power of the aristocracy. Untransformed, however, these materials represent what is outside the aristocratic body and most threatening to it.

The staging of a play within a play, say, in *A Midsummer Night's Dream* and *The Taming of the Shrew*, as well as in *Hamlet*, serves another purpose. Shakespeare makes these stagings part of the official rituals of state even when directed by pranksters and rude mechanicals. Furthermore, the dramatic performance so nested within the dramatic performance of the play as a whole invariably concerns itself with ruptures or disturbances within the aristocratic body itself. When Hamlet stages *The Murder of Gonzago*, it is his attempt to locate and purge a corrupt element within the aristocratic body. In this respect, he does not resemble Laertes playing the revenger of Senecan tragedy but acts in his capacity as would-be sovereign. Shakespeare gives Hamlet the state's power to discover and punish a crime against the sovereign's body. In refusing to display his power by staging some spectacle of punishment, we should recall, Richard II weakened his hold on the throne, while Henry IV strengthened his by taking such action upon acquiring the crown.

The play within the play is Hamlet's attempt to re-enact his uncle's assault on the sovereign body and thus establish the truth of regicide which would authorise Hamlet's claim to the throne. He explains:

> I'll have these players
> Play something like the murther of my father
> Before mine uncle. I'll observe his looks,
> I'll tent him to the quick. If 'a do blench.
> I know my course.
>
> (II.ii.594–8)

Hamlet means the play to 'tent', or probe Claudius as with a dagger that opens an infected wound. Thus he would inscribe upon his uncle's body the truth of his crime against the king. Of torture and confession which precedes the spectacle of punishment, Foucault writes, 'the secret and written form' – torture and confession – 'reflects the principle that in criminal matters the establishment of truth was the absolute right and the exclusive power of the sovereign'.[1] Let us make the statement still stronger and say that the monarch's ability to establish truth is as important as his ability to incorporate the state within his body politic. Both are means of authorising forms of violence which otherwise would have to be considered acts of insurrection and regicide. But Hamlet's play fails in two respects to materialise as a spectacle of punishment which would display the authority of Hamlet over Claudius. Because the play is only a play, first of all, and not an official ritual of state, its truth is bracketed as a supposition rather than a re-enactment of the truth. It is another instance of Shakespeare's giving Hamlet a mode of speech that cannot constitute political action because it automatically translates all action onto the purely symbolic plane of thought and art. Only here it is the Senecan mode of tragedy that turns the exercise of power into a purely symbolic gesture, not his use of Stoic discourse.

Even as a symbolic gesture, secondly, the play fails to hit its mark. Hamlet has chosen to produce *The Murder of Gonzago* for its political truth. The play he says will be 'something like the murther of my father' (II.ii.595). Indeed, the play does re-enact that fratricide in that it portrays the aristocratic body turning against itself to inflict a mortal wound. But Hamlet's gloss on the play gives us to understand he has chosen a play portraying the murder of an uncle by his nephew:

> This is one Lucianus, nephew to the king. . . .
> 'A poisons him i'th' garden for his estate. His name's Gonzago. The story is extant, and written in very choice Italian. You shall see anon how the murtherer gets the love of Gonzago's wife.
>
> (III.ii.244, 261–4)

Rather than a crime against a patrilineal system of descent, then, *The Murder of Gonzago* portrays a crime which would be precisely equivalent to fratricide in a matrilineal system of descent where uncle and nephew rather than first and second sons constitute the most competitive male relations. This is not to say that Shakespeare has the play betray Hamlet's intentions and reveal the secret wishes – thus the thought crimes – of its director. Quite the contrary, Shakespeare has carefully worked out the configuration of family relations within and without this play. As he did so, Shakespeare deviated from the source by casting the murderer as a nephew to the duke.[2] By this deliberate revision of his source, Shakespeare equated Hamlet's punishment with Claudius's crime. This is to say that both acts of violence assault the sovereign's body rather than establish the absolute power of the aristocratic body over that of its subject. Both turn out to be self-inflicted wounds. As the play concludes by heaping up the bodies of the royal family where the banquet scene should have been, this truth materialises: that the murder of one member of the aristocracy by another is an assault on the entire body, in other words, an act of suicide.

That Hamlet's act of vengeance against his uncle constitutes a crime against the state is dramatised in another way as well: in the language that Hamlet speaks. Where he spoke a Stoic discourse (e.g. 'To be or not to be ...') before staging his play, afterwards Hamlet speaks in the contrasting terms of Senecan tragedy:

> 'Tis now the very witching time of night,
> When churchyards yawn and hell itself breathes out
> Contagion to this world. Now could I drink hot blood
> And do such bitter business as the day
> Would quake to look on.
>
> (III.ii.387–92)

This is the language which Nashe identified a decade earlier as that of the 'English Seneca' which characterised earlier productions of 'whole Hamlets'.[3] By giving him this familiar stage speech, Shakespeare distinguishes Hamlet's exercise of authority from the rituals and processionals concluding the chronicle history plays. At the same time, such speech identifies Hamlet with Claudius whose exercise of force turns into Senecan tragedy, first in the murder of Hamlet's father which initiated the action of the play, and then in the murder of Hamlet with which the play concludes. Thus Hamlet's play figures out the power of the state on a symbolic plane in the very terms that Claudius uses to enact his authority. Neither can act in a way that establishes the family line according to the strategies of state governing the chronicle history plays.

One might be tempted to declare a generic difference between *Hamlet*, as a tragedy, and the history plays on just these grounds, but I will argue against the wisdom of doing so for those who want to understand Shakespeare's genres as political strategies. Even as he raises questions concerning the iconic relationship between the queen's two bodies, Shakespeare cannot imagine legitimate power in any other way. Given the fact that neither Claudius nor Hamlet could embody the state in a way that effectively hierarchised power – this, chiefly because each had equal claims to power – neither one could become the legitimate sovereign of Denmark. In light of their failure, the arrival of Fortinbras marks *Hamlet* as an Elizabethan play. Nowhere to be found in the sources, his name implies a natural ability to exercise force. Shakespeare also endows Fortinbras with aristocratic blood, though not that of the Danish line. In this, he obviously resembles the figure who emerges at the end of all the major history plays as the product of human history and providence as well. Most perfectly realised in *Henry V*, this figure acquires authority not only through material conflicts which display the effective exercise of force, but also through the metaphysics of blood which he embodies.

From Leonard Tennenhouse, *Power on Display: The Politics of Shakespeare's Genres* (London, 1986), pp. 88–93.

NOTES

[Leonard Tennenhouse's book on Shakespeare, *Power on Display: The Politics of Shakespeare's Genres*, is written from the perspective of New Historicist criticism. What Tennenhouse is interested in is the way in which political ideas about power are built into and displayed in Shakespeare's plays, and how these ideas link the tragedies and histories which traditional criticism has tended to treat separately. The extract printed here focuses on the rival claims to power of Hamlet and Claudius, and on their struggle to achieve sovereign authority. In particular, Tennenhouse analyses Hamlet's staging of the play-within-the-play not as a device to catch the conscience of the king but rather as a device which leads us to understand how revenge – no less than Claudius's murder – constitutes a crime against the state. To this extent, Tennenhouse concludes, neither Hamlet nor Claudius can become the legitimate sovereign of Denmark. As with the previous essay by Catherine Belsey, Tennenhouse sends us back to the play to think again about the political implications for its audience and what kind of debate the action prompts as we watch it.

Behind Tennenhouse's argument lies the work of the French philosopher and historian Michel Foucault, who is interested in the complex relationship between language, power and knowledge. Foucault argues that language is always an historical event rather than being outside history or politics, but he has also suggested how the state's control can work not only through language but also through theatrical display, such as public trials and executions. It is this second idea that Tennenhouse takes up here as he explores various ways in which different types and images of power are staged in *Hamlet*. All quotations in the extract are from *The Riverside Shakespeare*, ed. G. Blakemore Evans (Boston, 1974). Ed.]

1. Michel Foucault, *Discipline and Punish: The Birth of the Prison*, trans. Alan Sheridan (New York, 1979), p. 35.

2. See Geoffrey Bullough, *Narrative and Dramatic Sources of Shakespeare* (New York, 1973), vol. 7, pp. 30, 172–6.

3. Nashe writes, 'Yet English Seneca read by candlelight yields many good sentences, as "blood is a beggar", and so forth; and if you entreat him fair in a frosty morning, he will afford you whole Hamlets ... of tragical speeches'; *The Unfortunate Traveller and other Works*, ed. J. B. Steane (Harmondsworth, 1972), p. 474.

12

A Thing of Nothing: The Catastrophic Body in 'Hamlet'

JOHN HUNT

If Hamlet actually writes down moral lessons on his tablets as he studies his revenge, many of them surely have to do with how life is lived, and lost, in bodies. Far more even than in *Macbeth* or *Coriolanus*, the human body in *Hamlet* forms human experience, being the medium through which men suffer and act. But the body also deforms human beings and threatens ultimately to reduce them to nothing. The non-being lurking at the material centre of being announces itself everywhere in the play's corporeal imagery, and occupies Hamlet's mind as he tries to find his way from the regal death that initiates the action to the regal death that concludes it. This essay examines the problem in two parts, using an analysis of the imagery as an approach to the great mystery of the play, Hamlet's quandary about how to act. It suggests that Hamlet cannot adequately respond to the Ghost's commands until he learns to accept physicality, with all its dissolute inconstancy, as the image of mentality. Not until he finds his way out of a despairing contempt for the body can he achieve the wish of his first soliloquy and quietly cease to be.

I

At the end of *Hamlet*, all the remaining members of the two great families of Denmark lie crumpled about the stage. Meta-theatrically doubling this tableau, Horatio asks Fortinbras to 'give order that these bodies / High on a stage be placed to the view' (V.ii.379–80) – an order that is carried out as the play ends.[1] Polonius's 'guts' have already been hauled off the stage less ceremoniously; Ophelia's body has been brought on with truncated ceremony and lowered into the pit beneath the stage, from which skulls have come flying up to make room for it; and all the carnage has been set in motion by the pale, glaring 'dead corse' of King Hamlet. The eyes of the mind, if they are open, behold in the play's language a spectacle of ruined bodies fully as grim as what their physical counterparts behold on stage. Before hearing of and seeing the body's demise in the churchyard, we imagine an unorthodox autopsy when one gravedigger tells the other the results of the inquiry into Ophelia's suicide: 'The crowner hath sate on her, and finds it Christian burial' (V.i.4–5). Grotesque visions arise when he responds to the suggestion of his companion that the original spade-wielder, Adam, was a gentleman, 'the first that ever bore arms'. 'Why, he had none', the clown objects, only to be refuted in a manner that makes his statement monstrous. 'What, art a heathen? How doest thou understand the Scripture? The Scripture says Adam digged. Could he dig without arms?' (V.i.30ff.). Amputee gardeners, corpses used as sofas (perhaps two of the thousand natural shocks that flesh is heir to), and many kindred figures drive the play's physical violence deep into the minds of the audience.

The body thus represented is no mere vehicle or Platonic instrument for the soul; it incarnates spirit, as Christ, His Church, and the Host incarnate God. Shakespeare's metaphorical figures go to eery lengths to show man deeply rooted in a material substrate. Thus Hamlet takes the saying of Genesis and Matthew that man and wife become one flesh as authority for his mocking valediction to Claudius:

> **Hamlet**   Farewell, dear Mother.
> **King** Thy loving father, Hamlet.
> **Hamlet** My mother – father and mother is man and wife,
>   man and wife is one flesh, and so, my mother.
>   (IV.iii.50–3)

Claudius himself imparts a corporeal facticity to the old figure of horseman as Centaur, telling Laertes of a Norman rider who 'grew unto his seat' and seemed to have been 'incorpsed and deminatured / With the brave beast' (IV.vii.85–8). And Laertes warns his sister not to love the prince because his ambitious mind grows along with his young body and, as lord of the kingdom, he will be 'circumscribed / Unto the voice and yielding of that body / Whereof he is the head' (I.iii.22–4).

The body politic is more than a metaphor for social organisation in this play: it describes a tightly integrated world where reality stems palpably from the centres of political and religious authority. Francis Barker, describing the public, spectacular quality of *Hamlet* and other Jacobean tragedies, has argued that the abundant corporeal images used in texts of this period were not the 'dead metaphors' that they are now, but 'indices of a social order in which the body has a central and irreducible place'. 'With a clarity now hard to recapture', he says, 'the social plenum *is* the body of the king, and membership of this anatomy is the deep structural form of all being in the secular realm.'[2] The extravagant idea, examined by Ernst Kantorowicz three decades ago, that the king in fact has two bodies – his own plus a superbody equivalent to the corporate life of his nation – always threatened to revert to a mystical abstraction, and eventually disappeared from political theory. Discussing its role in *Richard II*, Kantorowicz observed that if the conceit 'still has a very real and human meaning today, this is largely due to Shakespeare. It is he who has eternalised that metaphor.'[3] There is nothing in *Richard II* to match the really astonishing concreteness that the metaphor acquires in one passage of *Hamlet*, when Rosencrantz and Guildenstern accede to Claudius's plan to 'dispatch' Hamlet to England:

> We will ourselves provide.
> Most holy and religious fear it is
> To keep those many many bodies safe
> That live and feed upon your Majesty.
> (III.iii.7–10)

Calling up pictures of a bloated insect queen covered by her sucking attendants, or a convocation of politic worms feasting on a corpse, or a communion more literally cannibalistic than most, this violently arresting image locates the king at the dark centre of a world dense with material significance. His universal Body, symbolising religious authority over a commonality, does not hover in some library of legal abstractions, but pulsates with grisly vitality.

The imagery that Shakespeare invents to establish man's corporeality startles most when isolated parts of the body function as metonymic or synecdochal equivalents for actions and states of being. Every audience remembers 'The harlot's cheek, beautied with plast'ring art'; Hecuba's 'lank and all o'er-teemed loins'; Fortinbras sharking up men 'For food and diet to some enterprise / That hath a stomach in't'; Osric complying with his dug before he sucks it; Hamlet beating his brains; and countless similar figures. This usage pervades so much of the play that one can hardly read or hear twenty consecutive lines without encountering it. To maintain the motif's impact in the midst of such copious use, Shakespeare occasionally resorts to violently pressured and improbable images. 'Let the candied tongue lick absurd pomp', says Hamlet to Horatio in an indictment of the flatterer so suggestively lewd that even the compleat courtier might blush to hear it. 'And crook the pregnant hinges of the knee / Where thrift may follow fawning' (III.ii.60–2). Shortly afterwards he asks Horatio to watch Claudius carefully. 'For I mine eyes will rivet to his face' (l.85). After this anatomical outrage has been performed upon him, Claudius decides that with Hamlet in Denmark he is not safe from the 'Hazard so near's as doth hourly grow / Out of his brows' (III.iii.6–7). In such images, strangely transformed parts of the body – the flatterer's glazed tongue and pregnant knees, Hamlet's bolted eyeballs and malignantly hypertrophic forehead – figure forth morbid states of mind typified in the pursuit of some compelling action. One thinks of certain punishments in the lower reaches of Dante's *Inferno*: Mohammad's riven trunk fulfilling his schismatic mischief, Ugolino gnawing his enemy's malevolent skull. Indeed, the Ghost hints that, were it not for the intolerable effects that such a tale would have on the living, he could tell of such a treatment of the body's parts in his purgatory: 'But this eternal blazon must not be / To ears of flesh and blood' (I.v.21–2).

It has, I believe, never been observed that these images of body parts in *Hamlet* add up to a virtual anatomical catalogue (or, to use the Ghost's grim little joke about dismemberment, 'blazon') of the human form. 'Considered curiously', as curiously as Hamlet considers the dust of Alexander, the play looks like a dissecting room, stocked with all of man's limbs, organs, tissues, and fluids. Certain parts are mentioned incessantly; eyes, ears, heads, hearts, hands, faces, tongues, brains. These major melodies in the carnal concerto are accompanied by numerous lesser themes. We hear (in varying degrees of frequency) of mouths, noses, lips, cheeks, jaws, teeth, eyelids, foreheads ('brows'), the crown of the head ('pate'), the skin, hair in general, beards, necks, limbs in general, arms, legs, knees, feet, heels, toes, fingers, the thumb, the palm, the wrist, the shoulder, the back, the loins, the waist, the breast in general ('bosom'), the mammary organ (Osric's 'dug'), genitals in general ('privates'), male genitals ('cock' and the 'long purple' flowers whose common name has been euphemised to 'dead men's fingers'), female genitals ('country matters'), and the anus ('bunghole').[4] Of internal organs, there is mention not only of the heart and brain, but also the throat, lungs, stomach, spleen, liver, guts, bones, marrow, nerves, sinews, spinal cord ('pith'), and arteries. Of the fluid products of the body, we hear of blood and tears incessantly, and also of sweat, milk, fat, and gall. The play also refers to various corrupting growths in the body – moles, cankers, warts, ulcers, abscesses, sores, scabs, and 'contagious blastments'. Finally, it alludes to such bodily functions as speech, hearing, sight, touch, taste, smell, eating, drinking, chewing, digestion, vomiting, evacuation, sleep, dreaming, hallucination, yawning, weeping, laughing, breathing, copulation, pregnancy, suckling, pulse, disease, fever, death, and decomposition.

More than simply painting a bloody backdrop for his tragedy of revenge, in the manner of Webster, Shakespeare seems to be methodically deconstructing the body. His universal cataloguing of particulars does to the human body what Hamlet tells Osric it would be hard to do to Laertes: 'divide him inventorially' (V.ii.114). Like Montaigne, who sought to examine the unknown totality of human experience through its genesis in many particular, irreducible phenomena experienced by the organism, Shakespeare seeks to reduce life to its corporeal elements. His characters in this play think of every psychological quality, every rational deliberation or spiritual choice, in terms of the physical equipment that locates them in a world of action. Claudius's unsuccessful attempt to pray is a good example, demonstrating as it does the limitation of human possibility implied by this procedure. He thinks throughout his soliloquy in corporeal images: the smell of his offence, the blood on his hand, the face of a reprobate and a penitent, 'stubborn knees' that will not bow down, a 'bosom black as death' hiding a 'heart with strings of steel', and so forth (III.iii.36ff). Claudius's 'limed soul' reflects conditions of corporeal limitation that Montaigne suggests, at the end of 'Raymond Sebond', man can overcome only through the extension of divine grace:

> For to make the handful bigger than the hand, the armful bigger than the arm, and to hope to straddle more than the reach of our legs, is impossible and unnatural. Nor can man raise himself and humanity: for he can see only with his own eyes, and seize only with his own grasp.
> He will rise, if God by exception lends him a hand.[5]

None of the angels whom Claudius begs to 'Make assay' offers him an incorporeal hand: caught within the paralytic compound of his heart, hands, brain, face, voice, he looks in vain for a way out of the dwelling that he has made a prison. Nor do any of the other characters in *Hamlet* find 'exceptional' release from their natural condition. In their variously less desperate ways, all struggle against the web of matter that life has woven round them and in which they implicate themselves further every time they act.

Montaigne's challenge, after sceptically weighing the particulars of human experience, was to put them back together in a living totality. Shakespeare's intention appears to be very different. Far from even attempting to present the life of the body as an organically function-ing entity, he portrays it more in the manner of Donne's *Devotions*, as a collection of pieces whose morbidity intimates their ultimate violent dissolution. The play's countless parts and functions, linked with various extreme and unhealthy states of mind, engender a disturbing sense of ontological dislocation. Things fall apart in *Hamlet* – or are torn apart. Shakespeare does not use the currently popular metaphor of anatomy here (as he does, for instance, for Jaques's lacerating intelligence in *As You Like It*), but throughout the play we are made to think of the fragmented state of a body that has been cut open, probed, dissected. When, in the first line of the play, Barnardo inappropriately demands the identity of Francisco, the sentinel he is replacing, Francisco responds, 'Nay, answer me. Stand and unfold yourself'. In the claustrophobic heart of Elsinore, the politicians try to make Hamlet stand still so that they can unfold him and find what lies within. Seeing Hamlet's disturbed behaviour, Claudius resolves to discover (surgically, as it were) 'Whether aught to us unknown afflicts him thus, / That opened lies within our remedy' (II.ii.17–18). Polonius, supposing that he has found the answer, points (according to the commonest editorial reading) to his head and shoulders and says:

> Take this from this, if this be otherwise.
> If circumstances lead me, I will find
> Where truth is hid, though it were hid indeed
> Within the centre.
>
> (II.ii.156–9)

Rosencrantz and Guildenstern, Fortune's privates, who make love to their employment, who would play on Hamlet's stops as on a pipe, reaching for the heart of his mystery, are themselves ground up in their obscene probings, doomed 'by their own insinuation' (V.ii.59). The king keeps them, as Hamlet tells Rosencrantz, 'like an ape, in the corner of his jaw, first mouthed, to be last swallowed' (IV.ii.19–20). Finally they become inert matter in Hamlet's own perversion of Claudius's plans.

Other insinuations of partition or dismemberment come in reference to 'parts' or 'piece', as in the fragmented lines that open the play. When two more figures enter, Barnardo asks, 'What, is Horatio there?' and Horatio answers – perhaps in numbness at the frigid weather, perhaps in disdain for the spooky proceedings, but certainly strangely – 'A piece of him' (I.i.19). Laertes, 'the continent of what part a gentleman would see' (V.ii.112–13), suffers often from such usages, several of them in the scene in which Claudius reduces him to a tool of his murderous intentions (IV.vii.57ff.). Laertes agrees to obey Claudius on the condition that 'you will not o'errule me to a peace', and Claudius replies 'To thine own peace'. Laertes is content, but wishes it could be arranged 'That I might be the organ' of Hamlet's punishment; and Claudius agrees that, of Laertes's courtly 'sum of parts', he will use one 'part', his fencing, to entice Hamlet to his doom. The ideas of incision and partition are combined in the closet scene, where Hamlet's promise not to let Gertrude go until he has made her see her 'inmost part' makes her fear that she is literally to be carved up (III.iv.20ff.). After her hasty exclamation has caused that fate to befall the vigilant Polonius instead, and after Hamlet has thrust his merely verbal daggers in her ears, the queen laments that her heart has been 'cleft in twain' and is told, 'O, throw away the worser part of it, / And live the purer with the other half' (III.iv.157–9). *Hamlet* teems with such figures of a body that has been dislocated, broken into its parts. 'The time is out of joint' in Denmark, and the young prince has been called upon to plant his foot in the socket and violently 'set it right' – an action that involves him in causing still more violation and dislocation.

All this imagery pertaining to the unmaking of the body bears some resemblance to the imagery of the *Henry IV* plays, which Neil Rhodes discusses in the course of his study of the Elizabethan tradition of isolating and distorting parts of the body for comic and admonitory effects.[6] Food metaphors in particular attach themselves to the person of Falstaff, alternately evoking joyous physicality and miserable corporeal degeneration. A similar emphasis on what Rhodes calls 'the mere materiality . . . of existence' inheres in the somewhat different corporeal metaphors of *Hamlet*, which derive ultimately from the Ghost who hovers behind the scenes and impels the action. Despite his relatively brief time on stage, the Ghost fills the linguistic fabric of his play with images of broken bodies, much as the fat knight generates images of sensory gratification and discomfort. 'Something is rotten in the state of Denmark', and he symbolises it. Since Wolfgang Clemen's book on Shakespeare's imagery, it has become a commonplace in *Hamlet* criticism that the motif of ulcerous infection and corruption that runs throughout the play centres on the speech in which Hamlet is told how poison was poured into his father's ears, coursed through his blood, and ate away his body from within, covering it with sores.[7] It could be added to Clemen's important observation that the figure of the dead king also organises corporeal imagery implying dislocation and dissolution. The physical undoing of King Hamlet accounts ultimately – in terms of both the structures of imagery and those of plot – for the physical, psychological, moral, and political undoing suffered by the play's living characters.

As the king was 'cut off' (I.v.76) from all that he loved, so Ophelia finds herself, in Claudius's words, 'Divided from herself and her fair judgment, / Without the which we are pictures or mere beasts' (IV.v.86–7). Deprived of the coherent form of reason, but still obscurely intelligible, 'Her speech is nothing. / Yet the unshaped use of it doth move / The hearers to collection: they yawn at it, / And botch the words up fit to their own thoughts' (IV.v.7–10). Claudius correctly says of this psychic mutilation. 'O, this is the poison of deep grief: it springs / All from her father's death' (IV.v.76–7) – just as he discerned earlier that some ruinous 'matter' in Hamlet's heart was distorting his appearance and behaviour (III.i.165ff.). Claudius can see that the same psychic recapitulation of King Hamlet's poisoned disfiguration is taking place in Laertes, who 'wants not buzzers to infect his ear / With pestilent speeches of his father's death. / Wherein necessity, of matter beggared, / Will nothing stick our person to arraign / In ear and ear' (IV.v.91–5). Noting all these changes, and the political trouble that they are bringing – Hamlet has just been sent to England, 'For like the hectic in my blood he rages', and Laertes is about to burst in upon the inner sanctum of the palace 'in a riotous head' – Claudius too succumbs to a feeling of violent psychological disruption. The swelling disaster in his kingdom, he tells Gertrude, 'Like to a murd'ring piece, in many places / Gives me superfluous death' (ll.96–7).

In the closet scene, Hamlet analyses in terms of corporeal disfigurement the moral depravity that reaches out from Claudius to all those who come under his sway. Gertrude's vice appears in her having abandoned the physical arrangement of parts that was King Hamlet – 'a combination and a form' that proclaimed manliness – for a demonstrably inferior form (III.iv.56ff.). 'Have you eyes?' Hamlet asks, suggesting that only some physical mutilation could account for such blindness. To choose Claudius indicates not merely sensual weakness, but sensory derangement:

> Sense sure you have,
> Else could you not have motion, but sure that sense
> Is apoplexed ...
> Eyes without feeling, feeling without sight,
> Ears without hands or eyes, smelling sans all,
> Or but a sickly part of one true sense
> Could not so mope.
>
> (ll.72–4, 79–82)

Hamlet continues his indictment of Claudius with a comparison to the dismembered body of the dead king. The new ruler of Denmark's government and Gertrude's affection is, he tells the queen, a sum of parts that do not make up a whole, a living body that has already been reduced to fragments: he is 'a king of shreds and patches', 'not twentieth part the tithe / Of your precedent lord' (ll.103, 98–9).

The physical imitation of King Hamlet's undoing that culminates in the play's final scene with four deaths by poisoning – five if Horatio could have his way – begins with the death of Polonius, whose corpse is made an emblem of physical decay. After Hamlet has rendered the old courtier 'most grave' and lugged his guts offstage, Claudius asks where Hamlet has gone and Gertrude replies, with echoes of dismemberment: 'To draw apart the body he hath killed' (IV.i.24). Claudius sends Rosencrantz and Guildenstern to 'bring the body / Into the chapel' (ll.36–7), but their persistent inquiries are parried by Hamlet, who makes the absent corpse a kind of absent prop for dramatising the mystery of undoing revealed by his father's ghost:

> Rosencrantz What have you done, my lord, with the dead body?
> Hamlet Compounded it with dust, whereto 'tis kin.
>
>   ...
>
> Rosencrantz My lord, you must tell us where the body is and go with us to the King.

Hamlet The body is with the King, but the King is not with the body.
The King is a thing—
Guildenstern A thing, my lord?
Hamlet Of nothing. Bring me to him.

(IV.ii.5–6, 26–31)

The death of kings is the beginning and the end of Hamlet's study in this play. Polonius offers him an imaginative link between the live king who attaches so much importance to bodies and the dead king who knows how little they amount to. Brought before Claudius and asked once more 'where the dead body is bestowed', Hamlet waxes philosophical about kings, beggars, and the worms that consume them both. Considering that even a king, whose mystically double Body represents the corporate being of all his subjects, 'may go a progress through the guts of a beggar', he recites the lesson of the play's corporeal images. The body personal and politic is a provisional structure, both a form that sustains human being and a shadow through which non-being beckons. As a composition of parts that will inevitably fall apart and decompose, human life is paradoxically 'a thing . . . of nothing', an existence constructed around the void.

II

In his famous subtilisation of the Romantic idea that Hamlet is unnecessarily and morbidly reflective, T. S. Eliot argued that Shakespeare himself failed in *Hamlet* to establish any clear correspondence between thought and action, idea and image. The play is 'full of some stuff that the writer could not drag to light, contemplate, or manipulate into art', Eliot suggested; and since nothing in the fictional occasion is sufficient to account for the protagonist's great apprehension and disgust, his thoughts and feelings cannot be expressed by 'a skilful accumulation of imagined sensory impressions'.[8] The morbid corporeality of the imagined sensory impressions described in the first section of this essay may provide an answer to Eliot's charge, in that they constitute something like an 'objective correlative' for Hamlet's obsessive withdrawal from the world of action. The attitude toward corporeal existence inherent in the play's imagery figures prominently in the protagonist's thinking as well; it contributes to his inability to 'act' by challenging what he regards as the integrity of his being.

In so far as Hamlet suffers from a psychological Problem distinct from the formidable moral and practical difficulties presented by his situation, it consists in questioning his own being; and this in turn has much to do with his inability to identify himself with that which decays, 'passing through nature to eternity' (I.ii.73). A small eternity of dramatic time must pass before Hamlet can think of himself as a creature of flesh without experiencing paroxysms of anguish and disgust. His observation that a king may pass through the guts of a beggar is intended as a thinly veiled threat against Claudius's life, but it attacks also his sense of himself as a dignified, purposeful, heroic being. Fearing that physical actions may never adequately embody virtuous intentions, he makes the doubt self-fulfilling by shielding his high sense of himself within an overwhelming contempt for the body – a contempt that sabotages meaningful action.

Mark Rose has observed how Hamlet is 'bound' to certain courses of action by his birth, by his uncle's calculating refusal to let him leave the corrupt 'prison' of Denmark, and by his loyalty to the Ghost ('I am bound to hear'; 'So art thou to revenge, when thou shalt hear'); he rebels against these constrictions, Rose argues, by becoming 'obsessed with the idea of freedom, with the dignity that resides in being master of oneself'.[9] But Hamlet is bound as well to his body, and obsessed with his contempt for it. Even before he is called upon to 'set right' the unnatural murder and the incestuous marriage, he laments his connection to the royal couple's physicality. His mother's lascivious 'appetite' prompts him to wish for a way out of the hateful body that can lead people to forget so quickly the spiritual goods that have sustained them for a lifetime:

> O that this too too sullied flesh would melt,
> Thaw, and resolve itself into a dew,
> Or that the Everlasting had not fixed
> His canon 'gainst self-slaughter.
>   (I.ii.129–32)

Claudius's rowdy behaviour with the boys becomes the occasion for another meditation on corporeal subversion of virtue. Denmark's 'heavy-headed revel', he tells Horatio, has taken 'from our achievements ... / The pith and marrow of our attribute' (I.iv.17–22) – hollowing out the bones, enervating the spine of a national reputation built up from the achievements of noble Danes. If an irruption of physical impulse can so damage the reputation of an entire nation, it is not surprising that some 'vicious mole of nature' or 'the o'er growth of some complexion' can undermine the reputation of individual men, to such a degree that their virtues 'Shall in the general censure take corruption / From that particular fault' (ll. 23–36).

The Ghost calls Hamlet deep into this world of disruption. Its invitation to decapitate the body politic seems a horrific charge ('O cursed spite'), and by the end of the play it will manifestly be so: Ophelia will have been emotionally brutalised and lost to lunatic distraction; the king and queen will have been pierced with hateful insight, their attempts to reconstitute a harmonious political entity shattered; the populace will have been raised to the brink of revolt; Polonius, Rosencrantz, Guildenstern, Ophelia, Gertrude, Laertes, and Hamlet himself will have fallen as more or less innocent victims before Claudius finally does; and Denmark itself will be put in the hands of the reckless young marauder whose hostile approach the sentries anticipated at the beginning of the play. In setting right two injustices, Hamlet will cause physical, psychological, moral, and political dislocations on a universal scale.

Nothing about the apparition gives Hamlet any confidence that the purposeful determination needed to persevere through the play's violence is grounded in substantial, lasting virtue transcending Oresteian futility. On the contrary, the Ghost is simultaneously insubstantial and a horrifying *memento* of all that rots, seeming to embody the very forces of corporeal ruin that Hamlet fears may be inimical to virtue. It recalls in appearance and dignity the majestic king who won honour destroying the Poles and conquering ambitious Norway. But the Ghost is a weak and ephemeral substitute for the king, referred to by Horatio and the guards as his 'image', 'this thing', 'illusion', 'this portentous figure', a 'horrible form', 'a figure like your father', something 'like the King'. Hamlet's astonished prostration before it in the closet scene contrasts with the queen's equally great astonishment that her son is gazing wildly into 'vacancy' and holding discourse with 'th'incorporal air' (III.iv.118–19). The Ghost seems very much 'a thing of nothing' when Hamlet's appeals for Gertrude to confirm its existence elicit only fears that her son is a victim of schizophrenic hallucination:

> Queen To whom do you speak this?
> Hamlet   Do you see nothing there?
> Queen Nothing at all, yet all that is I see.
> Hamlet Nor did you nothing hear?
> Queen   No, nothing but ourselves.

> **Hamlet**   Why, look you there, look how it steals away!
> My father, in his habit as he lived!
> Look where he goes, even now, out at the portal!
> > *Exit Ghost.*
> **Queen**   This is the very coinage of your brain.
> This bodiless creation ecstasy
> Is very cunning in.
> > (III.iv.132–40)

Hamlet answers his mother's charge of 'ecstasy' convincingly. We cannot believe that the Ghost is a figment of his imagination: Horatio has raised precisely this issue in the first scene of the play, and has been quickly convinced that the apparition is 'something more than fantasy' (I.i.54). But Shakespeare's stagecraft makes us feel poignantly how little Hamlet is able to rely on the Ghost as his justification for a murderous course of action. Cast on the defensive, forced to justify the right of a lunatic to catechise a sinner, Hamlet is in no way aided by the encore appearance that the Ghost makes to whet his 'almost blunted purpose'.

In addition to *being* 'incorporal', insubstantial, the Ghost dwells on the terrifying processes by which corporeal creatures are reduced to fragments of themselves. Its first words seem calculated to plunge Hamlet deep into thoughts of undoing. 'My hour is almost come,/ When I to sulf'rous and tormenting flames/Must render up myself', it begins, evoking visions of human flesh 'rendered' to its elements like animal fat (I.v.2–4). The Ghost may be Hamlet's 'father's spirit', but it is a spirit bound by 'foul crimes', doomed to wear away by fasting and fire the impurities that it acquired in nature (ll.9–13). The punishments of its 'prison house' are not less intense than what flesh is heir to; in fact, they are so much more intense that hearing of them

> Would harrow up thy soul, freeze thy young blood,
> Make thy two eyes like stars start from their spheres,
> Thy knotted and combined locks to part,
> And each particular hair to stand on end
> Like quills upon the fearful porpentine.
> But this eternal blazon must not be
> To ears of flesh and blood.
> > (ll.16–2)

The Ghost spares Hamlet the sympathetic undoing that would befall him if he heard this tale of the Almighty's purging fires, but it treats him to the next worst thing, an account of the effects of Claudius's poison. When he is told the manner of his father's death – cut off instantly from life, wife, and crown, with venom coursing through his body, his blood congealing and skin crusting, and unrepented sins weighing upon his head – Hamlet hardly requires the Ghost's accompanying injunction: 'O, horrible! Most horrible! / If thou hast nature in thee, bear it not' (ll.80–1). Reeling as beneath a physical blow, he feels that his own body may no longer cohere, no longer support his consciousness: 'Hold, hold, my heart, / And you, my sinews, grow not instant old, / But bear me stiffly up' (ll.93–5).

Earlier, the sight of the Ghost has left Marcellus and Barnardo 'distilled / Almost to jelly with the act of fear' (I.ii.204–5). The tale of how his father's body sank from admirable beauty to horrifying monstrosity in an instant, and how in the same instant invisible sins overwhelmed his father's soul, plunges Hamlet into a horror as much ontological as physical, into a world where man the effectual ethical agent seems distilled to utter inconsequence. Is ambition a shadow, as Rosencrantz and Guildenstern suggest in a feeble attempt to broach the topic of Hamlet's political intentions? 'Then are our beggars bodies, and our monarchs and outstretched heroes the beggars' shadows' (II.ii.267–9). Just as a king's body might be imagined going a passage through the guts of a beggar, his ambitious, 'outstretched' spirit may be nothing more lasting than a ghostly shadow. In this world, thoughts may be no more capable of transcending ruin than are bodies. The earth now seems 'sterile' to Hamlet, the firmament a morbid exhalation of infectious 'vapors', and godlike man a handful of dust waiting to return to its disorganised state (II.ii). The best things in himself – his fidelity to his father, and the love of Ophelia – are seen now as compromised by the old corrupt 'stock' of mankind that virtue can 'inoculate' but never supplant (III.i). Linking himself with men such as Claudius – and Ophelia with women such as Gertrude – by the corruptible material in which they are commonly rooted, Hamlet sees virtuous purpose and rational significance threatened everywhere by corporeal corruption.

This perception of bodily experience as corrupt and corrupting drives Hamlet into disdainful, alienated contempt: contempt for his own flesh, contempt for those parts of his experience that seem tainted by corporeality, contempt for people who threaten to harm or to compromise him by insinuating themselves into his thoughts. When Horatio warns him of the possible dangers of following the Ghost, he welcomes the destruction of his body: 'Why, what should be the fear? / I do not set my life at a pin's fee, / And for my soul, what can it do to that, / Being a thing immortal as itself?' (I.iv.64–7). Horatio's reasonable reminder that the soul is no more immutable or invulnerable than the body, but may itself be wrecked in madness as it hovers over the abyss, drives Hamlet into what seems to Horatio a 'desperate' violence: 'Unhand me, gentlemen. / By heaven, I'll make a ghost of him that lets me!' (ll.84–5). This violent withdrawal from his body and from his companions is augmented shortly by with-drawal from his own wordly self. Hamlet imagines that, in order to honour the Ghost's parting command, he must obliterate from memory all the experience and learning stored in his brain, uprooting past impressions until only those of the avenging spirit live there, 'Unmix'd with baser matter' (I.v.104). Forsaking for the moment the prudential considerations that his years of 'observation' would suggest to him, and also his trust in his companions, he contents himself with 'wild and whirling words', like a falcon towering high above the earth.

Hamlet's transcendent contempt is dramatised most powerfully in his treatment of Ophelia, the one creature who ties him inextricably, physically, to the corrupt world of Elsinore. His alienation from her begins soon after the encounter with the Ghost. At the end of II.i, she tells Polonius how Hamlet has withdrawn himself in ghostly silence from her society. The antic performance that Polonius takes for 'the very ecstasy of love' is indeed ecstatic, though hardly amatory. Hamlet, in Ophelia's description, resembles the literary figure of the distracted and dishevelled lover, but he more strongly evokes the corporeal ruin suggested by the figure of the Ghost. He has entered her room, Ophelia says, in a manner ominous enough to strike terror into her heart, very pale (as the Ghost was said to be), 'And with a look so piteous in purport, / As if he had been loosed out of hell / To speak of horrors' (II.i.82–4). Silently scrutinising the amazed object of his visitation, as the Ghost silently stood before his interlocutors before finally yielding up speech to Hamlet, and three times imitating its action of lifting its head up and down (described by Horatio at I.ii.216), he at last raises 'a sigh so piteous and profound / As it did seem to shatter all his bulk / And end his being' (II.i.94–6) – then drifts out of the room without the use of his eyes, they being constantly fixed on Ophelia, as the Ghost's were said to be on Horatio. In thus affecting the shattering of bulk and ending of being that tore his father from the queen, Hamlet declares his intention to tear himself from his erotic attachment to Ophelia.

A violent attempt to free himself from corporeality, resulting paradoxically in a deep immersion in it, characterises all of Hamlet's dealings with Ophelia. When he turns his assumed madness upon the unfortunate girl with full force in Act III, he reviles her as a pretty snare for the spirit – one of those creatures who substitute new faces for the ones God gave them, who jig and amble and lisp, who excuse their moral depravity by pleading their rational incapacity – and urges her to take herself out of sexual circulation. The next scene finds him attacking her body with ribald jokes about country matters, lying between maids' legs, and games of show and tell. In thus bitterly doing violence to the creature who most has access to his inner self, Hamlet does not find freedom from the danger of love, but only reduces himself and her to ruin. The deformation of his former self that Ophelia thinks she sees in his harangue – 'That unmatched form and feature of blown youth / Blasted with ecstasy' (III.i.160–1) – prefigures her own madness in the next Act. It foretells also Hamlet's distracted expressions of anguish at her death:

> 'Swounds, show me what thou't do.
> Woo't weep? Woo't fight? Woo't fast? Woo't tear thyself?
> Woo't drink up eisel? Eat a crocodile?
> I'll do't.
>
> (V.i.274–7)

Hamlet finds excessive and violent degradations of his own body the only adequate testimony to the falseness of his earlier contempt. All of his efforts to remove himself from the compromising infection of corporeality only drive him more deeply into the understanding of his dependence on the frail body.

Hamlet's violent, and ultimately futile, ambition to transcend bodily weakness can be seen not only in his dealings with Ophelia, but also in all of his attempts to respond adequately to the death of his father. In his first speech of the play, while manifestly acting the part of a mourner, he disdains dramatic action as being limited by the opacity of the flesh. No physical 'show', he insists, can adequately convey the immensity of his grief. His black clothes and the expressive corporeal actions that accompany them fall short of the indescribable state of suffering that resides within him. Hamlet's separation of 'actions that a man might play' and the invisible anguish of his alienated soul is an admission of futility, suggesting that no physical acts – whether dramatic or heroic – can serve the purposes of the spirit. And his words ring false when compared to the authentic alienation of Ophelia, whose mad meanderings and distracted gestures, while opaque to reason, nevertheless move their audience to anguished commiseration as coherent utterance never could – prompting Laertes to exclaim, 'This nothing's more than matter' (IV.v.174).

The Ghost's demand for vengeance requires some stronger resort to physicality, and when Hamlet asks the Player for 'a passionate speech' he seems briefly to have found a model for 'suiting' corporeal action to mental state. He admires the Player's capacity to so translate a fictional intention into dramatic action that all of his corporeal 'function' can be seen lending 'forms to his conceit' (II.ii.561–2). But it soon appears that Hamlet is not chiefly interested in the harmonious suiting of body to soul. Rather, he has asked for the speech in order to excite himself to a still more violent contempt for the body. He imagines that, given the magnitude of his wrong, he should 'drown the stage with tears', 'cleave the general ear with horrid speech', 'and amaze indeed/The very faculties of eyes and ears' (ll.567–71). He fixes obsessively on corporeal excitation as a standard for dramatic and ethical action, contemplating imaginary injuries to his own body in order to work himself up into violence:

> Am I a coward?
> Who calls me villain? Breaks my pate across?
> Plucks off my beard and blows it in my face?
> Tweaks me by the nose? Gives me the lie i' th' throat
> As deep as to the lungs? Who does me this?
> Ha, 'swounds, I should take it, for it cannot be
> But I am pigeon-livered and lack gall
> To make oppression bitter, or ere this
> I should ha' fatted all the region kites
> With this slave's offal. Bloody, bawdy villain!
> Remorseless, treacherous, lecherous, kindless villain!
> O, vengeance!
> Why, what an ass am I!
>
> (ll.577–89)

Hamlet's bitter self-hatred in these lines stems from his conviction that, in order to act the part of the revenger, he must plunge deep into the bodily passion that he so despises, and perhaps become a bloody villain himself. He quickly abandons the part, determining instead to have other actors enact a play that will determine the king's guilt or innocence.

His instructions to the players correct his bitter contempt for the body, assigning corporeality its due place in dramatic imitation. Renouncing his ecstatic exaggeration of physical violence, Hamlet says, 'O, it offends me to the soul to hear a robustious periwig-pated fellow tear a passion to tatters, to very rags, to split the ears of the groundlings' (III.ii.8–11). Use the body in your acting, he tells the players, but 'Suit the action to the word, the word to the action' (ll.17–18). He no longer disdains the capacity of bodily actions to execute ethical intentions. The purpose of acting, he says, is to mirror the lineaments of human experience on stage – 'to hold as 'twere the mirror up to nature; to show virtue her own feature, scorn her own image, and the very age and body of the time his form and pressure' (ll.21–4). Like a mirror that faithfully receives the physical forms of things, dramatic art takes the bodily impress of men and women and re-presents their moral nature in its living outlines. Hamlet achieves in these prescriptions for art a conception of its ethically effective function, and he manages to implement the conception when he uses other artists' works to probe the psyches of Claudius and Gertrude. The starkly mimetic tableau of courtly bodies played before Claudius literally shows the king the form of his actions, and achieves its intended effect of driving him from cover. The portraits of Gertrude's two husbands engage her conscience with similarly stunning effect, confronting her inescapably with the lineaments of her desires.

But artistic imitations of bodily action do not help Hamlet to accomplish his most important ethical action. He uses the artistic fusion of body and soul, form and intention, to do what art can do according to the Renaissance aesthetic: convey the intelligible order of experience to an audience and stir their moral responses. He cannot – or will not – use it to accomplish regicide. Indeed, he lets even his 'antic disposition' slip before and during the play, with the effect that Claudius understands exactly why the mousetrap has been sprung and determines to remove his enemy from Denmark.

Hamlet's explicit considerations of revenge, like his studies of models of dramatic action, suffer constantly from his ambition to transcend corporeal weakness. By associating heroic action with an escape from the flesh in the 'To be or not to be' soliloquy, he initiates a vain attempt to transcend the very conditions of action. He imagines that 'taking up arms' will somehow liberate his soul from the indignities of the body. But hearing the story of how his father died has made it impossible for him to imagine the process of leaving the body (so 'noble in the mind') in any terms except those of corporeal calamity. Eternal sleep suggests eternal nightmares. Casting his mind up and out of corporeal misery only leaves him 'sicklied o'er with the pale cast of thought', his face drained of 'the native hue of resolution' by a consciousness turned pathologically inward. Corporeality drags his heaven-seeking thoughts to earth; like the praying Claudius, he finds them miserably incapable of transcending the limitations of bodily existence.

His effort to draw inspiration from the soldiership of Fortinbras, like his very similar admiration for the Player, loses coherent ethical purpose as it sinks into violent disdain for bodily well-being. The Norwegian adventure against Poland seems to him a case of pathologically morbid violence, an 'imposthume of much wealth and peace, / That inward breaks, and shows no cause without / Why the man dies' (IV.iv.27–9). But he forces himself to admire it, because of Fortinbras's eagerness to abandon bodily concerns for the sake of the spirit. His own small sum of bloodshed, he decides, indicates a beast's dull maintenance of corporeal functions, while Fortinbras's admirable 'spirit', his 'divine ambition', appear in his willingness to expose the great 'mass' of his army to indiscriminate slaughter. Fortinbras's sacrifice of twenty thousand men for a piece of land not large enough to bury them outpaces in barbarity Laertes's willingness to cut his enemy's throat in the church, and his motives – 'a fantasy and trick of fame' – are more insubstantial. Hamlet recognises the monstrosity of the deed, and even the words that he calls up to defend it betray their ostensible purposes: 'Examples gross as earth exhort me' (can such examples be exemplary?); 'Rightly to be great / Is not to stir without great argument' (if he is affirming Fortinbras's action, does he not need another 'not'?). In yearning to pattern his own revenge on this senseless promotion of catastrophe, Hamlet abandons all realistic consideration of good and evil in an effort to overcome his dull animal maintenance of corporeal life. Instead of deploring Fortinbras's failure to use the body for substantial purposes, he celebrates the way in which he contemptuously smashes it, and thereby entertains thoughts of moral depravity.

In the prayer scene, we see Hamlet caught once more in the division that he would make between body and spirit, and once more cultivating the pathological corruption that he so fears. Seeing Claudius engaged, as he thinks, in 'the purging of his soul', making himself 'fit and seasoned for his passage' – whereas his own father died 'grossly, full of bread, / With all his crimes broad blown' – Hamlet waits for a moment that will have 'no relish of salvation in't', and leaves Claudius's 'physic' to give way to more 'sickly days'

(III.iii.80–96). An ill-intentioned consulting physician, he judges the alimentary system of the patient sufficiently free of obstruction to permit an unimpeded 'passage' of the soul to paradise, and prescribes a period of waiting so that the organism may worsen and clog the hateful soul within it before it is killed. His false assumption that any human soul, much less one so corrupt as Claudius's, could free itself from the conditions of corporeality leads him to seek a barbaric revenge incompatible with Christian virtue, and prevents him from enacting the simpler revenge that lies possible before him. The dramatic irony that Claudius has not been able to transcend his body and the things that it still loves urges the insufficiency of Hamlet's attitudes.

Purposeful action cannot coexist with Hamlet's effort to distinguish the invincible soul from the ruinous body. Such an effort seeks to rescue the self from something that it depends upon for its being and doing. Consciousness in *Hamlet* is, like the body, an entity poised between substantial presence and ephemeral absence. The body grows and decays according to its own laws; by the same inscrutable laws, men find achievement in the midst of loss, security in the midst of fear, power in weakness, significance in accident. Hamlet defies these laws so long as he attempts to remove the spirit from ambiguity and lodge it in simplicity. Instead of cultivating the compound of kindred elements that is a spirited body, he tries to split it into a duality, and wastes his energy contemning half of himself.

When Hamlet breaks out of his dualism and more confidently treads the stage as a duellist, it is because he has finally acknowledged, without dread or anguish, that princes, like their swords, accomplish their ends in 'passing'. A clown's tricks do not outlive his kicks: not only Yorick's lips have disappeared from the earth, but also his gibes, his gambols, his songs, his flashes of merriment. Nor, by the same token, can Caesar, 'that earth which kept the world in awe' (V.i.215), expect to remain a substantial and functional presence, save perhaps as a patch on a windy wall. The great personages who may have owned the graveyard's bones dance again in imagination as creatures who mistook their power for something more substantial than the body, and the fragments of their bodies mock their pretension by outliving them. Gertrude may have forgotten her husband after only two months, but a tanner's flesh is still keeping out water after eight years. As Hamlet persists (despite Horatio's objection) in his courageously reductive meditations on human vanity, he approaches the brash humility of the Gravedigger, who happily shovels aside pieces of bodies as he sings a ditty of age having 'shipped me into the land, / As if I had never been such' (V.i.71–4). The rustic's 'absolute' use of the terms 'man' and 'woman' comically relieves the anxiety generated since the beginning of the play by Hamlet's effort to distinguish mankind from corporeality:

> Hamlet   What man dost thou dig it for?
> Clown   For no man, sir.
> Hamlet   For what woman then?
> Clown   For none neither.
> Hamlet   Who is to be buried in't?
> Clown   One that was a woman, sir; but, rest her soul, she's dead.
> Hamlet   How absolute the knave is!
>
> (ll.130–6)

Hamlet's taking solace in the provisional 'absolute' that men and women are more than their bodies, but not different from them, suggests that he accepts as well the fact that man's strength consists in acceding to corporeal accidents, rather than in trying to transcend them.

While it is clear that Hamlet adopts a new kind of understanding in Act V, and that he undergoes some beneficial change as a result, criticism has long been notoriously vague about precisely what this saving knowledge consists in. Hamlet does not learn simply to accept death: indeed, he seems always to have desired it. Nor are his words about the 'divinity that shapes our ends' and the 'special providence in the fall of a sparrow' sufficient foundation on which to base a religious ethic or cosmology. What seems to be on his mind more essentially than either death or God is a preoccupation with the possibilities and conditions of purposeful human action. But even here the understanding seems to be more negative than positive. Hamlet begins to embrace accidental occasions – seeing them under the aspect of Providence rather than Fortune – and to renounce his earlier need to understand and control every aspect of his revenge. Discussing the importance of chance occurrence in the final action, William Warner has recently observed how reluctant the critics of various schools have been to accept limitations on Hamlet's importance, and how they have been driven to ingenious or vague arguments in attempts to rescue his purposeful intentionality.[10] What Hamlet learns, Warner suggests, is precisely the insufficiency of his own attempts to make final and coherent constructions of reality: he learns, in effect, by unlearning what he has thought earlier in the play.

One thing that Hamlet unlearns is his contempt for his physical nature, which has persistently reduced this spirited and capable exemplar of active virtue to acting not at all, or in spurts of blind rage. Hamlet's identity throughout the play has depended upon his wish to exceed the conditions of vulnerability and incompleteness that inhere in an animal body. But reality has repeatedly contradicted this assumed identity, insisting that the body must be central to his being, not something inessential that can be thought into irrelevance and violently discarded. All of Hamlet's efforts to transcend corporeality have only implicated him amorally in its ruinous violence. Finally he abandons the fruitless attempt. He sees in the graveyard not simply the bodily 'nothingness' that has so distressed him before, but an inescapable connection between that nothingness and his own being. As James Calderwood has put it, 'For Hamlet fully "To Be", it seems, he must experience in the graveyard, under the tutelage of the Gravemaker, What it is "Not To Be". For his own identity to crystallise, he must come to the place where all identities dissolve.'[11] The Hamlet who kills the king is a man who has accepted radical limitations on his being, leaving the orchestration of his revenge to Claudius ('I am constant to my purposes; they follow the King's pleasure'), the understanding of his death to God ('Since no man of aught he leaves knows, what is't to leave betimes?'), the telling of his tale to Horatio ('Horatio, I am dead; / Thou livest; report me and my cause aright'), and the continuation of his life to Fortinbras ('He has my dying voice'). In asking forgiveness of Laertes for the imprudent violence that took Polonius's life, he detaches himself – with diplomatic mendacity, but also with evident sincerity – from the arrogant and tormented self that he has been:

> If Hamlet from himself be ta'en away,
> And when he's not himself does wrong Laertes,
> Then Hamlet does it not, Hamlet denies it.
> Who does it then? His madness.
>
> (V.ii.236–9)

Hamlet has not in fact killed Polonius in a fit of 'madness', but the word may be taken as a tactful way of referring to an assumed self that has been all but insane. Calderwood calls it a metaphor: 'As a metaphor for Hamlet's bond to his father – for that sense in which Hamlet as revenger is "possessed" by the ghost of his father – Hamlet's madness is truly no part of himself, and is in fact "poor Hamlet's enemy".'[12]

Secure in the less ambitious and less anxious self that remains when he has cast out the demon of transcendent power, Hamlet comes into his own as an actor on the national stage, easily and confidently submitting himself to the 'pass' of swordplay. He accepts Claudius's invitation to let Laertes's poisonous hand pass into his own: 'Come, Hamlet, come, and take this hand from me' (V.ii.227). His body informs him with sick misgiving that Claudius is arranging his exit from this life, but it assures him at the same moment that he has the physical means to act as he purposes:

> Horatio   You will lose this wager, my lord.
> Hamlet   I do not think so. Since he went into France I have been in continual practice. I shall win at the odds. But thou wouldst not think how ill all's here about my heart. But it is no matter.
> (V.ii.211–15)

Hamlet suggests that, in order to act, human beings must accept the fact that their achievements go hand in hand with failure, and find their integrity in the welcoming of fragmentation. Accepting that he will himself sooner or later be 'no matter', Hamlet consents to make up one frangible part in a larger body, as an actor performs one role in a play. In his final words before the cushions and courtiers and daggers and drinks appear – 'Let be' – he overcomes the distinction between spiritual fixity and corporeal flux that has plagued him throughout the play. Things will be as they become, his death will come when it arrives, and he can at last leave off his effort to define himself in opposition to what Maynard Mack has called his 'imaginative environment'.[13]

Most of Shakespeare's tragedies tell the story of an arrogant man who mistakes his grandiose constructions of reality for reality itself. From Richard II to Coriolanus, his heroes attempt forcefully to impose a deluded conception of reality on the world, and reality brings them down. Hamlet differs from these vain and power-mad men in being adolescent, uncertain, victimised, self-hating. But he shares with them the presumptuousness of believing that he can transcend the laws by which other men and women think and behave. The futility of his attempting to be something other than a body is comically asserted by the madcap ramblings of the Grave-digger; it assumes tragic grandeur in the final catastrophe, as newly ruined bodies litter the stage, awaiting the Gravedigger's services. Having finally consented to act the modest part of the duellist, a disciplined corporeal agent who confines his thoughts to the play of physical circumstances, Hamlet submits with grace and dignity to the limitations of his kind.

From *Shakespeare Quarterly*, 39 (no. 1, Spring 1988), 27–44.

NOTES

[John Hunt's discussion of *Hamlet* starts from the idea put forward by Francis Barker in his influential book *The Tremulous Private Body* (London, 1984), that the body imagery in the play is part of the whole idea of the state as a 'body politic' in the Renaissance. In *Hamlet*, however, the body politic, like the language of the play, 'pulsates with grisly vitality' even as it is dissected by Shakespeare into limbs, organs, tissues, to impress upon us the very corporeal nature of life. It is this very corporeality, Hunt argues in the second part of his essay, that Hamlet must come to terms with before he can act and fulfil the Ghost's commands. Like other critics, Hunt sees Hamlet adopting this new kind of understanding in Act V, but what his analysis also shows is how it is possible to combine contemporary critical ideas and methods with a very traditional subject like imagery in Shakespeare to produce a new reading of the play. Ed.]

1. All quotations are from the Signet text edited by Edward Hubler (1963; reprinted New York, 1972).

2. Francis Barker, *The Tremulous Private Body: Essays on Subjection* (London and New York, 1984), pp. 23, 31.

3. Ernst Kantorowicz, *The King's Two Bodies: A Study in Mediaeval Political Theology* (Princeton, 1957), p. 26.

4. The *OED* identifies the anus as a contemporary figurative sense of 'bung-hole', citing an entry in Cotgrave's *Dictionarie of the French and English Tongues* (1611) for the *cul de cheval* or sea anemone: 'a small and ouglie fish, or excrescence of the Sea, resembling a mans bung-hole, and called the red Nettle.'

5. Donald Frame, trans., *The Complete Works of Montaigne* (Stanford, 1957), p. 457.

6. Neil Rhodes, *Elizabethan Grotesque* (London, 1980).

7. Wolfgang H. Clemen, *The Development of Shakespeare's Imagery* (Cambridge, 1951).

8. T. S. Eliot, *Selected Essays: 1917–1932* (London, 1932), pp. 144–5.

9. Mark Rose, '*Hamlet* and the Shape of Revenge', *English Literary Renaissance*, 1 (1971), 132–43, especially 132–4.

10. William Beatty Warner, *Chance and the Text of Experience: Freud, Nietzsche, and Shakespeare's Hamlet* (Ithaca, 1986), pp. 268–75.

11. James L. Calderwood, *To Be and Not To Be: Negation and Metadrama in 'Hamlet'* (New York, 1983), p. 103. [An extract from Calderwood's book is reprinted in this volume – see p. 68. Ed.]

12. Ibid., p. 44.

13. Maynard Mack, 'The World of *Hamlet*', *The Yale Review*, 41 (1952), 502–23, especially 502.

Further Reading

The reading list below essentially follows the pattern of the Introduction and puts books under broad critical headings, including those of 'Critical Theory' and 'Editions' of *Hamlet*. First, however, some very obvious advice.

The best place to begin any further reading is with the text. All the essays in this volume start from and assume a close reading of the play. Indeed, one of the marks of modern writing about *Hamlet* is an almost fierce interest in every aspect of the text, including details of plot, staging, textual variations and past criticism. A good, annotated edition of *Hamlet* is, therefore, essential to any serious work on the play. There is, though, another reason for using a modern edition of the text. The editions listed below all include substantial critical introductions to the play and in many ways sum up the traditional critical view of *Hamlet*. There are, of course, differences of interpretation between the editions, but not of critical approach. Because modern critical theory is, in part, a reaction against such traditional criticism, it is important for students to familiarise themselves with the way traditional critics have approached the play so that they can think about their ideas for themselves.

Under the heading of traditional criticism I have included a number of books to do with staging and performance, again for straightforward reasons. First, such books provide a good deal of useful factual information. Second, most critics of *Hamlet*, regardless of their critical stance, make it their business to know about the Elizabethan theatre, and often write with the assumption that their readers are aware of the practices and conventions of the Renaissance stage. Most, too, seek to convey in their writing about the play a sense of the play as something acted before an audience. The political and social implications of theatrical performance have become increasingly important to modern discussions of *Hamlet*, but students also need to know the 'ordinary' things about staging, such as the use of spectacle, boy actors, disguise and so on.

It might seem from the above that in order to get to grips with *Hamlet* it is first necessary to read an enormous amount of criticism. This, however, is to miss the point. Criticism is not a substitute for reading and thinking about the play. What it does do is open up possible ways of rereading the text which can enlarge our understanding of the relationship between text and reader, text and audience. Sometimes it is argued that modern theoretical criticism is not really interested in Shakespeare but is simply using the plays to clarify points of theory. In one or two cases this might seem to be true, but such accusations have to be weighed against the fact that many of the most exciting discussions of Shakespeare over the last two decades have come from critics who are at the forefront of critical theory. Again, one of the benefits of modern critical theory has been to make traditional critics much more self-conscious of their critical stance and ready to defend their position and values. Set against such benefits are some obvious drawbacks: occasionally modern criticism can prove hard to understand; its critical terminology can seem alienating or obscure; and, because it is opposed to traditional ideas, it can appear difficult to grasp its relevance.

This, however, should not serve as an excuse either to reject or not to read modern critical writing. The best way into modern criticism and modern critical theory is to read those books which seem most immediately approachable (such as Catherine Belsey's *Critical Practice* or Terry Eagleton's *Literary Theory: An Introduction*) and to use these, along with such works as Roger Fowler's excellent *A Dictionary of Modern Critical Terms* (revised edition 1987), or M. H. Abrams's *A Glossary of Literary Terms* (5th edition 1988), as a starting-point. Though, initially, it may prove hard work to follow their arguments, after a while you will begin to see what they are saying and why.

EDITIONS

The following are the standard editions of *Hamlet*. As I noted in the Introduction, there are significant, indeed radical differences between them that raise a number of important questions about what we mean when we speak of 'Shakespeare's *Hamlet*':

Philip Edwards (ed.), *Hamlet*, The New Cambridge Shakespeare (Cambridge: Cambridge University Press, 1985).

G. Blakemore Evans (ed.), *The Riverside Shakespeare* (Boston: Houghton Mifflin, 1974).

Alfred Harbage (ed.), *The Complete Pelican Shakespeare* (Baltimore: Penguin, 1969).

George Hibbard (ed.), *Hamlet*, The Oxford Shakespeare (Oxford: Oxford University Press, 1987).

Edward Hubler (ed.), *Hamlet*, The Signet Shakespeare (New York: New American Library, revised edn 1987).

Harold Jenkins (ed.), *Hamlet*, The Arden Shakespeare (London: Methuen, 1982).

T. J. B. Spencer (ed.), *Hamlet*, The New Penguin Shakespeare (Harmondsworth: Penguin, 1980).

A full account of the problems involved in editing Shakespeare's plays can be found in:

Stanley Wells and Gary Taylor, *William Shakespeare: A Textual Companion* (Oxford: Clarendon Press, 1987).

TRADITIONAL CRITICISM

It would obviously be possible to provide a very long list at this point. The following, however, are likely to prove most helpful:

R. M. Frye, *The Renaissance 'Hamlet': Issues and Responses in 1600* (Princeton: Princeton University Press, 1984).
G. K. Hunter, 'The Heroism of Hamlet', in G. K. Hunter, *Dramatic Identities and Cultural Tradition* (Liverpool: Liverpool University Press, 1978), ch. 9, pp. 230–50.
Mark Rose, '*Hamlet* and the Shape of Revenge', *English Literary Renaissance*, 1 (1971), 132–43.

The following are collections of essays on the play.

John Jump (ed.), *Shakespeare: 'Hamlet'* (London: Macmillan, 1968).
Kenneth Muir and Stanley Wells (eds), *Aspects of 'Hamlet'* (Cambridge: Cambridge University Press, 1979).

The books below provide valuable information and ideas about staging and performance:

Andrew Gurr, *The Shakespearean Stage, 1574–1642*, 2nd edn (Cambridge: Cambridge University Press, 1980).
Michael Hattaway, *Elizabethan Popular Theatre: Plays in Performance* (London: Routledge & Kegan Paul, 1982).
Peter Thomson, *Shakespeare's Theatre* (London: Routledge & Kegan Paul, 1983).
Glynne Wickham, *Early English Stages 1300–1660*, vol. 2 (London: Routledge & Kegan Paul, 1963, 1972).

CRITICAL THEORY

These are general books about current critical theory rather than about Shakespeare or *Hamlet*. Many of the ideas they discuss, however, lie behind modern writing on Shakespeare. The first two deal with structuralism:

Jonathan Culler, *Structuralist Poetics* (London: Routledge & Kegan Paul, 1975).
Terence Hawkes, *Structuralism and Semiotics* (London: Methuen, 1977).

The next group discuss poststructuralism and deconstruction:

Catherine Belsey, *Critical Practice* (London: Methuen 1980).
Christopher Butler, *Interpretation, Deconstruction and Ideology* (Oxford: Clarendon Press, 1984).
Christopher Norris, *Deconstruction: Theory and Practice* (London: Methuen, 1982).
John Sturrock (ed.), *Structuralism and Since* (Oxford: Oxford University Press, 1979).

The following provide good introductions to feminist criticism:

Catherine Belsey and Jane Moore (eds), *The Feminist Reader: Essays in Gender and the Politics of Literary Criticism* (London: Macmillan, 1989).

Mary Eagleton (ed.), *Feminist Literary Theory: A Reader* (Oxford: Blackwell, 1986).

Gayle Greene and Coppélia Kahn (eds), *Making a Difference: Feminist Literary Criticism* (London: Methuen, 1985).

Kate Millett, *Sexual Politics* (New York: Doubleday, 1970).

Elaine Showalter (ed.), *The New Feminist Criticism: Essays on Women, Literature, and Theory* (London: Virago, 1986).

The best general introduction to modern psychological criticism is:

Elizabeth Wright, *Psychoanalytic Criticism* (London: Methuen, 1984).

The following group deals with Marxist criticism and what is sometimes called Cultural Materialism, a type of Marxist criticism associated with Raymond Williams, Jonathan Dollimore and Alan Sinfield, and which has much in common with New Historicist criticism (see the introduction to their *Political Shakespeare*):

Terry Eagleton, *Literary Theory: An Introduction* (Oxford: Blackwell, 1983).

Terry Eagleton, *Marxism and Literary Criticism* (London: Methuen, 1976).

Frank Lentricchia, *After the New Criticism* (London: The Athlone Press, 1980).

Raymond Williams, *Marxism and Literature* (Oxford: Oxford University Press, 1977).

Raymond Williams, *Problems in Materialism and Culture* (London: Verso, 1980).

The last group here is concerned with New Historicism:

Stephen Greenblatt, *Renaissance Self-Fashioning From More to Shakespeare* (Chicago: University of Chicago Press, 1980).

Stephen Greenblatt (ed.), *Representing the English Renaissance* (Berkeley: University of California Press, 1988).

Jean E. Howard, 'The New Historicism in Renaissance Studies', *English Literary Renaissance*, 16 (1986), 13–43.

Harold Veeser (ed.), *The New Historicism* (London: Routledge, 1989).

In addition, useful brief discussions of several of these approaches and theories appear in:

M. H. Abrams, *A Glossary of Literary Terms*, 5th edn (New York: Holt, Rinehart & Winston, 1988).

Roger Fowler (ed.), *A Dictionary of Modern Critical Terms*, revised edn (London: Routledge & Kegan Paul, 1987).

Ann Jefferson and David Robey (eds), *Modern Literary Theory*, 2nd edn (London: Batsford, 1986).

Raman Selden, *A Reader's Guide to Contemporary Literary Theory* (Brighton: Harvester Press, 1985).

RECENT CRITICAL APPROACHES TO SHAKESPEARE

As with traditional criticism, it would be possible (but pointless) to give a very long list here. This selected list contains several collections of essays on

Shakespeare which all include material on *Hamlet*, as do all the books. (Modern criticism is much less interested in the single text than traditional criticism and so studies of individual plays are rarer.) The various groups should not be taken as totally exclusive – for example, Catherine Belsey's book *The Subject of Tragedy* combines a Marxist approach with feminist criticism together with an interest in history and theatre.

The first two books focus on structuralism, semiotics and language:

Keir Elam, *The Semiotics of Theatre and Drama* (London: Methuen, 1980).
Malcolm Evans, *Signifying Nothing: Truth's True Contents in Shakespeare's Text* (Brighton: Harvester Press, 1986).

This second group reveals something of the variety of feminist approaches to Shakespeare:

Juliet Dusinberre, *Shakespeare and the Nature of Women* (London: Macmillan, 1975).
Marilyn French, *Shakespeare's Division of Experience* (London: Cape, 1982).
Lisa Jardine, *Still Harping on Daughters: Women and Drama in the Age of Shakespeare* (Brighton: Harvester, 1983).
Coppélia Kahn, *Man's Estate: Masculine Identity in Shakespeare* (Berkeley: University of California Press, 1981).
Carolyn Ruth Swift Lenz, Gayle Greene and Carol Thomas Neely (eds), *The Woman's Part: Feminist Criticism of Shakespeare* (Urbana: University of Illinois Press, 1980).
Kathleen McLuskie, 'The Patriarchal Bard: Feminist Criticism and Shakespeare', in Jonathan Dollimore and Alan Sinfield (eds), *Political Shakespeare* (Manchester: Manchester University Press, 1985), pp. 88–108.

The following all offer radical political readings of Shakespeare:

Francis Barker, *The Tremulous Private Body* (London: Methuen, 1984).
Catherine Belsey, *The Subject of Tragedy: Identity and Difference in Renaissance Drama* (London: Methuen, 1985).
Jonathan Dollimore, *Radical Tragedy: Religion, Ideology and Power in the Drama of Shakespeare and his Contemporaries* (Brighton: Harvester Press, 1984).
Terry Eagleton, *William Shakespeare* (Oxford: Blackwell, 1986).
Kiernan Ryan, *Shakespeare* (London: Harvester Wheatsheaf, 1989).

The following collections of essays include several different modern critical approaches:

Jonathan Dollimore and Alan Sinfield (eds), *Political Shakespeare: New Essays in Cultural Materialism* (Manchester: Manchester University Press, 1985).
John Drakakis (ed.), *Alternative Shakespeares* (London: Methuen, 1985).
Jean E. Howard and Marion F. O'Connor (eds), *Shakespeare Reproduced: The Text in History and Ideology* (London: Methuen, 1987).
Patricia Parker and Geoffrey Hartman (eds), *Shakespeare and The Question of Theory* (London: Methuen, 1985).

The next two books focus on the politics of theatre:

Michael D. Bristol, *Carnival and Theatre* (London: Methuen, 1985).
Robert Weimann, *Shakespeare and the Popular Tradition in the Theater* (Baltimore: Johns Hopkins University Press, 1978).

Terence Hawkes's book examines the way traditional criticism has created the 'canonical' Shakespeare:

Terence Hawkes, *That Shakespehearian Rag: Essays on a Critical Process* (London: Methuen, 1986).

Finally, a full discussion of modern approaches to Shakespeare can be found in Hugh Grady's book:

Hugh Grady, *The Modernist Shakespeare* (Oxford: Clarendon Press, 1991).

It goes without saying that no one expects students to read their way through long lists of books such as this. The best course, as I suggested above, is to try those that seem most approachable. Do not, however, be put off by the occasional unusual term or obscure passage, but rather try to stand back and see what larger case the writer is making, and how that bears upon your own critical practice.

Notes on Contributors

Nigel Alexander is an Emeritus Professor of English of the University of London. He is the editor of the Macmillan edition of *Hamlet* (London, 1973), and the author of *Poison, Play, and Duel* (London, 1971) and *Shakespeare: Measure for Measure* (London, 1975).

Catherine Belsey is Professor of English at the University of Wales, Cardiff, where she chairs the Centre for Critical and Cultural Theory. Her publications include *Critical Practice* (London and New York, 1980); *The Subject of Tragedy: Identity and Difference in Renaissance Drama* (London and New York, 1985); and *John Milton: Language, Gender, Power* (Oxford and New York, 1988).

Stephen Booth is Professor of English at the University of California, Berkeley. He is the editor of *Shakespeare's Sonnets* (New Haven, 1977), and the author of *An Essay on Shakespeare's Sonnets* (New Haven, 1969) and *'King Lear', 'Macbeth', Indefinition, and Tragedy* (New Haven, 1983).

James Calderwood is Professor of English and Associate Dean of Humanities at the University of California, Irvine. His publications include *Shakespearean Metadrama* (Minneapolis, 1971); *Metadrama in Shakespeare's Henriad* (Berkeley and Los Angeles, 1979); *To Be And Not To Be: Negation and Metadrama in 'Hamlet'* (New York, 1983); *If It Were Done: 'Macbeth' and Tragic Action* (Amherst, 1986); *Shakespeare and the Denial of Death* (Amherst, 1988); and *The Properties of 'Othello'* (Amherst, 1989).

Peter Davison was formerly Fellow of the Shakespeare Institute and Professor of English at St David's University College and the University of Kent. His many publications include *Popular Appeal in English Drama to 1590* (London, 1982); *Hamlet: Text and Performance* (London, 1983); and the Facsimile edition of Orwell's *Nineteen Eighty-Four* (London, 1984). He is editor of *The Complete Works of George Orwell* (Penguin, 20 vols).

Philip Edwards is King Alfred Professor of English Literature at Liverpool University. He is the editor of the New Cambridge edition of *Hamlet*

(1985). His many publications include *Shakespeare and the Confines of Art* (Methuen, 1968) and *Threshold of a Nation: a Study in English and Irish Drama* (Cambridge, 1979).

Marilyn French is one of America's leading academic writers and also an international best-selling novelist. Her major academic publications include *The Book As World: James Joyce's 'Ulysses'* (Cambridge, 1976); *Shakespeare's Division of Experience* (New York, 1981); and *Beyond Power: On Women, Men and Morals* (New York, 1985). Her novels, *The Women's Room* (New York, 1977), and *The Bleeding Heart* (New York, 1980), were both best-sellers. Her most recent novel is *Her Mother's Daughter* (New York, 1988).

John Hunt is Assistant Professor of English at the University of Montana.

David Leverenz is Professor of English at the University of Florida, Gainesville. He is co-editor of *Mindful Pleasures: Essays on Thomas Pynchon* (Boston, 1976), and the author of *The Language of Puritan Feeling: An Exploration in Literature, Psychology, and Social History* (New Brunswick, 1980) and *Manhood and the American Renaissance* (Ithaca, 1989).

Elaine Showalter is Professor of English at Princeton University. She is the editor of *The New Feminist Criticism* (London, 1986), and the author of *A Literature of Their Own: British Women Novelists from Brontë to Lessing* (Princeton, 1977) and *The Female Malady: Women, Madness and English Culture 1830–1980* (New York, 1986).

Rebecca Smith is Director of the Intensive English Language Institute and Adjunct Associate Professor of English at the University of North Texas, Denton.

Leonard Tennenhouse is Visiting Professor of Comparative Literature at the University of Minnesota. His publications include *Power on Display: The Politics of Shakespeare's Genres* (London, 1986).

Index